When I was
Done Dying

REQUIEM

A Memoir of Sex, Madness, and Self-Destruction

FREDY ESPINOZA

ISBN-10: 1466254971
ISBN-13: 978-1466254978

I dedicate this memoir to my mother, Alma Fabiola Espinoza

CONTENTS

ACKNOWLEDGMENTS

I wish to thank several people. I would like to thank Michael Griffin for his support and patience over the three years it took me to write this memoir. I would like to thank Sherri Starr for believing in me. I would also like to thank Ricardo Delvie for the book cover. Last, but not least, I would like to thank my editor, Mark Rhynsburger.

∞ PROLOGUE ∞

MY NAME IS Fredy Espinoza—that is to say Fredy of the thorns, or better yet, protected by thorns.

Every family has a dark secret, even the picture-perfect ones.

My family has many.

These white-sepulcher secrets disguise themselves as decrepit skeletons, forever entrenched in whispers lingering in unkempt closets. They are drenched in crimson blasphemous sin—dripping with ghastly splattered blood—and one would be wise to keep them silenced in the guttural scream of shattered memories.

I choose to unveil these treacherous secrets that have haunted me for so long; I have carried them in my heart for far too long.

The oldest of four, I perched myself beneath the wings of my mother and witnessed horrifying acts that ultimately catapulted all her children into the depths of darkness and self-destruction. It came in tumultuous waves, gradually galvanizing every one of us until all there was left in its harrowing

aftermath was a bludgeoned carcass of lost innocence.

Born in Redwood City, California on a cold night in January, I would soon be followed by my brother, Eduardo, a year later, and my only sister, Bianca, another year later. I grew up being the apple of my mother's eye and my father's American dream. My parents, Alma and Ambrocio, spoiled me to pieces and kept me extremely sheltered. Yet I prepared myself early in life to be perfect. I had to be the perfect son, the perfect role model, and the perfect embodiment of the American dream. Everything I touched had to be perfect.

Seven years later, my youngest brother, Alexander, came into being in Mountain View, California.

Ghostly spirits chased my family from one town to the next. We were gypsies escaping a past threatening to catch up to us. No town was ever good enough for my mother. She was running away from the life she never wanted; she was constantly yearning for something unattainable, something better than what the present moment could give her. And even though fate had bestowed on my mother bewitching beauty, a demure smile, self-possessed dark-brown eyes, a slim model physique, and pitch-black rivulets of curly hair, she wanted more.

We left Mountain View in the dust to live in Sunnyvale. It was in Sunnyvale that my mother's preoccupations with being followed slowly manifested; in Sunnyvale that my mother first told my father of her belief that there was someone watching us in the middle of the night. I'd awake to see her slowly pacing back and forth outside my bedroom. Her eyes pierced the night as she would timidly approach the curtains, part them slightly, glance outside, and just as quickly, step furtively away from the window and continue her pacing.

I always asked myself who it was she believed was watching us.

Indeed, from the outside, we were a picture-perfect family, living the

picture-perfect American dream—until the Devil appeared before my mother, arriving in a bejeweled golden chariot full of fire and brimstone.

And one by one, the Devil whisked us all into his dark embrace, consumed our souls, and left behind whispers in the wind. Haunting whispers that to this day flicker in the wind, churning in angst, mourning over stolen childhoods, displaced dreams, and lost innocence.

The Devil left behind a requiem.

∞ PART ONE: DEVIL AT THE DOOR ∞

"-Michael: There's nothing here to fear.

-Lucifer: Well, there's always the truth."—Mike Carey

∞ CHAPTER I: WHISPERS IN THE WIND ∞

A FEW WEEKS into my freshman year of 1999, I can't help but feel like a demigod.

Mingling among my classmates in the science hallway, I beam brightly as sixth period descends upon Washington High School in Fremont, California. I recently threw a successful party at my house, attended by several seniors, football players, cheerleaders, and the in-crowd. It is just one more step to securing my spot within the circle of the elite.

"Good luck, Fredy!" Brittany Boliba, a very attractive and blonde fourteen-year-old gymnastics classmate, shouts out to me as she strolls by.

"Thank you," I say, smiling seductively as I consider dating her to further propagate my passing as a straight guy.

Jonathan Smith walks up to me, slaps me on the back, and says, laughing, "You know you got it, man! All the guys voted for you. You have it in the bag. Hey, have you signed up for frosh football? First practice is around the corner."

"Of course, man! I'm getting fitted later this evening," I reply nonchalantly.

Traipsing into Ms. Raymond's science class, I casually linger at her desk before randomly sitting at an empty chair near the windows. I glance around and become aware of my classmates acknowledging my presence. Giddiness accentuates the air as the clock ticks closer to revealing whether or not I become the class vice president. In the back of the classroom, someone cheers out my name.

"Good luck, Fredy," Ms. Raymond whispers to me before calming the class down. "Okay, everyone, please open your text-book to page thirty-four. We're going to review the formation of sedimentary rocks."

The class discussion flies past me in a blur.

Toward the end of the class period, a knock at the door quiets everyone. Two representatives of the Associative Student Body step into the classroom and approach the teacher. Holding my breath, I wipe the sweat glistening on my forehead as several eyes turn in my direction.

"First of all, we want to express our gratitude to those of you who voted in this year's election. Your class president is Leanel Liwanag, vice president is Fredy Espinoza—"

The class erupts in cheers as several students cry out, "We knew you'd get it!"

Ms. Raymond mouths, "Congratulations."

After school, elated from the victory, I rush to the gym to sign up for frosh football. I am only signing up as another stepping stone to securing my position within the popular crowd. Nothing matters more to me in the world than my assured spot within the in-crowd. Frankly, I couldn't care less for football and, in fact, I dread the impact of bodies colliding into me.

Just then, I run into my opponent, Emma Sandoe.

"I'm glad I ran into you. I just want to say congratulations in person,"

she says graciously.

"It was a good race!" I extend my hand and shake her palm.

Slipping past her, I dash into the locker room and feign disinterest as the seniors unclothe themselves around me.

∞

AFTER A ROUGH football practice, I slowly trudge down Peralta Boulevard to my house. Just as quickly as elation had come, sadness and fear now trickle down the back of my spine as each step weighs heavier and heavier. In school, I successfully created the perfect image of myself; but no one, not even my closest friends, knew what was happening behind the closed doors of my home.

The sun burns orange embers across the warm September evening, casting long shadows across the pavement. Cars whip pass me as I lose myself within the ghosts of a life I pretend to escape from. Grasping to maintain my state of elation, I force a smile on my face and hope, just hope, that this evening I will be able to celebrate my victory with Bianca. Yes, I can imagine it now… Coming home to Dad hugging me and taking me out to celebrate, to Bianca pouncing on me in excitement as she asks questions about what my role entails, and to Mom sedated in bed. And just like that, my smile evaporates as my mother dominates my mind and I am tossed back into the past…

Crossing the lawn of parched grass, I pass the cherub statue with its umbrella held high, and jump over the white steel fence. I come to a dead halt as shattered glass lies sparkling across the pebbly footpath between a tall hedge and the side of the house. Laced within the shattered glass are remnants of a broken microwave.

"What the—?" I cautiously step onto the patio and find the door ajar.

My heart sinks to the pit of my stomach as I see the black leather couches slit erratically from one end to the other. White cotton decorates the beige carpet like patches of snow. The television is smashed in and a butcher knife stares menacingly at me.

"Bianca! Alexander!" I yell out.

Knots of fear strangle my heart as I step into the kitchen.

Dropping my book bag, I dash down the hallway and peer into our bedrooms.

"Eduardo!" I yell, but only silence answers my call.

Evidently no one is home.

Confused and terrified, I slowly make my way into the living room and then into the den. Coming upon my bed, I pull down the bed-covers, sink into a fetal position, and cry softly into the pillow.

Several hours later, I wake up to my father standing over me.

"What happened?" I ask him groggily.

A grim look constricts his face. "Your mother has lost her mind. She's been admitted into a mental facility and will be staying there for a few weeks."

"What's wrong with her?"

"I don't know. The doctors will find out."

"Where's Bianca, Eduardo, and Alexander?" I whisper in trepidation, afraid to hear the answer.

"They're with your grandmother in Newark. Nothing happened to them. I'm heading out to pick them up. Did you want to come along?" His face is taut with deep sorrow.

"No, it's okay. I'll clean up here. I'll clean up everything. Don't worry about the mess, it'll all be cleaned up by the time you guys come back."

Without another word, my father nods, briefly looks at the couches, shakes his head, and steps out...

A car honks, shaking me out of my reverie.

Across the street, I see Uncle Martin pull up and he waves at me. What is he doing here? I notice multiple cars parked alongside the driveway in front of my house. Hmmm, I wonder what is going on. I am certain it's no one's birthday today. Jetting across the lawn, I hop the fence. Through the window I see figures moving across the living room. From behind me, Uncle Martin darts across the street, walks around the hedges, and makes eye contact with

me. I cringe at the sight of a Bible in his hand.

"You've stopped attending Bible study," he states with admonishment.

"Been ridiculously busy with school," I interject nervously.

"Jesus Christ is never too busy for you," he says with a smile.

I give him a dead-pan look as I open the door to the house and walk into several religious relatives huddling together, praying. Uncle Martin strolls over to Mom, who has her eyes closed shut. Surrounding my mother I see several aunts with their palms facing outward toward her and praying.

Like a ghost, I flutter past them into the kitchen and run into Bianca.

"What's going on?" I whisper.

Disgust crosses her soft dewy brown eyes as uncertainty shrouds her porcelain face. Her hair cascades in curly brown ripples onto her tender shoulders. Twirling a strand of hair with her fingers, she softly mutters, "Mom begged Dad to call Uncle Martin to tell them that the voices are getting worse again."

"I don't get why she doesn't just stick to the medication the doctors had prescribed her. It's like, hello?! Don't they realize she's paranoid schizophrenic?!" I reply sharply.

Bianca grimaces and stops twirling her hair.

"I'm sorry, it just frustrates me that they"—I point toward the living room—"can't see she's paranoid schizophrenic. Ugh. So Mom's voices are getting out of hand?"

"She believes the Devil is in our house"—Bianca bites her lip and glances down—"and how demons and witches are telling her that the witching hour is upon us, and that it's only a matter of time before the Devil takes our souls." She slides her fingers through her hair. Whenever Bianca gets upset or anxious, she unconsciously slides her fingers through her hair. It is something she has done since she was a little girl.

Staring at her, it hits me how grown-up she looks. At thirteen years old,

she could easily pass for a young woman in her early twenties. Her shimmering white blouse further accentuates her maturing body. I wonder how it feels for her to be the only girl among a family of guys. Does she feel special being the only girl, or does she wish she had another sister whom she could confide in? And what of her bond to our mother? I once heard that the strongest bond is that between a mother and daughter.

The door pops open and Dad strides in.

"The both of you—get in here now. We're having an exorcism," he says gravely.

My jaw drops open as I try to utter a sound. I can't believe what I'm hearing. "A what?" I ask him, finally attaining my voice as I incredulously swallow my father's words.

"You heard me—an exorcism. This house is having an exorcism to get rid of the evil spirits."

"But there is no such thing as evil spirits!" I spit out.

"That's not what your mother thinks. Now, stop arguing with me, get in here, and pray with the rest of us." His hairline is receding, showing a bald spot on his forehead, and dark shadows puff beneath his eyes as he glares at me sternly.

"I hate praying," I mutter beneath my breath as I slam my backpack onto the dining table with revulsion and look at Bianca. A part of me urges me to revolt and run out the door; especially on this day when I have just been declared class vice president. Why can't I just have a normal functional family? Why can't I come home to my parents smiling and celebrating with me the marvelous news? Instead, I am forced to consort with the rest of my extremely pious family.

"Father in Heaven, we pray to you to release the Devil's demonic hold over this house. Jesus Christ, our Savior, we beg you to rein in the Devil and banish him once and for all from this saintly home, from your children whom

you will not forsake, and whom you will give mercy to! In the name of the Father, the Son, and the Holy Spirit, we banish you, Lucifer, from this home of God!" Uncle Martin's voice rises louder and sharper as he fiercely pulls me into the circle. In the background, my aunts tremble and shake as they pray alongside Uncle Martin. Behind Mom, my grandmother sobs quietly, clenching her rosary beads tight.

Closing my eyes, I imagine pulling my hair out, screaming, and shouting at the top of my lungs that everyone in this room is deluded. And you know why everyone is deluded? Because I prayed in vain every night for the past two years for God to heal Mom from her illness. Every night I asked God to heal her, and in exchange, I would leave school behind and enter a monastery. I swore I would have. I would have given my life to God and preached his Word if only He'd heal Mom from her mental illness. But alas, I am beginning to believe there is no God.

Fluttering my eyes open, I make eye contact with Alexander.

He stands between our mother and grandmother, dazed and confused. He is only six years old, but his eyes are disconsolate and shadowed with phantoms. I can tell Alexander doesn't understand anything that is happening around him. My poor little lost brother. My eyes darken as I see his shaved head. I can't believe Eduardo shaved Alexander's head to make Alexander look more like him.

Eduardo's little doppelganger.

My eyes shift toward Eduardo, whose face is grimly taught with angst. My brooding sight lingers over his bald head, his eyes squeezed shut, his mouth moving quietly as he prays along, and his rippling muscular body. For the first time, I pay close attention to him without him noticing me. Eduardo may look twenty five years old, but in reality, he is only fourteen, one year younger than me. I also can't believe he chose to drop out of school. What does he do in his spare time? Where does he go? I desperately want to judge

him, but how can I judge him when Mom is constantly losing it before our very eyes? How can I blame him for his choices if this is the path he is choosing in order to deal with the pain our mother has bestowed upon us?

And then there's Bianca.

I feel her getting distant from me. Nothing used to separate us, but now a gulf has widened between us. She catches my eye and I smile at her, rolling my eyes. Bianca looks away, uttering a sigh. I fear Eduardo will influence her choices. If only there is a way to show her that school is the answer to this insanity. She leans on Eduardo, locks hands with Alexander, and lowers her head.

Suddenly, Mom breaks into tortured sobs.

"God, please help me in this time of need! The Devil wants to take my children away! Don't let the Devil take them away from me! Can't you hear them, God! They're telling me that they're here at the doorstep waiting to take them away from me! God, please! Don't take Ambrocio and my children away from me! I beg you!"

Staring at our mother, I pity her. Gaunt, with bones protruding from her skin, Mom's face looks hollow. Her black hair is disheveled, her nails are long and yellow, and her eyes are drenched in blackness. It's as if death has already taken her essence, leaving behind a frigid corpse.

Terrified, Alexander shakes his shoulders and cries.

Bianca leans down and picks him up into her arms.

Our aunts break into hysterical sobs as they beg God to listen to Mom's calls.

Our grandmother exits into the kitchen and returns with holy water in her hand. Another aunt slips into the kitchen and appears behind my grandmother with lit sage. The air smells crisp and sharp. As night descends, flickering flames from votive candles cast shadows across ghostly barren white walls.

"In the name of the Father, the Son, and the Holy Spirit, we denounce you, Devil! We denounce you, evil spirits!" Uncle Martin's voice booms over everyone's prayers as he motions us to gather into a line. He leads us into the kitchen, and as we pass the doorway, Uncle Martin tacks holy grass in the shape of a cross onto the doorway.

Our grandmother sprinkles holy water all over the place and utters, "Hallelujah!"

"If you exist, God, you'd strike me down with lightning right here in this very spot," I say, seething through clenched teeth.

Dad gives me a chastising look.

The house is full of moans, sobs, and shrieks of prayers as every entryway is tacked with holy grass crosses. Uncle Martin fervently demands the Devil and his evil spirits to loosen their grip over this home.

I turn to Bianca and whisper into her ear, "I think we should have an exorcism on Uncle Martin and *his* minions."

She bursts into quiet giggles as Dad scowls at us.

Around midnight, the house clears up.

One by one, each aunt gives us blessings, whispering among themselves that the house held God's spiritual presence. Releasing a sigh of relief, I head down the hallway to the bathroom. In my parents' bedroom, I see my mother and grandmother prostrating themselves near the bed, praying diligently.

If forces of good and evil exist, why has Satan come to us now?

What is it about our family that has attracted Satan so?

∞

I QUIT FOOTBALL right before the first game. My friends are shocked and upset over my decision, but I feel it necessary for my own sake. Ever since the exorcism, I have been having the most awful nightmares. I wake up drenched in sweat, paralyzed with fear, and gasping for light as I shudder away remnants of the Devil coming for me. It is always the same nightmare

night after night...

Fluttering my eyes open, I am paralyzed by a malevolent force on my bed. In the darkness, I make out the outline of a two legged beast staring at me at the doorway. It seems as if it has been standing there for eternity waiting for me to wake up. I open my mouth to utter a scream but no noise comes out. The beast jerks forward and slowly approaches me...

Taking a deep breath, I remind myself that it is only a nightmare. Turning on my desktop computer, I glance at the clock and it is seven in the evening. I turn on Radiohead and hum along to the lyrics. *"I'm a creep, I'm a weirdo, what the hell am I doing here? I don't belong here..."*

I shift my eyes to the walls and find myself satisfied for having painted them a light shade of blue over the weekend. The den looks better this way, I sigh. The bed is meticulously made, the room clean of any debris, and at the entrance, a two-step stairway leads into the adjacent living room. African American beads dangle from the ceiling, creating the illusion of an elongated doorway separating my room from the common area.

I grab *Romeo and Juliet*, prop it open, and open up a document containing my essay for Honors English class. Not only do I have to write an essay, but I also have to memorize a monologue.

Alexander storms into my room with tears streaming down his face.

"What's wrong?"

"Fredy! Mommy... Mommy!" he cries and jumps into my arms.

"It's okay, Alexander. I'm right here. She won't harm you while I'm here, okay?"

"You're conspiring with the Devil, Ambrocio! I know it!" Mom's accusatory voice carries into the room.

Turning down the music, I hold tightly onto Alexander as we hear our parents fighting in the kitchen.

"You're talking nonsense, Alma!" Dad replies tensely.

"You made a pact with the Devil! You want to take my children away from me! I won't let you, Ambrocio! I won't let you and those whores of Satan take my children away from me! Do you hear me?!"

I flinch as I hear a plate crash against the wall.

"What the hell, Alma! Listen to yourself! Listen to what you're saying! It's just plain ridiculous!" Dad reasons with her.

"I know what you all think of me! I won't give in to those lies! No, I won't give in to any of it! To Hell with you and your motherfucking lies! That's all they are, Ambrocio, lies! Despicable lies, you cheating bastard! I'm not crazy! You hear me, Ambrocio! I'm not fucking crazy!"

"Put that knife down, Alma! What do you think you're going to do with that knife?!"

I gasp, swiftly pick up Alexander into my arms, and dash to the entrance of the kitchen. His arms in the air, Dad is pleading with Mom to put the knife down. She flings the knife at him.

"Daddy!" Alexander buries his face in my neck.

The knife misses him as it slices through the air, hits the refrigerator, and clatters onto the linoleum floor.

The blood drains from my face as Dad sprints, grabs Mom, and holds her immobile in his arms. Struggling in his arms, she curses, strikes him in the face, and thrusts about for several seconds before becoming a limp doll. She leans into his arms and breaks down into sobs.

"What's happening to me, Ambrocio? You believe me, right, Ambrocio? Tell me you believe me, please, oh God, tell me I'm not crazy."

"You're not crazy, Alma. I'm right here," he assuages her. Picking her up off the ground, he walks her back to their bedroom.

Half-way down the hallway, Mom halts and pivots her head toward a corner of the wall.

"Do you hear that, Ambrocio?"

"Hear what?" Dad's voice strains as he turns to look at what she is seeing.

"Shhhh…" she hushes him.

She cranes her head so as to see better, throws her middle finger out, and spits, "Fuck you! You're not taking anyone away from me! Damn you, Lucifer! You have no idea who you're messing with!"

"Alma, come on… Let's get into the bedroom. You need to take your medication." He pulls at her.

"I'm not taking it, Ambrocio," she says, resisting his arms.

"The medication will help."

"The Devil will kill my children once I fall asleep… How am I supposed to protect them if the Devil's waiting for me to fall asleep, Ambrocio? I can't fall asleep. No, I can't. I just can't. I have to stay awake. That medication makes me fall asleep. I-I am not sick, Ambrocio. Can you hear the witches? Please, tell me you hear them too. Ambrocio… They're laughing. Listen— they say you're with them. Please, tell me you're not with them, Ambrocio. For the love of God, tell me it's not true!"

"Enough! Damn it, Alma! You're taking that medication right now whether you like it or not," Dad replies harshly.

He yanks her into the bedroom and closes the door.

Holding Alexander, I whisper into his ear, "You see, nothing bad happened. Everything is okay. Want to sleep in my bed tonight?" Alexander trembles and nods his head in trepidation.

A bad odor fills the room as Alexander defecates in his underwear.

"I'm sorry," Alexander moans, shame filling his eyes.

"It's okay, Alexander. Want me to join you in the bathroom while you take a bath?"

"Yeah." He casts his eyes to the floor.

I return to the den, grab *Romeo and Juliet*, and head to the bathroom.

Passing our parents' bedroom, we hear our mom softly sobbing in the background. We also overhear our dad's muffled voice as he says, "If you don't take the medication, Alma, I will send you away to your mother's house."

Inside the bathroom, I close the door behind us, turn the faucets on, splash some soap to create bubbles for Alexander, and then wait patiently until the water is warm enough before unclothing Alexander and allowing him to jump in. Sitting on the toilet seat, I stop my heart from racing, prop open the book, and concentrate on memorizing the lines of the scene where Romeo first comes upon Juliet at her bedroom window. Out of the corner of my eye, I see Alexander peeking at me, as if inquiring what hell he was born into. His eyes haunt and trouble me. Uncomfortable, I put down the book and glance back with a smile, hoping that my smile will lift his mood.

"Why does Mommy hear the Boogeyman?" Alexander asks softly, his eyes wide with fear and curiosity.

I get off the toilet seat, approach Alexander, lean over, and gently caress his hair.

"I wish I knew the answer to that," I reply quietly.

"Bianca says she's paraschenic. What's paraschenic mean, Fredy?"

"You mean paranoid schizophrenic—that's what doctors and psychologists call people like Mommy who have the ability to hear the Boogeyman."

"Is the Boogeyman real?" Alexander sinks lower into the bathtub afraid to hear the answer.

"No, the Boogeyman doesn't exist. And if he does exist, he'll have to get through me first."

"You promise?"

"I promise."

∞

WAKING UP THE following morning, I peer through the curtains and watch Dad get into his car, back out of the driveway, and shoot off into the dawn. I creep back into my bedroom, throw on a pair of jeans and a fitted Abercrombie & Fitch shirt, and feign a smile as I shake away last night's memories.

I calmly tell myself that in school, I am someone else. I can pretend to come from a wealthy family, with doting parents, and an ordinary background. In school, I am a role model and all the teachers adore me and my classmates vie for my attention. Among my peers, I can pretend I am one of them.

It is an illusion, but one that helps me cope with reality.

Entering my sister's bedroom, I see Bianca nervously brushing her hair as she glances at me.

"What about Alexander?" she asks.

"Eduardo will be here. He'll watch over him."

"But what if Eduardo leaves?" She bites her lower lip and slides her hand through her hair.

"He won't. Eduardo has nothing better to do anyway. He'll make sure that nothing happens to him. I'm sorry to hear about you and Ryan."

"How did you find out?" she asks me quizzically.

"I heard through the grapevine."

"Don't be sorry. I'm not thinking about him. It wasn't meant to be." She continues to brush her hair.

"Well, I hope things get patched up between you because I really like him. He's a nice guy, has his head together, and isn't like the other guys who only care about—"

"Where do you two think you're going?" Mom's voice cuts the conversation short.

"To school," I say, my eyes tarnishing with anger as I turn around and face her.

Bianca shrinks behind me, avoiding her icy glare.

"No one is going anywhere, you hear me, Fredy?!" She threatens us with a leather belt in her hand.

"Actually, no, I don't hear you one bit," I tell her.

"Don't talk to me like that! I'm your mother! I am not letting you children leave my presence! Satan's witches are out there, conspiring to take you away. And I won't let that happen. Don't you understand? Can't you see I'm only doing this for your own good? I love you children too much to let you step out of this house and into the arms of Satan."

A dirty black shirt hangs loosely over her emaciated body and the stench of cigarette smoke reeks from her foul hair.

"Bianca, go," I say tensely.

Bianca walks to the door, only to stop in her tracks as Mom lifts the belt into the air. I step between them just as the belt whips down and strikes me across the chest. Disregarding the pain, I push up against Mom and grab her wrists.

"Go now, Bianca!"

Bianca rushes past us and flees the house.

"Bianca! Get back here!" Mom desperately screams at the top of her lungs as she struggles vehemently, digging her nails into my arms and biting my shoulder. Yelping, I release her. She pivots and chases after Bianca. "Bianca! The Devil is out there! Bianca! Don't leave this house! The Devil! The Devil!" I run after Mom and grab her just as she steps outside.

"It's too late! There's nothing you can do! We're going to school whether you like it or not," I retort defiantly.

"You listen to me! I am your mother, damn it! You're not leaving this house! I won't let you go out there into the Devil's lair!"

Without hesitation, I shove her and make a run for it. Mom lunges from behind, grabs me, and drags me back into the house.

"Let go of me," I cry, "You can't stop me from attending school! It's against the law to stop me from attending school!" I wince in pain as her nails draw blood across my back. Holding onto the door, I cry out as she yanks my hair. I try to elbow her but she suddenly grabs my hand and bites deeply into it, tearing my flesh.

"Like hell you're leaving. Over my dead body!" she huffs, straining to pull me further back into the house.

"You witch!" I scream in anger as I kick her to the side with all my strength, slam the door behind me, and run as fast as I can down the street. From behind, I hear Mom's distant screams. Wiping tears off my face, I tell myself it's all over. I tell myself it is just another day in the Espinoza household and life goes on.

It has to go on.

It will go on.

For my sake.

At the corner, I meet up with Bianca.

"Are you okay?" she asks.

"Yes, I'm fine," I whisper.

∞

THAT EVENING, EDUARDO smokes pot in the living room. Alexander sits next to him, his eyes glazed over in a misty hue.

"What's up, faggot!" Eduardo leers at me with a crooked smile on his face.

"Is Alexander high?"

"Yeah, I got him high." He breaks into squeals of laughter. "Alexander is high! He needed it, bro! I mean, just look at the crazy shit we're going through... I'm helping Alexander deal with this crazy-ass shit. He don't

mind"—he nudges Alexander—"do ya?"

"Look, you pathetic piece of shit! Alexander is only six years old! Six years old! I can't believe you got him high!" My voice rises as I open the kitchen door and call out Dad's name.

"Dad's not home, asshole," Eduardo's voice ices over with anger.

"Fuck you, Eduardo! Can't you see this isn't helping the situation at all?"

"Yeah, well, being a faggot doesn't help either!"

"Stop calling me a faggot!" I snap.

"Well, that's what you are! You're a fucking sissy. Always have been and always will be! I see right through you, cock-sucker. You can't hide that from me." Eduardo gets up from the couch and slowly paces toward me. His knuckles cave into fists as he jeers his lopsided smile in my direction.

He comes at me quickly and slams one hard on my chest.

"Come on, you fucking fudge packer! What you gonna do about it? Huh? Huh?" He socks the side of my face with the other fist.

"Stop it, you fucking bastard!" I push against him as hard as I can before making a dash for it into the garage. With tears flooding my vision, I try to make out anything that will protect me from Eduardo. I grab Dad's hatchet on the cement floor and brace myself for another assault as I make my way back into the kitchen.

"Ohh, what you gonna do with that, huh? You ain't got balls, bro! You chicken shit!" Opening the refrigerator door, he takes out a beer bottle and hurls it at me. I duck and it sails past me and shatters against the wall; shards of glass fly across the linoleum floor as beer spews over my back.

All the pent-up anger I've kept hidden for these past few years spills over as a black rage possesses me. A force of heat crackles within my hands as I lift the hatchet high above my head. Gritting my teeth, I shake with fury as the blood boils in my veins and a strong desire to kill him overcomes me.

"Don't threaten me, Eduardo! I'll fucking kill you! I swear I will!" I snarl

in rabid anger.

"You're a fucking coward, Fredy! You don't have the fucking guts to kill me, you faggot!" He grabs another beer bottle and throws it at me, this time striking my shoulder. "Come on, faggot! Kill me! Kill me, you fucking faggot!" he throws another beer bottle and it flies above my head, slamming into a cabinet door.

"I FUCKING HATE YOU!"

I drive the hatchet at Eduardo just as Dad storms in and yells at me to stop. His voice doesn't register. I slice the hatchet through the air and miss Eduardo by inches. It strikes the wall, leaving a nasty gash.

Eduardo jumps on top of me and punches my face. I fall onto the ground and protect myself as he kicks me, but then Dad yanks Eduardo off me and slams him against the refrigerator.

"WHAT THE HELL IS WRONG WITH YOU!" Dad shouts.

"He tried to kill me!" Eduardo cries out in shock.

Tears streaming down my face, I lash out. "I can't take this anymore! I hate him, Dad! Hate him! He's a monster! He got Alexander high on weed!"

"I didn't do nothing wrong," Eduardo whimpers defensively as Dad socks him in the shoulder.

"I told you to keep that shit out of this house!" Dad yanks him into the living room, hastily opens the door, and throws Eduardo out, and barks, "Don't come back until you shape up!"

From outside, Eduardo yells, "What the fuck! I didn't do nothing!"

Trembling, I run past Dad into my room.

Dad appears at the entrance, parts the beads dangling from the ceiling, and struggles to come up with something to say.

I turn my back against him and whisper, "Please, leave me alone."

He steps back, picks up Alexander, and closes the door behind him as he returns to the kitchen. I quickly get up from the bed and blast on Radiohead

to muffle the constricted sobs emanating from my throat.

Opening the window, I undo the screen, set it aside, and slip out of the house. Sobbing silently, I walk for miles, not knowing which direction to go. It isn't until I get to Niles Canyon Bridge that I realize I've walked for over an hour.

Exhausted, I fall to the ground as fresh waves of sadness penetrate my soul. It's my freshman year of high school, I've been elected class vice president, have straight-A's, succeeded in becoming part of the popular crowd—I have it all going for me. But if I have it all, then why am I feeling this agonizing pain?

It's not Mom's mental illness that is at the source of this pain, but Eduardo's words. The notion of the world finding out I am gay mortifies me. I'd rather jump off the bridge, commit suicide, and die a thousand deaths over than to have anyone find out. All I crave is acceptance, but the truth crucifies my bleeding heart. And the last thing I need now is for Eduardo to be my worst enemy; where is my brother when I need him the most?

Getting off the pavement, I sit on the edge of the bridge.

Dry heaving, I squeeze my eyes shut and beg for this throbbing pain to go away. It's as if I'm descending into an inferno of torturous flames; damning fires of Damascus devour my rotting flesh as ravenous vultures peck endlessly away at my chest, shred apart skin, and splatter boiling blood across jarring beaks; excruciating pain nails my pulsating heart down into a perpetual state of cascading agony; putrid maggots flow forth from a strangled throat, squirm across blackened cheeks, and slowly slither into the slits of blood-shot eyes, blinded by a carousel of demented and maddening images.

I scream into the night, "I just want to end it all!"

Craning my neck, I peer behind me into the darkness below the bridge.

Jagged rocks protrude from the ground, like stakes awaiting to impale me.

Leaning back into the black abyss, I pray a better life awaits me on the other side.

"It will only take a few seconds, Fredy," I say, convincing myself, "and then…it will all be over. It will all be over and I won't have to deal with any of this bullshit. I won't have to deal with life any longer and I can be free from all of this pain. And no one will ever know I'm gay." I cry out, wincing as the pain explodes, ricochets in my chest. "Oh, God, I hate my life so much! I hate it! I just want to be free!"

I dig my nails into the cement and prepare to lunge off the bridge head first, when suddenly, rose petals flutter across my blurry vision, and stillness ripples across my heart. A soothing voice whispers, "Look to tomorrow. It will be better tomorrow."

Flinging myself forward, I crumble into a fetal position on the sidewalk. An anchor of loneliness sweeps across my body as I heave out, "I don't know if I have it in me to live another day like this."

After countless hours of lying in pitch darkness, I get up and tread back home; back to the horror and terror that awaits within the walls of my enslavement, to the descending madness that threatens to consume me within its deathly embrace, and to a house full of broken lives and shattered promises.

∞ CHAPTER II: TEARS OF LAMENTATION ∞

FIVE MONTHS HAVE passed since my near suicide attempt. I never shared with anyone about that night. After I returned home late that night, I forced my mind to create two towers in my head and locked away any emotions of despair and depression.

All my dark secrets are bolted shut deep within the trenches of these two cobblestoned towers. I have found the secret to dealing with anything that comes my way; nothing will affect my state of mind and keep me from succeeding at school in order to get to the top. I will attend a university; it is my ticket out of this hell.

Standing in front of the mirror, I style my hair with gel, brush my teeth, and gargle with mouthwash. Spitting it out, I smile as excitement bubbles inside. For tonight's event, I purchased raver pants, bracelets, and a bright orange shirt from Hot Topic. I have never attended a rave in my life, but Eduardo's girlfriend, Victoria Huerta, has invited me to one.

I like Victoria.

She came into Eduardo's life just at the right moment. Victoria keeps him in check. Then there's her sister, Alicia. As much as I care for Alicia, I try to keep my distance. I've known her since the end of seventh grade. We dated throughout eighth grade and I broke up with her after being elected vice president. Alicia admitted to falling in love with me, but how could I love her the way she wants me to when in the back of my mind I know I could never love a woman that way. It hurts me to see the pain I cause her because she is the closest person to me in my life, but I also don't want Alicia to fall deeper in love with me than she already is.

If I come out, I will lose everyone.

No, it is not something to consider.

Stepping out into the hallway, I hear laughter trickling out of Bianca's room.

I frown in disapproval.

Lately, Bianca has been associating herself with runaway girls from broken homes. All they care about is making trouble. Bianca is precariously following Eduardo's footsteps. If she had only stuck to playing soccer and intermingled with the popular crowd, she wouldn't be influenced by negativity. I worry for her, but then again, maybe I only care about my own image and how it affects me as opposed to understanding my sister's pain.

"Hey, Dad, I'm going out tonight with Victoria and her friends. I won't be back until tomorrow morning," I tell him as he looks up from the couch.

"Have fun. Tell Victoria and Alicia hello for me," he says before taking a swig from a bottle of beer. He sits there on the couch amused with a Spanish soap opera, a *telenovela*. Recently, Dad has been coming home late in the evenings. And the second he gets home, he kicks off his work boots, saunters into the kitchen, grabs a few bottles of beer, turns on the television, and lounges in the armchair. Sometimes it gets to the point where I'm left wondering if he is ever at home.

Another reason why I'm looking forward to the rave is that Mom returns from Newark tonight. After another fight broke out between my parents, he took her to her sister's house and left her there. He told her not to come back until she took her medication.

For my sixteenth birthday, Dad bought me a sleek black two-door Nissan sports car. I named her Marilyn, after Marilyn Monroe. I blast Britney Spears as I pull out of the driveway and into the cool night.

Driving into Niles Canyon, I briefly glance at the bridge where I almost ended my life. I still wonder whose soothing voice it was that brought a stillness into my heart for a few seconds. Whatever happened that night, I can say for certain that at least I got my two towers out of it—the towers where I can store all my pain, anger, and sadness.

Driving onto Victoria's street, I turn the music down and find a parking spot. I step out of the car and feel a warm breeze kiss my skin. I love California weather; it's only February and yet it feels like summer.

"Hey Alicia, what's up?" I smile as I open the door to her house and see her sitting on the couch with her new boyfriend.

"I can't believe my sister's taking you to a rave," Alicia mutters. She gets up and comes over to me.

Alicia's hair is naturally dark brown, but as I stare at her, I notice she had dyed it pitch black. And her eyeliner makes her luminous hazel eyes pop out as she smiles and embraces me in her arms. She's very beautiful, but it hurts me whenever I overhear any of the girls from school call her fat.

"It's only a rave, Alicia—nothing bad will happen." I walk over and give her boyfriend a hug. "What are you guys planning tonight?"

"We're staying up and watching a list of movies we compiled," Alicia replies.

"Fredster!!!! Oh my god!!! You're going to love it tonight! I promise!" Victoria jumps out of the bathroom and slams herself into my body, hugging

me fiercely. I notice how short she is, about five feet four. "Richard and Jake are on their way. We're taking Richard's truck so you don't have to worry about driving your car. I'm so happy you're coming!"

"Me too. I'm so looking forward to it," I say with a laugh.

∞

HORDES OF PEOPLE trudge pass me as Victoria, Richard, Jake, and a few more of their friends congregate in a tightly knit circle outside an enclosed brick dome. From inside, hypnotic music sounds in the cool air.

"Here, take this," Victoria says, placing a white tablet in my palm.

"Is this what I think it is?" I glance at everyone and notice they are swallowing the pills.

"It's called White Buddha. It's an ecstasy pill. I'll take care of you all night long, okay? I promise this will change your life forever." Victoria smiles as she hands me a bottle of water.

"What happens when I'm on it?" My voice shakes slightly.

"For several hours, you will feel connected to every human being tonight, and you will feel so much love from everyone. Just make sure that every half hour you drink water. I don't want you to dehydrate."

Suddenly everyone stares at me as Richard and Jake cheer me on, "Do it, Fredster! We'll be right here for you!"

Slipping the pill into my mouth, I sip water and swallow it. I wait, expecting to feel something, anything, at that moment, but nothing arises.

"I don't feel anything," I say, flustered.

"Fredster, it'll take about twenty minutes. You will know the minute it hits you."

Victoria and I walk around the venue.

Suddenly, I catch my breath.

People's voices around me sharpen and the clatter of a spoon magnifies tenfold.

"Victoria," I whisper, coming to a dead stop and holding my hand out.

"OMG, are you feeling it?"

"I think so," I giggle, taking a step forward into a bubble of high energy. My paradigm shifts as every sound and sensation intensifies around me. A surge of happiness explodes over my body. I focus my eyes on glow sticks, whose fluorescent green light gives off a power of its own, captivating my attention. My brain goes into overdrive as the light consumes my visual field.

"You *are* feeling it! You should see your face, Fredster! You're beaming so wide!" Victoria laughs and hugs me. "Remember, I love you! We all love you and this is a safe environment. No one will harm you, okay? You can trust everyone!"

"I can trust everyone?"

"Yes! You can trust everyone with whatever is on your mind! What's on your mind?"

"Dance! I want to dance, Victoria! Let's go dancing!"

Meeting up with the group, I find myself in a whole new world. We all hop and skip into the main dance room. I am instantly infatuated with an attractive white guy; giving him the widest smile, I confront him with dance moves as he watches me. Nodding his head, he waits until I am done before going into his own jam. His beauty keeps me transfixed in my spot and his sparkling blue eyes send me over the edge into a state of pure bliss. He motions at me to follow him, and for a second I look behind me to catch sight of Victoria and the crew dancing in their own world. I tell myself I will be back. Darting through the crowd, I follow him into the cool night.

"Here, want some water?" He smiles at me.

"Yeah, thanks!" I accept his bottle of water and take several gulps.

"You having fun, bro?" He asks me.

"It's my first time here."

"Whoa, dude... And it's your first time doing ecstasy as well."

"How did you know?" I give him a sheepish smile.

I lean over and caress his arm.

"It's obvious," he says with a laugh, gently grabbing me. "You're rolling hard. Whatever pill you took must be some good stuff. Here, sit on the grass. I'm going to give you a massage."

Closing my eyes, I reply, "They call it the White Buddha..." My words lose all meaning as I succumb to pleasures never spoken of before. Moaning, I feel deeply connected to this handsome stranger. His fingers rub gently against my temples, then his hands nudge my shoulders, move down my lower back, and finally rest on my neck as I feel his skin make contact with mine.

"That's amazing," I whisper in awe.

"Thanks, man."

Sitting there, I think briefly about how it's a complete lie that when one is on ecstasy all you want to do is have sex. Feeling his hands on me and connecting with him on a level beyond sex is euphoric, ten times better than anything else in the world. To be so connected, linked, at one with another guy my age is pure bliss.

"All right, I'm going back inside. You want to come?" he asks.

"I'll be right in. I'm just enjoying this moment," I reply slowly, watching two guys stroll by with the brightest glow sticks I've ever seen.

"See you inside." He walks back into the main dance room.

Getting up, I follow the two guys with the glow sticks.

"I love you guys!" I yell at them.

They turn around and yell back, "We love you too, man!"

Smiling, I feel as if I am in Heaven. Is this what Heaven feels like? There is no pain, no sorrow, nothing. Just pure bliss. I walk and walk, not knowing where I am heading, until I hear good trance music emanating from a small white circular building. Dashing in, I feel euphoria intensifying over my body

as I feel the music in my bones.

The music pulsates in my bones!

I unleash all my inhibitions and dance among complete strangers. At one point, I accidentally bump into another guy. He turns around with a frown on his face, but smiles the second he notices I am rolling.

"I love you!" I cry out to him.

"I love you too, man!" he says before disappearing back into the crowd of people. No wonder people do ecstasy; it lets them transcend to a state of an abundance of love. It makes you feel intimately connected to every human being as every illusion of separation falls away.

I step out into the cool air and notice the sky brightening.

Suddenly, I hear someone screaming my name.

Up ahead, Victoria is waving her arms frantically.

"What's wrong?" I ask, running to her.

"What happened to you?! We lost you! You could have died!" She shrieks.

At the word *"died"* my face crumbles in tears.

I wail, "Oh my God! I'm dead?! I'm dead! Is this what being dead is like?! Am I in Heaven? But if I'm dead, then you must be dead too!"

"Oh crap, Victoria, he's still rolling," Jake says, grimacing.

Victoria throws her arms around me.

"Shh, you're not dead, Fredster. You scared us. You're not dead."

"I'm not?" I sniffle.

"You're not. Look around you. Where's that smile of yours?"

I give quizzical looks to Victoria, Jake, and Richard before bliss slowly trickles back in. Breaking into laughter, I hug all of them. "I can't believe you told me I was dead!"

"Dude, it's been over seven hours and Fredster's still rolling hard," Jake says, nudging Richard.

"This stuff is awesome! I met so many friends! I love every one of you so much! You guys mean the world to me!"

<center>∞</center>

A FEW DAYS later, I am still aglow from the evening at the rave. I am certain it is due to having felt full self-expression, being able to stand up knowing I am gay and not worrying about it. If I did anything questionable, Victoria and her friends never mentioned it. Although, thinking back on that evening, Victoria's eyes conveyed that she knew my secret.

Turning on *Days of Our Lives*, I sit down on the couch and relax. It's a day off from school. "Like sand through the hourglass, so are the days of our lives." The theme song plays as I look forward to Bo and Hope's love triangle with Billie. In my bedroom, Alexander plays with car toys.

Mom walks into the living room and quietly talks to herself.

She paces back and forth, halts in front of the television, and mutters something beneath her breath while smoking two cigarettes at the same time.

"Bo, are you okay? How's the case going in Italy? Did you find Billie?" Hope *questions Bo over the phone.*

"Hope, I'm fine. Just a bit hurt. Stefano DiMera all over again," Bo *whispers lovingly into the phone from Italy.*

"I feel your pain, Bo. Even though you're so many miles away, I feel your pain."

"Shows how connected we are, Hope. You will always be my one true love, Hope. And nobody can ever take that away."

"Why are you talking like this Bo? Bo… Bo, are you there? Bo!" Hope *cries out as the phone goes dead.*

Mom disappears into the kitchen and comes back with a towel. Staring at the ground, she spits out profanities as she throws the towel over an imaginary demon. She picks up the towel and tosses it to another spot in the living room. She goes back and forth several minutes, jerking to a stop as she doubles over, drops the towel, steps on the towel, and then repeats this ritual.

Alexander looks up from his car toys and stares at our mother.

"You bastard, I won't let you, you bastard! Making everyone think I'm crazy, well, I'm not, you bastard! I know he's conspiring with everyone to take them away from me…" Mom mutters beneath her breath as she picks up the towel and tosses it onto the couch. Standing still for a few seconds, she takes a huge puff from her cigarette, then curses at the wall.

I pretend she isn't there.

"Turn that damn television off!" she snaps, walking up to the television and turning it off.

"No! If you don't like it, go into your room! And take your medication!" I retort defiantly, getting up from the couch and turning the television back on.

I hate her.

No, loathe her.

I loathe how her black eyes watch me, how they dart back and forth, hold me in her insane gaze. Her bony wrist periodically swooshes back and forth as she puffs and puffs smoke.

Bianca enters the living room with a look of contempt on her face. She slips past Mom and leans down to distract Alexander. Our mother yells and curses at me for not obeying her.

I refuse to acknowledge her.

She paces into the kitchen, picks up the cigarette carton, and lets out a small whimper as she finds it empty. Storming back in, she demands I buy her cigarettes.

"I can't," I say, straining to focus on the plot of *Days of Our Lives.*

"Here, I have money." She throws a twenty-dollar bill at my face.

"No, I'm not going to buy you cigarettes. I don't believe in supporting smokers, and second of all, I'm only sixteen! *Days of Our Lives* is on. Why don't you go buy them yourself?"

"Damn it, Fredy! Didn't I tell you to turn that shit off! Why don't you ever listen to me?" She rushes to the television, grabs it with her cadaverous bony hands, and hurls it across the decrepit room, smashing it against the wall. Her eyes flash with fiery coals of uncontrollable fury as she spits out, "I hate you miserable brats!"

"Well, I fucking hate you too!" I hiss between clenched teeth.

Slap.

Blood rushes to my face. Pain etches itself across my cheek.

"Fredy!" Bianca cries out in alarm.

Alexander freezes, one hand dangling a race car in midair. His eyes become expressionless.

"I wish you little bastard were never born from my womb!" Mom yells, lunging at me. She grabs my hair, pulls me into her grasp, and nicks my arms with her long pointy nails. She spews, "I hate you, you bastard!" Her heavy breath reeks of cigarettes.

"Bianca! Grab Alexander and run into your room!"

Bianca's eyes widen in horror as I throw Mom across the floor.

"NOW!" I demand. I grab my paralyzed brother, clutching him to me, and push my sister through the kitchen, down the hall, and into the last bedroom at the back of the house.

Slamming the door shut, I press a chair beneath the doorknob.

We hear Mom cursing loudly in the kitchen. Cabinet doors slam shut, dishes crash on the floor. Then the sound of the dining table overturning, making a huge bang.

"Little bastards of Satan! Satan's children! That's what you are! Fuck you! Fuck you! I'll show them! I'll show them once and for all! They're demons! Demons! Satan's bastards!" She bellows endlessly as pots and pans rattle down the hallway in our direction.

Alexander throws himself into our sister's arms, buries his face, and cries

silently, trembling profusely in horror.

"It's okay," Bianca whispers apprehensively.

STAB!

Bianca and Alexander let out horrifying screams as Mom stabs the door with a butcher knife.

"OPEN THE GOD DAMN DOOR! OPEN THE GOD DAMN DOOR, YOU FUCKING BASTARDS!"

STAB!

The sound of wood splintering.

STAB!

Holding onto Alexander, Bianca rushes to the corner of her bedroom and shudders, staring at me with her jaw agape as I press the chair tighter against the door.

STAB!

STAB!

STAB!

STAB!

"OPEN THIS GOD DAMN DOOR! DAMN IT! OPEN IT! OPEN IT RIGHT NOW! RIGHT FUCKING NOW!" Mom howls at the top of her lungs, over and over again, as the butcher knife stabs the door relentlessly.

Bianca and Alexander hold tightly to each other.

"Fredy," Alexander cries out, extending his little hand to me. I want to run to them and hold them fiercely in my arms. But I am petrified—no, I am scared shitless. I can't show them fear. I am the man of the house. I took on Dad's role, so I need to keep my cool in these extreme circumstances. I have to keep it together. It'll all be over soon.

I'm so sorry, my eyes plead to him.

"OPEN IT! YOU FUCKING DEMONS! OPEN IT SO I CAN SAVE YOUR FUCKING SOULS!"

Then, silence.

The knife clatters to the floor.

I ease out of the chair and tensely hold my stance, unsure of what to expect.

From the other side of the bludgeoned door, we hear Mom break into quiet sobs.

"Please, Fredy, let me in. Just let me in. I just want to be near my children. Please, forgive me. I don't know what is happening to me. Let me in," she whimpers.

"Go away!" Alexander cries out.

"Oh God, I'm so sorry. I'm so sorry. I could never hurt you." The doorknob twists as she tries to open the locked door. "Please let me in! I love you. Fredy! Bianca! I'm scared! I need you—please open the door and let me in. I need to hold you, please!" Her words become muffled, her sobs penetrating the cold room.

After a few more attempts to twist the doorknob, she retreats. Down the hallway, we hear the sound of a door closing and stifled sounds of crying.

Releasing the chair, I edge over to Bianca and Alexander and sit down beside them in the corner. The three of us remain in the bedroom for several hours. As night descends upon us, I finally nudge the door open, peek into the hallway, tiptoe out, and whisper to Bianca to lock the door behind me. Alexander opens his mouth to persuade me to stay, but I glance at him sternly and put my finger to my mouth, hushing him.

Door closing behind me, I look down and see a gleam of moonlight reflecting off the silver butcher knife. A visceral chill knocks my breath away. The hairs on the back of my neck stand up. The knife gleams clandestinely at me.

Stepping across the knife, afraid to touch it, I quietly follow the hallway to the kitchen. The door to Mom's bedroom is cracked ajar. Peering in, I see

her lying down on her bed, facing away from me, weeping silently into the pillow. The sight of her catches me by surprise, stopping me in my tracks. I find myself yearning to enter the room; to crawl up next to her and hold her in this moment of vulnerability; to soothe her fears while whispering into her ear how much I love her; to comfort her and understand what it is that she is going through. Why are you going crazy? Why are you hearing voices? I just don't understand. I want to, but I have no idea how. Was it due to your involvement with psychics? I recall you taking me to see a psychic one evening when I was seven years old and she told you something you didn't want to hear. I remember you getting up immediately from the chair and snapping at the psychic. Did the psychic mention that something like this would befall us?

"Fredy," I hear her whisper.

Startled, I stop breathing.

I see her reflection in the mirror. She extends her arm toward my image and beckons me to join her. "Fredy, please come in here and hug me. Don't be afraid. I'm so lonely, Fredy. I need you. You know I would never hurt you. The Devil wants us, but I won't let the Devil come near any of us. Please, come in here and hold me." Her bloodshot eyes gaze deep into my soul and tears cascade down her face.

I nudge the door open.

Smiling, she whispers, "Please, I need you more than ever, my handsome son."

I step forward into the bedroom and act as if I'm about to lie down next to her, then suddenly, I grab the door handle, jerk back into the hallway, and slam the door shut.

Wailing, she sobs, "Please, son! Don't leave me alone! Fredy, I'm so alone in here! No one understands me! Please, come back! Please!"

Standing still, I place my cheek against the door and wait there a few

seconds, conflicted about what I have just done. Struggling back tears, I swallow my sorrow and toss it into the tower, turn around, and return to Bianca's bedroom.

Like slaves in a maniacal holocaust, we lower our heads and silently trudge down the hallway. Chains of anxiety and unsettling fear wear us down as each heavy step feels as if it leads us to our untimely deaths. We proceed through the kitchen and disappear into the living room. Without a single word, I shove the brown sofa against the door.

Better to be safe than sorry.

Mom's depressing sobs drift across the deafening silence, filling up every corner, every pocket of this desolate, maddening house. Her uncontrollable sobs heave and unfold like a heavy sea, crashing and ricocheting into one another as misery anchors itself deeply into our hearts.

We sit there in silence.

We sit there in denial.

We sit there numbed, embraced in the blanket of our mother's agonizing tears of lamentation.

∞ CHAPTER III: DEVIL AT THE DOOR ∞

IT DIDN'T TAKE long before Bianca caved into Mom's demands that she not attend school. I also noticed Bianca withdrawing into her own world as everything around us fell apart. I wanted to be there for her, but I didn't know how.

"I noticed you hanging out with some girls the other day," I prod her. She puts on heavy eyeliner and stains her lips with crimson-red lipstick. Then she grabs a matching coloring pencil and etches it around her lips. Her blue shirt hangs loosely over her cleavage. She crunches her hair and sprays copious amounts of hairspray all over it.

"And?" She rolls her eyes dismissively.

"I think they're a bad influence on you," I say, biting my lip.

"You're not Dad, Fredy. Stop acting like him," she puts down the hairspray and trots over to the door. "In fact, you're invading my privacy right now."

She slams the door in my face.

"Whatever," I mutter beneath my breath as I creep down the hallway. I knew better than to argue with her. She can be very stubborn and I knew it would only be a losing battle trying to dissuade her from hanging out with her new friends.

Entering the kitchen, I open a drawer and pull out a long white candle. A few seconds later, in the bathroom, I close the door and from my back pocket unfold a gay magazine. Opening it, I stare transfixed at the two men giving each other blow jobs. Undoing my pants, I lower my underwear and masturbate. Licking the candle, I imagine myself giving head to the guy in the magazine. I close my eyes, bend over, and slowly press the candle into my butt. I moan in pleasure as it enters me. Penetrating myself with the candle in one hand, and masturbating myself with the other, I ask myself why I have never experimented before. Ejaculating onto the toilet seat, I jerk and hear a snap as the candle breaks in half.

"Great," I whisper as half of the candle falls onto the floor.

Grabbing the string, I pull at it until the remainder of the candle pops out.

"Maybe I should try a pickle next time?" I say out loud.

Suddenly, Eduardo is knocking at the door, yelling, "Hey fag, what are you doing in there? I need the bathroom! Fuck, man!"

My face flushes in embarrassment as I look at the broken candle pieces in my hand.

"Just wait a minute, I'm…ah… Taking a dump!"

Turning the faucet on, I toss the candle pieces into the trash can and unravel toilet paper over the pieces. I wash my hands and smell my fingers to make sure no trace of odor is left behind.

"Hurry up in there, you fucker!" Eduardo yells.

"Geesh!" I open the door and step out into the hallway.

He glares at me with his glazed eyes. I can tell immediately he is on

something. He doesn't smell like marijuana, but I am certain it is a drug. A Mongolian tail protrudes from the back of his head, making him look oddly fascinating. A red bandana hangs from his back pocket. A white tank top is visible beneath his gang-affiliated red shirt.

"Sick, bro! Were you just wanking it?"

"What?! N-n-no!" I gasp and stammer as I stare into his eyes.

"Then what's this white goop all over the toilet seat?" he asks me, pointing at my ejaculation.

"Uh…soap?" I feign stupidity as I grab a towel and quickly wipe it off.

I can't believe I forgot to wipe the toilet seat clean.

Eduardo raises an eyebrow and fixes his eyes on me. It's indiscernible what he is thinking at that moment, but I am certain he can smell a fib when I tell him a fib. That is what always annoyed me about him. He could see right through me, even the whitest lie.

"There! It's clean," I say in a high-pitched voice.

I dash out of there, hoping that whatever drug Eduardo is on will make him forget this whole incident.

∞

LATER THAT EVENING, Dad asks me why Bianca and Alexander haven't been going to school.

"After you leave to work, Mom gets up and holds them hostage. She threatens them. She also threatens me, but you know me, I go no matter what the consequences."

"Damn it." Dad opens the refrigerator and cracks open a beer. "The administration is calling me, asking me why your sister and brother haven't been attending any classes. I need you to make sure they go to school on time."

I carefully reply, "I don't think Bianca cares for school anymore. The other day, she wouldn't wake up, so I threw cold water all over her. She

screamed profanities at me. And Mom keeps a close eye on Alexander. She threatens to hurt him if I even dare try to make him go to school. I figured it's best to let him stay here with Bianca as opposed to having him get hurt in the process."

Downing the whole beer, he opens another one, looks up at me, and says, "Well, thank you for doing what you can do. You've always been a good son."

Uncomfortable at the sudden display of affection, I mumble, "No worries." I'm not used to Dad being affectionate. He's always been distant. It's not that he's cold-hearted, no; he just never expresses his emotions to any of us.

I slip out of the kitchen, into the living room, and close the door.

Glancing at my watch, I see it tick toward eight in the evening. *Queer as Folk* comes on in a few minutes. That show has been my guilty pleasure. All I have been desiring lately is the flesh of another guy. I am so frustrated, and yet terrified because I have no idea what it feels like to be with another guy my age. Most of my friends have already lost their virginity with girls, but I still hold onto mine because I want to experience my very first time with a guy.

I am not sure how Dad would take it if I told him that the girls I have been dating were just for show. I didn't enjoy breaking up with them, nor did I feel happy about using them, but how can anyone blame me. This is how society has raised me. When a girl initiates wanting to do more than kiss, I immediately break up with her. And I move on, quickly. There is always another girl who is willing to date me. It doesn't surprise me that my nickname at school is the "heart-breaker."

Watching the show, I wonder what it would be like to be out of the closet. What would it be like to have supporting parents and friends? What is gay culture like? Is it truly the way it is portrayed on television? Is gay culture

only about sex?

"Brian, I love you," Justin *moans as Brian pounds his ass.*

"Shh, don't talk." Brian leans over and kisses him fiercely on the lips.

"Brian…"

"What the hell are you watching?!" Dad demands to know, entering the room.

"It's a gay show I'm watching because there is a girl in class who loves this show. Jenni Gebhart… You've met Jenni, right? Well…uh… She keeps talking about this show and I thought if I started watching it, I could…uh…get closer to her. Dad, I think I'm in love with this girl. I'd do anything to find a common link. I want to impress her by saying that I've been watching this show." The lie rushes out of my mouth in seconds.

Thank goodness for acting classes.

His eyes narrow to slits as he sits down on the couch.

He doesn't say a single word.

Brian and Justin continue having sex on the screen and my face turns beet red. I can't believe I'm watching this with Dad. I eye him nervously and notice his eyes darken by the second.

"So, Jenni's into this crap?"

Exasperated, I say, "Well, it is the twentieth-first century, Dad." I play it cool, making sure my voice sounds as deep as usual.

"She better be worth it because that's satanic shit you're watching there."

Stiffening, I ignore him.

"Don't tell me you're one of *los otros*!" he spits out.

Rolling my eyes, I snap back, "I am not one of *the others*."

Dad has never called homosexuals by their name; he thinks of them as an *other*, something outside of our society. If he only knew, I wonder what he would do. I just want to come out of the closet right here, right now. I want to blurt out, "You're right, damn it! I am one of *los otros*!"

and see his reaction. But I wouldn't dare do that.

After several minutes of silence, Dad rises from the couch and leaves without saying another word. The door closes behind him. In the kitchen, I hear the refrigerator door slam shut and the sound of another beer bottle opening.

Knock.

Knock.

Knock.

Pressing Mute on the remote control, I get up from the couch, walk to the door, and peer into the keyhole.

"Who is it?" I ask, flipping the light switch.

The patio remains in darkness.

Opening the door, I gaze outside and see no one.

With a shrug, I close the door, settle back into the couch, and shudder as a chill creeps down my back. A memory of my grandfather when I was a little child registers in the corners of my mind...

"There's an old saying in Mexico," my grandfather whispers as I wrap my arms around him and place my head on his chest.

"What kind of saying?"

"If you hear knocking at the door and no one's there, don't open it."

"Why?" I ask him.

"Because the Devil will be let in."

BAM!

"Fuck me!" I jump several feet off the couch as the door slams open. The wind howls into the living room. With a quick leap, I slam the door shut and bolt it.

I swear I locked the door a few seconds ago.

Turning the lights on, I briskly glance outside the window.

And I slip into another childhood memory...

It's a cold November night in Newark, California.

Sitting between Eduardo and Bianca, I pop a tape of Richie Rich's newest single, "Let's Ride," into the stereo as I excitedly say, "You guys have to listen to this."

"Something about the West Coast..." Richie Rich's voice croons into the room.

Suddenly, a hoarse, low, guttural voice, "Frrrreeeddddy."

"Shhh... Don't tell nobody," Richie Rich whispers.

Jamming the Off button, I stare wide-eyed at Eduardo and Bianca to see if they heard exactly what I heard. Their expressions mirror my horror as we all cry out, leap from our spots on the floor, and race to the door. One second, Bianca is ahead of us, then in the next, she is tossed to the side as I push her out of my way.

"Dad! Dad!" Eduardo and I cry.

From behind, we hear Bianca's shrill, horrified screams.

"What's going on!?" He sits up in alarm as the three of us jump into his arms.

"We heard someone call Fredy's name out," Eduardo says. He shudders.

"Someone called my name out," I whimper, pushing my weight into his arms.

Eduardo, Bianca, and I fight for his muscular arms, burying ourselves in his armpits.

"Ambrocio, I'm telling you, it must be the Devil," Mom whispers frantically as she gets up and holds herself.

"Not in front of the children, Alma. They're terrified." Dad's voice drops an octave.

In the kitchen, the phone rings.

Tensing, we direct our gaze to the dark kitchen.

"You have to be kidding me," Dad whispers.

He slowly gets up and waits to see if the phone continues to ring.

Ring.

Ring.

Ring.

"Well—go answer it," Mom says meekly.

We all look at Dad as he exits the living room into the kitchen.

"Hello. Yes, everything's fine. No, no one made any phone calls. It's impossible, we

just moved into this apartment a week ago and the phone line is not connected yet. I see. No, no, there is no need to send anyone over. Thank you, bye."

Dad enters with a puzzled expression on his face.

"Who was that?" Mom inquires.

"The police. They say a girl called crying for help."

Ring.

Ring.

Ring.

Eduardo, Bianca, and I grab each other tightly as Dad calmly returns to the phone.

"Hello. I'm telling you, everything is fine here. The phone is not working, so it's impossible that anyone made a phone call. Service won't be on for another few days. I see. Uh, yes. Thank you."

He hangs up the phone and reenters the room.

This time, his face is even more troubled. "The police dispatched someone to come over. They keep insisting a girl is calling for help from this line."

An hour later, after a police officer has stopped by and spoken to Dad, we huddle in the living room and sleep together.

It was the first of many nights when we slept together...

Reminiscing about that night in 1996, I retreat to the long beige couch against the wall facing the window and the television in the corner. Lying down, I wrap my arms around myself and ruminate about how it was then that I noticed Mom acting more unusual than normal. Mom stayed up late every night, became more withdrawn, ate less, and didn't care to attend any social functions. I recall having just enrolled in sixth grade and Mom telling my siblings and me that it would be okay if we chose to remain home instead of attending school. Eduardo and Bianca happily obliged and took advantage of Mom's request. Furthermore, after the incident in the bedroom with my siblings, Mom's anxiety peaked, leading her to chain-smoke. It's as if the very notion of the Devil being in our presence evoked a need to assuage her

nerves, but the more convinced she became that the Devil was around the corner, the more she justified her actions and the accusations she made toward Dad by ensuring that our pious family believed her.

And yet, thinking back on that night, it dawns on me that if Mom is sane and rationally right, maybe the Devil has been among us since that night in Newark. He obviously desires our souls—or maybe just my own.

I close my eyes, shudder, and descend into a deep restless sleep.

∞

LAUGHING, I SWING into the air. The sandbox is desolate. A translucent veil of blue skies stretch perpetually across the horizon. Turning my face upward toward the sun, I imagine flying into the light.

"Fredy," an ominous dark voice desecrates the sandbox.

My hands clench the silver bars tight as the swing set propels me higher and higher, swaying faster and faster.

Suddenly, the sky above me turns into liquid fire and a vein of darkness rapidly shrouds the grounds beneath me.

"I've finally found you. Your soul is mine," the nefarious voice booms around me.

"MOM! MOM!" I scream.

In the distance I hear Mom's voice, a faraway whisper carrying the notes of her promise: I'll protect you, my son...

I stir awake and find myself paralyzed.

Mom sits on top of me.

"In the name of the Father, the Son, and the Holy Spirit, I will save his soul," Mom whispers.

My heart drops at the sight of a long butcher knife moving erratically in the sign of the crucifix inches away from my face. The knife hovers menacingly over me as Mom's face spasms in fury.

"Lucifer! Fuck you! I will not let you have my son's soul! I am doing God's bidding, you hear me!"

From the corner of my eye, I notice a flame held high and wonder if it is an angel summoned to take me into the afterlife. Is this the light at the end of the tunnel that people speak about on their deathbeds? No, it is merely a white votive candle wavering in Mom's other hand. It flickers above me, casting demonic shadows to dance around us as sweat breaks across my forehead. Paralyzed, I tell myself it must all be a horrible nightmare. Maybe if I pinch myself I will wake up.

"As you say, God! I will save Fredy's soul!" Her voice rises in pitch.

She extends her arm back and with a lunge shoves the butcher knife straight toward my face.

Reacting instinctively, I toss her off of me and scream bloody murder. The candle whiffs out and covers us in darkness. Dread ripples down my spine as death's shadow kisses me briefly. I'm terrified of getting up from the couch. My eyes dart back and forth, trying to see where she fell. In the background, I hear irregular breathing, but I can't tell whom it's coming from. Then I see a slight movement in the middle of the room as she flings her arm about the floor, searching for the knife.

"I won't let you stop me, Lucifer! God's will is stronger! I have to save Fredy's soul! I won't let you! I won't let you take my son's soul!" she gasps, suddenly arching her back and stealthily standing up, preparing to attack.

The lights flood the living room.

Dad enters, and before he can demand to know what the commotion is, like a tigress Mom pounces, plunges the knife into his back, and gashes him.

Dark crimson blood splatters across the white walls.

Bianca dashes in her pajamas, her eyes wild with terror as she quickly processes everything.

"Stop it! Stop it!" Bianca screams, throwing herself onto Mom and yanking Mom's hair.

With a monstrous blow, Mom smacks Bianca on the side of her face and

hurls her across the room. Bianca hits the wall with a sickening thud and crumples like a porcelain doll on the floor.

"The Devil's here! Lucifer is here! You're with him, Ambrocio, aren't you?! I won't let you take my son's soul! Fucking bastard!" Mom screams horridly, as if possessed by the Devil himself. Her face winces in deep pain and her eyes flash emptily about the room.

Alexander appears at the doorway, blanching.

Mom sees Alexander and rushes at him. Alexander throws his fragile hands into the air as she demonically drives the knife at him.

Dad tackles her onto the floor, knocking the bloody knife out of her hands.

"Fredy!" he yells, wrestling with Mom, "Call the police! Call the police!"

Shaking, I snap out of denial, run to the phone, and dial 911. Like a rabid dog, Mom struggles and convulses on the floor.

"We have an emergency," I cry hysterically into the phone, "Please, hurry! My mother's gone crazy!"

∞ CHAPTER IV: LOST INNOCENCE ∞

"YOU'RE SEVENTEEN YEARS old, a sophomore excelling in all your studies, maintaining leadership positions in school politics, taking on the role of your father at home, doing community theater, and taking on extra-curricular activities." Ms. Cunningham pauses. "And yet, with all that you've been through, none of it has affected your external environment. Why is that? Why is it that in spite of these traumatic incidents, you continue to excel? What drives you, Fredy?"

Her beautiful blue eyes pry at me through her black-rimmed eyeglasses, which further accentuate her wisdom and heighten the perception of making her look younger than her age. Shoulder-length golden hair drops in waves, giving her face an angelic glow. For being in her early thirties, my therapist easily passes as someone in her twenties.

Lying on the couch, I close my eyes and ponder the question. What drives me? What makes me keep going when all I desire is to sink into the arms of darkness, to allow this tide of emptiness to consume me, to commit

suicide and get it all over with? Why do I insist on continuing to be perfect rather than giving into the rage and losing myself to a life of drugs, as Eduardo has done? How easy it sounds to lose myself in my family's insanity, yet, something deep inside propels me forward, tells me that beneath this chaos there is beauty waiting to be revealed.

But how much longer must I suffer before I get there?

"I tell myself there are people who have it worse than me," I answer softly, "and what drives me is the belief that I need to look toward tomorrow. After all, tomorrow will be a better day."

"Do you know what minimizing is, Fredy?"

I shake my head.

"It's when you make your problems seem less serious than what they truly are. What has happened to you is extremely traumatic. How have you been coping with your mother's mental illness and your brother's physical abuse?"

"I lock them away in my two towers." My chest constricts as a wave of feelings threatens to overcome me.

"What's happening right now?" she asks, leaning forward in her chair.

"I feel like the world is closing in on me. I feel like I am on the precipice of a cliff and I am perilously close to slipping into madness. As if my life can collapse at any moment, but I can't let that happen. No, I won't let it happen."

"And when you feel this state of being, do you feel like the world is spinning and you're short of breath?"

"Yes."

"What you're experiencing right now, Fredy, is a high dose of anxiety. Anxiety occurs when your body has suffered a traumatic episode and doesn't know how to fully acknowledge the magnitude of that experience. And when this happens, it can lead to panic attacks. How many times does this happen

to you?"

"Ever since my m-m-mom almost succeeded in killing me, I feel at any moment that the world will kill me. I will be walking down the hallway to a classroom when suddenly I feel everything tilting and I feel short of breath. Most of the time I am able to push myself past it, but sometimes, sometimes I feel like I will faint, but I'm terrified of what will happen to me if I faint. I'm afraid to faint, afraid to black out."

"Take deep breaths. Take as many as you need," Ms. Cunningham assuages me.

I take several huge long breaths.

"I feel slightly better."

"What I am hearing is that you are experiencing panic attacks. I am going to prescribe Paxil to you. Take one pill a day and it will ease the anxiety you are currently experiencing." Ms. Cunningham scribbles on her prescription pad.

"Will I have to be on Paxil for the rest of my life?"

"No, every month I will check on you and when the time comes I will gradually lessen the dosage until you no longer need it."

∞

A WEEK LATER, Ms. Cunningham sits in her chair, gazing at me with inquisitive eyes.

"Last week, you mentioned that you cope with all that has taken place by locking it away in a tower. Can you elaborate for me?"

"There are two towers in my head. They are circular, with multiple padlocked rooms, bolted with chains. Every time something horrible happens to me, I throw that incident into one of the towers and lock it away. For good. I think this is why I am able to function so well at school and in my community. I lock everything away."

"What happens if the towers collapse?"

"They won't."

"Do you ever consider unlocking any of those rooms to see what lies behind?"

Shifting on her couch, I picture the two towers. One of them is bulging and pulsating with fire and blood. A fire burns at the base of it. Behind it, another tower awaits many more dark secrets. So many dark secrets.

"No, I'm afraid to open any of those doors."

"What are you afraid of, Fredy?"

"I'm terrified that if I open one of those doors, every single door will unlock, causing my towers to collapse."

"What if I told you that nothing horrible will happen if they collapse?"

"I won't allow myself to go there," I reply sharply.

"It's a very powerful defense mechanism you created for yourself, Fredy, and we don't need to go there now, but when you do, know that you will be fine. Nothing horrible will happen if you allow yourself to come face to face with whatever lies behind those locked doors."

"I haven't told you everything that has happened to me," I whisper as a wave of grief overcomes me. My eyes become moist as I choke on my own words. Why do I feel like this suddenly? Where did this emotion come from? I never allow myself to feel these kinds of emotions, especially in front of other people.

Ms. Cunningham lurches forward in her chair, causing her rosy perfume to waft into my nostrils.

"Here, take a tissue, Fredy. What do you mean, you haven't told me everything?" Ms. Cunningham asks softly in a very soothing voice. "Did your mom or brother do anything else that you haven't mentioned?"

"No, it has nothing to do with Mom or Eduardo," I whisper.

Heaving, I break down crying.

"That's good, Fredy. Just allow yourself to feel your grief. Whenever

you're ready, Fredy. Whenever you're ready."

Sniffling and maintaining composure, I tell her about the red-brick house...

<div align="center">∞</div>

I LOCK THE door behind me as my cousin Rodrigo rummages through his father's cabinets, tossing aside clothes in pursuit of our little secret. We're just children—young and innocent—at the tender age of eleven. Rodrigo and I are inseparable. We do everything together.

Rodrigo lives with his father in a one-story red-brick house on the wrong side of the tracks in Union City. Three red steps lead to his red patio. A rusty rocking chair, covered in cobwebs and dust, settles against the backdrop of the patio, with empty beer bottles scattered across the soiled floor.

A mariachi band plays Spanish music in the background.

In the kitchen, beer bottles slam against a stained table as men cajole each other and bet money in a game of cards. My younger cousins pound through the living room, chasing one another, screaming and laughing as they run past the main bedroom, out to the unkempt patio, and down those three red steps.

"Did you find it?" I ask quietly.

A smirk spreads across Rodrigo's face.

Blood rushes to my head.

"Here it is." Whispering with excitement, Rodrigo clutches a videocassette. Shutting his father's drawer, he moves to the television and turns it on. He is the same height as me, about five feet four, but his eyes are a lighter brown. His muscles protrude from his shirt as he inserts the video into the VCR.

"Do you know where Fredy is?" I hear Mom ask outside the bedroom.

"Alma, just leave him here. He's with Rodrigo," my aunt replies.

Rodrigo places his hand on my thigh. Startled, I turn my head to see a mischievous smile curl on his lips. The blood pounds louder in my ears as I notice his hand slowly rubbing himself inside his jeans. Nodding, I give a goofy smile and turn my attention to the

television screen. How many times have Rodrigo and I gotten together to watch porn? Countless times. It is our secret—a form of brotherhood, sharing intimate moments, jerking off together as if it were an everyday thing among boys.

A naked brunette waits patiently on the couch, smacking her lips and massaging her Pamela Anderson breasts. Her sultry stare captivates me more than anything. She seems to be a siren, hooking in any man who makes eye contact with her. It is this look that I imitate whenever I make eye contact with my fifth-grade teacher, hoping to get his attention. It's gross watching a straight couple have sex. I truly don't get the same fascination my cousin gets when the camera zooms in on the vagina. My fixation is on the man's genitalia.

Suddenly, the camera zooms in on a blonde, blue-eyed, Caucasian man dressed in a doctor's outfit. A look of surprise appears across his face as he comes upon the naked patient. Moving in on her, he unzips his khaki pants and whips out his penis. The camera cuts to the woman's eyes growing wide with excitement.

My eyes slit into anger, frustration aching across my tingling body.

"I don't understand why they just don't show more of his penis," I complain.

"Who cares? It's the woman we want to stare at," Rodrigo whispers condescendingly. "Why, are you gay?"

"No, just wondering." I quickly abandon it, feigning interest in the woman's breasts as the guy goes down on her.

Unable to maintain interest in the film, I close my eyes and imagine the doctor operating on me. It's useless. I hear Rodrigo whacking off in the background.

A yawn escapes my mouth.

"I'm so tired, I think I'm going to pass out here," I whisper.

"Go ahead and pass out," he mumbles.

Falling into a deep sleep, I think about my cousin's comment. Why, are you gay? Why didn't I admit to him that yes! I am gay! But what would happen to our friendship? The whole time we watched porn, I kept wishing it was me being operated on instead of that whore. I crave kissing a boy instead of pretending to like kissing girls. I just don't see what all the commotion is about girls. Rodrigo and my friends talk about all these girls who are

in the process of maturing and all I can think about is wanting to see how we mature.

It isn't fair!

I desire the touch of another man's hand. I yearn for the intimacy of two male bodies colliding. I want it so badly that I silently wish for it to happen. I don't care how, but I just want to feel a man's penis.

If I only knew that whatever I want, I always get.

I wake up with a start.

Pitch darkness blankets the bedroom except for bright red lights from an alarm clock blaring out two in the morning. The red-brick house sleeps in deathly silence while, outside, the wind picks up and howls ferociously. It angrily smacks against the windowpane, whips branches against the side of the house, and screams into the roof shingles. Heaviness settles deeply across the bedroom, and sweet innocence seeps out through the cracks of the window.

And it is this heaviness that takes my breath away as a hand slides underneath my shirt, glides down my back, and gently slips into my white Hanes underwear.

Intoxicated wafts of alcohol scent the air around me as hot breath flows like lava across my neck, scorching my skin with scarlet sin. My eyes glaze over with fear as a hand caresses my buttocks and slowly makes its way across my pubescent genitalia.

I squeeze my eyes shut.

Terror paralyzes me.

Please, don't let him know I'm awake. He can't know that I am awake. Flames of violation skyrocket up my spine like ice. Is this actually happening? I don't want to believe it. His hand grabs mine and I feel his penis in it. Is this what manhood feels like? It feels cylindrical, intricately aligned ribs on top of one another. His hand directs mine, up and down, up and down, in endless motion as his warmth vibrates into my hand. Like a double-edged sword, I am torn between pleasure and pain.

His hand stops directing mine.

I freeze, not sure what to do.

Should I continue to masturbate him?

Or should I feign sleep?

He makes the choice for me.

He lifts my hand and places it back to my side. Then he slides my underwear off and gently massages my buttocks. My cheeks clench and unclench in his fingers. I want to let out a moan, release the pent-up tension of my tortured excitement, but it would expose our dark clandestine act. I do not know which is more frightening, opening my mouth to give voice to this event, or remaining in silence as he uses me as his inflatable doll.

Suddenly, scorching heat shoots up my spine.

A whimper escapes me and hot tears sting my eyes.

His hard cock penetrates me, slowly at first, then speeding up as he approaches the final act. His scrotum smacks against my inner thighs as he rams himself into me. His sweat caresses my back. He nails my innocence harder and harder, faster and faster, deeper and deeper, panting and groaning.

And like a smack of thunder, it hits me that this is not what I meant when I wanted to be with a man for the first time! It's not meant to be like this! Not my first time! No— my first time was meant to be with a guy my age, the tenderness and innocence of two young men who are deeply devoted to each other losing their virginity together. I want to scream out loud: STOP! STOP! I CAN WAIT!

But it is too late.

He pulls out, too quickly.

Grunting, he lets out a sigh and becomes still.

Then his hand jerks over my face and he forces his fingers into my mouth. He grinds my teeth shut, smearing a thick salty substance on my gums.

Then he pulls away, turns over, and passes out.

I stare in shock at the alarm clock.

Blood-stained numbers scream three in the morning.

Frozen for an hour, I finally pull the blanket aside, step out of my uncle's bed, and tiptoe into the bathroom. Closing the door, I snap the lights on. I glance into the mirror over the sink. My face is a pale, ashen mask. Bloodshot eyes stare back at me. I no longer see a boy, but a man with demons at bay. And these demons howl and gnaw my insides out as

the pain ricochets up and down my lower abdomen. Lifting the toilet seat up, I barely manage to sit down, the pain lacerating my insides. Grimacing, I hold tightly onto my stomach as putrid gas blows out. I shake my head in horror as the agony sharpens. Bringing my palms to my face, I hide it as I desperately fight back sobs.

For all I know, it seems as if time itself stops.

It seems like minutes, hours, days pass by as I remain there on the toilet in a fetal position. I can't go back into that bedroom—not the way I feel right now.

Wiping myself, I stand up and let out a gasp as my legs undo themselves and I fall onto the cold linoleum floor. Grabbing the toilet seat, I pull myself up. Reaching across the toilet seat to push the handle down, I glance into the bowl.

A stream of dark crimson blood ripples across the surface.

Now I understand completely the meaning of being deflowered.

<div align="center">∞</div>

"AND HOW OLD were you when this happened?" Ms. Cunningham whispers in shock as I imagine locking that memory away into the tower, abating my sadness.

"Eleven years old," I whisper hoarsely.

"Does anyone know?"

"No, no one knows. Except for you. You're the only one who knows." I grimace.

"And for how long has this been continuing?" Ms. Cunningham stares at me with an empty expression on her face. I can't tell what to make of it. What is she thinking?

"It only happened three times." I sink lower into the couch and close my eyes...

<div align="center">∞</div>

I CHOOSE TO return to the one-story red-brick house with its red steps that lead onto the red patio. Maybe I return out of guilt, or is it out of shame, or possibly the memory of being touched for the very first time. In a weird way, it's as if I yearn for my uncle's touch. I

yearn for him to molest me again and again.

After the first incident of our indiscretion, I would sit in my bathroom and masturbate to the sensation of his phallus in my hand. And just as soon as I ejaculated, I would break down crying because it's all so wrong. But if it's so wrong then why am I here again, in his bedroom, in his bed?

It's a bright Sunday morning.

I should be in church praying to Jesus, but instead, I am anticipating my uncle's tutelage. I frown as I ponder why he didn't just take me by force like the previous two occasions.

The bathroom door opens, revealing a naked man in his mid-thirties, belly hanging out, covered in ringlets of black hair. His troubled bloodshot eyes catch mine. He approaches my side of the bed. Butterflies knot in my stomach as I reach out and masturbate him. I stare at his penis, marveling at its atrocity and its beauty. What fascinates me even more is his scrotum; it's hairier than mine and his balls are huge.

"Do you like it?" he whispers down at me.

With disbelief, I thickly reply, "Yes, I like it."

It's the first time he's spoken to me throughout our sexual encounters.

He moans.

"Want to give me a blow job?" he looks down at me.

I nod, tensing up because I have never given a blow job before.

Getting over me, he flops onto the bed, lies down on his back, and holds his erect penis, motioning me to put my mouth around it. It has no particular taste as my mouth pulsates up and down around his luminous shaft. At the same time, he masturbates himself in unison to the rhythm of my mouth lapping up and down.

"That's right," he moans, "you're doing it good. Oh, fuck yeah."

I fondle his sac, imitating the blonde bimbo in the porn video I last saw with Rodrigo, and notice the soft ripples of layered skin. I grab his huge testicles in my palm and massage them.

Slap!

I yelp out, the sting reddening my face.

"Not like that! You need to suck it like a girl," he demands as his nostrils flare. A disgusting look crosses his face. He grabs my head and forces it back to his phallus. "That's not the way you're supposed to give head," he lectures me. "You have to put your lips over your teeth so that your teeth won't scrape my dick."

Another slap turns my skin bright red. Yanking myself from his grasp, I stumble off the bed and hover over him. I grab my white Hanes, slip into them, and slit my eyes into fiery orbs of anger.

"Get back into bed!" he growls in a threatening tone.

"No!" I retort defiantly. "You hit me! Twice! No one hits me and gets away with it!"

Pivoting around, I throw the door open and storm into the kitchen. My uncle's roommate is sitting at the dining table. His jaw drops, eyes widen in confusion, and he stammers something as I pull out a chair and sit down next to him. I cross my arms and glare at my uncle's bedroom.

My uncle appears at the doorway naked.

"Fredy! Get back in here, NOW!"

"No!"

My uncle notices his roommate, looks at me, then slams the door to his room.

"What's going on?" his roommate asks, baffled.

"You ask him." I shrug my shoulders.

Seething in anger, I promise myself I will never return to this house.

<center>∞</center>

"AND I KEPT my promise," I say, shivering on the couch.

"Do you realize what needs to happen, now that you've told me this?" Ms. Cunningham looks at me with a twinge of sadness, anger, and remorse.

"What?" I look at her quizzically.

"I have to inform your father. Due to the nature of what you just revealed to me and being that you're underage, I am required to—"

"No! You can't! No one can know! You promised! You promised

everything would be kept confidential!" I jump out of the couch and grab her wrist. "PLEASE!"

She glances down at my hand tightening around her wrist, then looks deep into my eyes for several seconds. I can see she is mulling over a decision that could affect the rest of my family's lives. If there is anything that would destroy my life it would be Ms. Cunningham telling my father. If he were ever to find out, I *would* jump off the bridge. Should I tell her what I am thinking right now? No, best to keep it a secret.

"Well, there is another possibility," Ms. Cunningham says, looking to the door as if unsure whether she should tell me what is in her head.

"I will do anything! Anything! But for the love of God, don't tell my father! Don't tell him! No one can know about this! No one!" I desperately plead as I let go of her wrist and sink softly into her sofa.

"You'll have to notify the police."

"What?" I look at her in horror.

"I have a confidential number you can use to report this incident. If you do that, then I won't tell your father."

I sit there numbed, petrified by the choice at hand.

If I don't call the police, my whole family finds out. Or I can report my uncle and suffer the consequences. Biting my lip, I fight back tears. This is all stupid! So stupid! Why did I have to open my mouth?!

"Do you ever think that if your uncle did this to you, he might be out there doing it to someone else? Don't you want to hold him accountable for what he did?" Ms. Cunningham asks me softly.

"I never considered that he could be doing it to anyone else."

"And your cousin, Rodrigo. Do you know if his father is molesting him as well?"

"No, I don't think so."

"I will leave it up to you whether you want to report him, or have me

report this information to your father. But if you choose to report your uncle, you will need to do it before you leave. I promise I will be right here for you. You have the strength, Fredy. Trust me, I know it is a difficult choice, but think about the lives you could possibly save."

"I'm scared," I whisper.

"It's okay to be scared," she says.

Sitting there, I notice the clock ticking away. We are ten minutes past my scheduled time slot. Outside, my father sits in his car waiting for me to come out. The thought of Ms. Cunningham telling him my darkest secret motivates me to get up and say, "I'll report him."

Stunned, Ms. Cunningham leans back in her chair as if I just whip-lashed her. I guess she wasn't expecting me to make that choice under such pressure. Getting up, she beckons me to follow her into another room. On the desk, I see a red telephone with its cord disappearing behind a potted plant. Picking up the phone, she dials a number from heart and hands it over to me.

"Ah, yes, hello? I am calling to—" I glance at Ms. Cunningham as the words get stuck in my throat. She smiles at me as if to say that she's not going to go back on her word. "—Uh, calling to report a molestation. Yes. I don't know if he's molesting anyone else. Six years ago. No, I won't tell you how old I am."

Hanging up the phone, I throw myself into Ms. Cunningham's arms.

Breaking down into sobs, I hold onto her tightly, wishing she never lets me go.

"I am so proud of you right now, Fredy Espinoza. So very proud of you."

∞

POPPING A PAXIL into my mouth, I close my eyes and listen to the silence around me. Dad tries to fix me dinner, but I inform him that I can't stomach eating. He retreats to his bedroom with Alexander. I can tell Dad is extremely

worried, because he hasn't opened a beer in a few days. One would think it would be the opposite, Dad binge-drinking to forget our family problems. But I can tell Bianca's been on his mind a lot.

Bianca ran away.

She's been gone for over a week now and hasn't phoned to let Dad know where she's gone. The house has been quiet since then. Another reason why Dad hasn't gone straight to the bottle is that Social Services has been coming around and threatening to take us away. Maybe Bianca ran away because she's afraid of being taken away from the only environment she knows.

And Eduardo hasn't been around either.

It's as if he just disappeared off the face of the planet. Eduardo and Victoria broke up. He can't control his anger and it has upset her parents so much that they forced him to end his relationship with her. Alicia tells me it's because he has become friends with a guy named Rudy who has been giving him more powerful drugs than weed and ecstasy. I've only done ecstasy a few times, but I won't allow myself to become dependent on any of it, mainly because of the way it affects Eduardo.

Eduardo becomes a monster on drugs.

I feel like I want to cry, or scream, or bang my head against the wall demanding why this is happening to us, but this little pill numbs all my emotions. Not only does the Paxil numb my emotions, but I no longer have nightmares about the Devil coming for my soul late at night. Who knew that I could allow myself to sleep in darkness?

Lying in bed, I pretend I am floating on the ocean and all I see is stars. My fingers linger at the edge of the water and I imagine sinking into its soothing abyss. And the stars fade as I forget having told Ms. Cunningham about being molested, Mom's desire to kill me, and my awakening sexuality.

No, in this black abyss I can fall asleep and never wake up.

I can pretend that I don't exist, that I am no one.

<p style="text-align:center">∞</p>

MY REPRESSED HOMOSEXUAL desire for men intensifies throughout the remaining time of my sophomore year. Paxil's ability to quiet all anxiety leads me to reconnect with my feelings for men. With Mom gone, Dad lost in work, Eduardo up to no good somewhere in the neighborhood, Bianca being AWOL, and Alexander being watched over by our grandmother, I find myself with ample time on my hands. At night, I log onto gay chat rooms and chat with guys from across the country. I don't dare meet anyone from Fremont, for fear of being caught, so chatting away until four in the morning suffices for now.

Trying out for the swimming team doesn't help make me forget my awakening sexual urges. Diving among my peers in their Speedos always keeps me distracted from focusing on my laps. I want to feel the flesh of someone my age. With all my friends losing their virginity to girls, I feel it's time for me to lose mine to a guy. But how do I go about it if I am the only gay guy on my whole campus?

If anything has kept me afloat, kept me from sinking deeper into depression, it is drama class. It's a paradox: I consider myself well known and popular, yet I feel like a complete outcast and an outsider. But in drama class, there is a freshman who captures my eye and makes me feel something beyond labels and the need to be accepted. For the longest time I have been able to distract myself from making eye contact with him, but lately, he has persistently and unwaveringly held my stare without backing down.

He isn't popular or someone I'd hang out with. Yet his being an outcast is exactly what draws me to him. It's Jacob Lee, Jenni Gebhart's best friend. Norwegian, with the most captivating and mysterious blue eyes, Jacob stares right through me every afternoon. He's tall, lanky, and awkward looking. I'm not usually attracted to lanky guys; I tend to fall head over heels for guys like

Casey Roberts, the hot muscular football senior in our drama class; but Jacob has a quality that Casey doesn't, and that's the ability to make me feel something deeper than looks.

I nonchalantly befriend Jacob and muster the courage to do an assignment with him for a class project. The more I hang out with him, the more I find myself at ease, laughing and falling for him. Jacob makes me forget about my therapy sessions with Ms. Cunningham, the ongoing troubles back at home, and the pressure of needing to be perfect.

One day, he invites me to his house to complete our drama class project.

"I am so excited about this film," Jacob says in a high-pitched voice.

"Yeah, me too," I reply with a deeper tone.

"Gosh, you have to tell me everything about you. I want to know what it feels like to be Fredy Espinoza." He smiles sheepishly as we enter his bedroom. He throws his backpack onto his bed and then motions me to drop mine on top of his.

"There isn't much to know about me, Jacob." I lower my gaze to the floor as his eyes pierce into mine, as if seeing something there that no one else sees.

"No, I bet there is a lot about you that no one knows. You're, like, so mysterious. All my friends think that, you know. Like, you act and behave as if you are hiding something." He casually picks up our script to the short based on *Double Indemnity* and pretends to glance through it.

"Ha!" I laugh nervously. "What makes you and your friends think I'm hiding anything?"

"You're a good actor, Fredy, but we all notice how you never talk about your family life. You have a lot of girlfriends, but you never commit to them. You keep yourself so busy that it's hard for you to ever go out with anyone." Jacob looks up from the script and smiles apologetically as if these observations might hurt me.

"It's hot in here," I mumble as I shift uncomfortably onto my other leg and pretend to look at the slasher film posters plastered over his walls. Am I that obvious? I need to put more effort into ensuring that I make it out of high school without anyone finding out any of my secrets.

"Would you like a glass of water? Wait right here, I'll be right back." He rushes out of the room without even waiting for a response.

In one corner of the room I see many videocassettes stacked on top of one another. Picking up one, I read the title, "*A Nightmare on Elm Street.*" I didn't realize Jacob loved horror films.

"Fredy?" Jacob's voice calls out from far away.

"Yes?"

"Can you come out here, please?" His high-pitched voice sounds breathy.

"Where are you?" I ask, stepping out of his room and walking into the kitchen.

"In here," his voice lingers in the air as I trace it to the garage.

"What are you doing in there?" I step into the garage and search for the light switch.

"Don't turn the light on." His voice drops an octave. "Do you trust me?"

"I-I do?"

"Just close your eyes."

"Okay." I close my eyes and wonder what the heck he is up to. I am not one for surprises and I just hope it's not a sick joke he's playing. After several seconds pass, I consider opening my eyes when suddenly I feel rough lips kissing me gingerly.

"Do you still trust me?" Jacob whispers as his hot breath flows against my chin.

"Yes," I whisper back. He kisses me harder.

So this is what it feels like to kiss another guy. His tongue intertwines with mine. It's more rough and sensual. All the girls I have kissed pale in comparison to this moment.

His hand touches my crotch and I instantly get a hard-on.

"Mmm," Jacob moans as he fumbles with my belt, undoes it, unzips my pants, and masturbates me. At first, I am frozen, but then I reach over and feel his erection tightly outlined in his denim jeans.

Jacob kisses me one more time before lowering his head and giving me my very first blow job by another guy. I squeeze my eyes shut and a pleasure unknown courses through my body as I realize Jacob can do whatever he wants with me.

Ejaculating into his mouth, I freak out.

"Oh, my God!" I push Jacob away from me.

"What's wrong?"

"Oh, my God! Oh, my God!" I quickly zip up my pants, rush into his bedroom, grab my backpack, and jet out before Jacob can get at me.

"Fredy, wait! Come back!" Jacob cries out in alarm, shocked by my reaction.

<p style="text-align:center">∞</p>

I ALWAYS COME back to Jacob.

At first, I always had the same reaction when he sucked me off and I ejaculated—a feeling of shame and guilt. But overtime, I recognized that it came from a place of deep denial about my homosexuality.

"Can I make love to you?" Jacob asks me one evening.

"Yes, but be gentle," I whisper as I throw my clothes off and jump onto his couch. Jacob follows suit. Jumping on top of me, he spits onto his seven-inch penis and begins to insert himself inside me. Grimacing, he stops and asks me if I'm okay. "Yes, keep going," I reply, holding onto his smooth elongated back. I let out a small whimper, and this causes Jacob to stop and

e. "I'm sorry," I say, "I don't think I can let you do me." I

ng him to look at me with disapproval.

"Maybe we can do it another time, Fredy. I love you." He pauses. "Will you be my boyfriend?"

The idea of Jacob being my first boyfriend frightens me. This has gone too far. What if everyone finds out at school? My reputation! But I've never had a boyfriend before and I want one.

"I will be your boyfriend on one condition: as long as no one ever finds out about us," I say, gazing into his blue eyes.

"I promise," he pinky-swears. He leans in and we kiss for over an hour.

Leaving Jacob's house, I get into my car, pick up my cell-phone and call him.

"Hey, Jacob." I bite my nails.

"Hey, Fredy, did you forget something? I can bring it to you if you're still outside." Jacob's breathy voice almost stops me in my tracks.

"No, I didn't forget anything. I'm breaking up with you."

"What?! But we've only been boyfriends for like an hour!"

"It's not you, it's me. I'm not ready to have a boyfriend. I'm not even out to anyone," I tell him, closing my eyes as I feel a migraine coming on.

"Then come out!"

"I can't come out, Jacob! And I just can't be your boyfriend—at least, not right now. I'm sorry."

"Does this mean you don't want to see me ever again?"

"I still want to see you."

Jacob Lee becomes my closest ally, confidante, and best friend.

I confide in him everything, every secret, from my mother's attempt to kill me to Eduardo's drug usage and how he's been caught getting Alexander high several more times, from Bianca dropping out of high school and never being home to Dad begging me to keep everything a secret because, as he

says, "This is the family's business and no one has the right to know what is happening behind our closed doors!" Jacob promises me he'd never tell anyone about any of my secrets.

In many ways, Jacob keeps me afloat when I choose to run for the position of Associative Student Body vice president in my junior year of high school—an ambitious race, since only seniors hold those positions overseeing and leading the whole student body. And, of course, I win.

I need to keep myself busy, keep everyone's attention away from the truth, thereby allowing me to hide behind an illusion of perfection. How can anyone question the traumatic events occurring in my own life when all my external manifestations point otherwise?

∞ CHAPTER V: HIS DARKEST SIN ∞

MOM ALWAYS RETURNS from the mental institution. After going through a psychotic episode and being locked away for an interim of time, she always returns looking healthy and sane. To everyone else, she passes for a shy middle-aged woman who keeps to herself.

But it is an illusion.

I witness Mom walking among us like a zombie. Whatever drugs she takes, they make her feel nothing. From anorexia to ballooning up, gaining an extra hundred pounds, she is constantly eating. If she isn't eating, she's chain-smoking. I never hear her speak, and then only to whisper feebly that she loves us before retreating to her bedroom, locking herself in, and falling into a deep sleep. Mom does express an emotion when the nurse stops by to make her weekly routine. Mom will break into a smile and chitchat away while the nurse injects her with the medication. Sometimes, when I happen to catch Mom unawares with the nurse, I am taken back to a memory of when I was a little boy...

"Mijo, rise and shine, handsome! Breakfast is on the table! Now, hurry along and remember to take your bath!" I jump out of bed and race into the kitchen.

Grabbing my bowl of cereal, I creep up to the bedroom and gaze in on her.

She sits in her boudoir, facing a mirror, humming to herself as she brushes her long silky black hair, then smiles as she applies red lipstick to her lips. She's so beautiful with her honey milk skin, her stunning cheekbones, her sultry figure, her Chanel nightgown. Her cappuccino eyes are luminous. She reaches down to pick up an eyeliner pencil and then very leisurely takes her time as she puckers her lips and contently continues to hum.

As I stare at her I think how much I want to be just like her.

"Mijo, what are you doing?" She turns around and looks at me lovingly.

"Watching you," I say, smiling and chowing down on my cereal.

"Come in here." She beckons me into the bedroom.

Putting the bowl on the nightstand, she picks me up and I sit on her lap. A waft of Chanel perfume intoxicates my nose as I sigh and lower my head into her breasts. Squeezing her, I take in her perfume and feel at home.

Kissing the crown of my head, she hums and continues to apply powdered foundation to her face. Closing my eyes, I am about to nod off into sleep when she suddenly stops humming and raises my chin to her face. Blinking away sleep, I become captivated by her eyes.

"Mijo, I just want you to know this. No matter what happens, I will always love you. Never forget this, mijo, okay? Te amo mucho con todo mi vida." She kisses both of my cheeks. "No matter what happens, never forget how much I love you."

What happened to her between that moment and now? Why is it that she is diagnosed with paranoid schizophrenia? Based on my own research, it turns out that Mom has a chronic mental illness that has caused her to lose touch with reality; she has paranoid delusions accompanied by auditory and perceptual hallucinations. It is a lifelong illness without a cure. The best treatment for her is medication, but even then, there will always be the possibility of episodic remissions if she goes off her medication. Nothing

scares me more in life than the fear of being diagnosed with Mom's mental illness.

Ms. Cunningham relocated to an office in Southern California. She persuaded me to see another therapist in her place, but after one session, I freaked and dropped out of therapy. In the meantime, Paxil works for me until I choose to stop altogether.

As my junior year began, Eduardo officially initiated himself into the Norteño gang. Unbeknown to him, Bianca found solace with new girlfriends who had been initiated into Eduardo's rival gang, the Sureños. Turns out Bianca had been running away with girls from this gang, and now that she's back home, she has transformed from a shy sweet-natured girl to a feisty hard-edged fifteen-year-old.

The second Eduardo found out Bianca spent her time with his nemesis, explosive fights shook the very foundation of our house. Many nights I'd awaken to Eduardo's friends clashing with Bianca's as turf battles raged. Bodies would hurl against one another and girls would scream at the top of their lungs, "Sur for life! Sur for life, motherfuckers!" as rival counterparts shouted back, "Norte! Norte!"

And what do I do?

I sit back, make popcorn, and munch on it before dialing 911.

∞

MY EIGHTEENTH BIRTHDAY comes and goes without any excitement.

Jacob Lee and I stop hanging out as rumors circulate around school that we slept together. I furiously deny them and accuse Jacob of being a heinous liar. Furthermore, a few classmates have been spreading lies about Bianca for dropping out halfway through her freshman year, only to show up for two weeks of her sophomore year and drop out again. For many, Bianca was the girl who was supposed to follow in my footsteps, but when she reappeared, rumors flew left and right that she had been sent off to boarding school for

getting pregnant, for sleeping around too much, and for who knows what else. When Bianca chose to drop out of school, I kept my mouth shut. Yet Bianca's reemergence from obscurity has only shed more light on the backstage scenes of my life.

My peers are beginning to question what it is that I am hiding from everyone.

If they only knew. But fear has held me back from confiding in anyone. How can I be the school leader I purport to be if everything else in my life is going to hell?

<div align="center">∞</div>

"THE MOST MAGICAL place in the entire world is Disneyland! We're going to have so much fun this weekend, Alexander!" I kiss Alexander's head and kneel down to help him with his sneakers.

"Is Mommy coming with us?" Alexander's eyes wander past the hanging beads into the living room.

"No, she's staying here with Eduardo. It's just going to be you, Dad, Bianca, and me." I step back and look into his eyes.

"I don't want to go to school," Alexander says, folding his arms defiantly.

"Why? School is good for you, Alexander." I frown. "You get to learn about the world, learn how to be a big boy, and then one day go to a university and make something of yourself."

"I'm stupid," he says, looking down in shame.

"Hey, don't say that. You're not stupid."

"I am stupid!" Alexander gets up, runs to the wall, and bangs his head against it, "I'm stupid! I'm stupid! I'm stupid!"

"Alexander! Stop it!" I grab him and pull him into my arms. "You're smart! Why do you say this?"

"Eduardo tells me I'm stupid." Alexander's eyes water.

"Well, he's the stupid one, Alexander. Not you." I pick him up, carry him into the living room, and sit down on the couch with him.

"Please, don't make me go to school, Fredy. I hate school. I don't want to learn," Alexander pleads with me.

"What are you going to do?"

Alexander's eyes shift to the door as it smacks open and Eduardo stumbles in. He laughs loudly as his friend, Rudy, bursts in behind him. Their eyes are glazed over. Once they settle on me, mischievous grins break out on their faces.

"What's up, fag? Yo, my brother's a fucking fag!" Eduardo spits out to Rudy.

"Nah, man, are you fucking serious?" Rudy replies with a thick Mexican accent. His face is marked with acne scars and his shaved head is covered with a red bandanna.

"We're just leaving," I say, seething as I quickly get up and approach the door.

"Nah, you ain't going nowhere, fool." Eduardo steps toward me and pushes me hard. "I think you need a lesson, bro."

"Fuck you, Eduardo," I spit out as I regain my balance and brace myself in defense mode.

"What kind of lesson are you thinking?" Rudy chimes in as he and Eduardo slowly make their way to me.

"Let's beat the gay out of him," Eduardo snarls. They gang up on me and start throwing punches. "You fuckin' fag! Where's Dad to help you, huh? Fuckin' faggot!"

Punching back, I scream, "Stop it, you fucking assholes! What the fuck!" I force myself between them and try to run out of my room when suddenly Eduardo grabs me, throws me back into the room, and commences to kick me.

Eduardo lets out a squeal of laughter as I try to curl into a ball and protect my face and stomach from the blows.

From behind them, Mom appears with a broomstick. "Eduardo! Stop it right now! Leave Fredy alone!"

Eduardo stops kicking me and steps away.

"Isn't your mom supposed to be fucking sick in bed?" Rudy asks, nudging Eduardo.

Through the hanging beads, I see Mom glaring at Eduardo and his friend. Alexander has disappeared from the couch and the living room.

"Get out of the house, now! Leave, Eduardo!" Mom yells as she threateningly comes forward with the broom.

"Fuck!" Eduardo whispers beneath his breath. He spits out a noogie and it lands on my face. "You got lucky this time, faggot." He looks at Rudy and motions him to follow him out of the house.

Mom stands there for a few seconds staring at me.

"Alexander is in my bedroom, Fredy. He's not going to school today." Her words drop without any affect or intonation.

I nod my head as I struggle not to reveal any emotion on my face.

She turns to the kitchen and leaves.

Gasping, I let out a low sob as I get up and dash out of the house. Tears streaming down my face, I run past my car and down Peralta Boulevard. I run as fast as I can, hoping to shake off the physical and emotional pain. Not being able to see anymore, I duck behind a hedge along the side of a fence and break down crying. I remain there shaking and sobbing for half an hour, until I can't feel any more tears. Every interaction with Eduardo is like this. I hate him, loathe him, wish him death. I don't understand why he hates me so much! I've never done anything to him to make him hate me so!

I take my time returning home.

Not wanting to go back inside, I get into my car, turn on the radio, sit

there for a few minutes as I recompose myself. Then, starting the ignition, I reverse the car, pull out of the garage, and drive off to San Francisco for the day. No need for me to go to school looking like this. I deserve a day off.

<div align="center">∞</div>

THE TRIP TO Southern California ends too quickly. We spend it at Knott's Berry Farm, Six Flags, and Disneyland. I ditch Dad, Bianca, and Alexander at Six Flags needing to be by myself and pretend that my real family was out there somewhere among the crowd of anonymous people.

"Did you guys have fun?" Dad asks as we pull into the driveway of our house.

"Yes!" Alexander chirps. "I want to go again, and again, and again!"

Bianca rolls her eyes and steps out of the car. She grabs her luggage and trudges back into the house. Alexander follows behind closely. I look at Dad and tell him I'll get the rest of the luggage.

I think to myself about the outfits I will wear for the week. Should I wear the outfit I bought from Structure, or the one from Abercrombie & Fitch tomorrow? I definitely need to wear my new jeans I bought from Hollister in Anaheim.

Entering the house, I let out a sigh and think about plopping down on bed. In the kitchen, I notice Bianca's horrified face and Dad paralyzed with dread. Uncle Manuel, Mom's brother, stands at the table, solemnly saying something to them. He stops as he notices me eavesdropping with a curious look on my face.

"What happened this time?" I ask, letting out another sigh, expecting to hear Uncle Manuel reveal that Mom had another psychotic episode.

"Alma turned herself into the police," Uncle Manuel says.

"I don't get it. Why would she do that?" I furrow my brow.

"She persuaded Eduardo to have sex with her." The revelation falls on my ears like a rushing sea, churning me in its waves.

"No?!" I gasp.

"Yes, Alma called the police and told them she had sex with Eduardo."

"And Eduardo?"

"He's locked away at Santa Rita jail."

∞

BIANCA AND ALEXANDER stare at me with petrified glances as I sit next to Dad inside the courtroom. Child Protective Services took them away the day after we learned about Eduardo's sexual relationship with Mom. The judge's voice snaps my attention back to the hearing.

"Mr. Espinoza, what an accomplished student you are! Your record here reveals so many good things about you: student body vice president, a straight-A student, on the swimming team, involved in many hours of community service, playing the lead role of Lysander in Shakespeare's *A Midsummer Night's Dream*, working part-time at both Structure and Starbucks, and on top of that, involved in minor roles for your local community theater. Very impressive, Mr. Espinoza."

"Thank you, your Honor," I whisper.

"Due to the unfortunate events, Mr. Espinoza, your sister and brother have been placed in foster care, but seeing that you have just recently turned eighteen, I feel that the choice of foster care should be left up to you. Mr. Espinoza, if you choose to enter foster care, even if for a short period of time, you will be a ward of the state of California. Furthermore, you will be living with Mrs. Richardson."

"Mrs. Richardson, your honor?" I reply with surprise.

"Mrs. Richardson has kept tabs on you since seventh grade. As I understand, she mentioned to the court that there was something special about you since she first met you. Mrs. Richardson was impressed with how you chose to attend summer school and assist her as a volunteer in her office, even though you were at the top of your class. Is this true?"

"Yes, it is true, your Honor," I answer softly as I glance at Dad.

His work clothes are stained with tree sap. A painful broken smile lingers on his face as he musters the courage to stay strong before the judge. He wants Bianca and Alexander to return home, but the judge won't allow it.

"Mrs. Richardson specifically asked to become your guardian. She will ensure that your transition is effortless and she promises to ensure that you get into a top-notch university. Although her children attend Mission High School, you will be granted permission to remain at your home school. However, being that you are eighteen, Mr. Espinoza, I leave the choice to you."

I look at Dad.

His eyes plead, *Tell them you'll stay with me. Don't let the court take you away from me. Stay with me, Fredy. You're all I have left, my son.*

Dad doesn't have to say anything.

I read it in his eyes.

Biting my lip, I whisper, "I choose to stay with my father."

Concealing my emotions by tossing them into the towers in my head, I shake my head as I think about Bianca and Alexander. I wonder what they think of me for having the opportunity to stay at home, and I wonder what their new homes must be like. And what of Mrs. Richardson's home? She lives in a beautiful small version of a mansion in the Mission Hills. Am I sacrificing a connection that could ensure my entrance into a top-notch university by choosing Dad over her? After all, her sons got into good schools because of her. But I don't know what home is like outside my own home.

Will I ever get to know what home is meant to feel like?

∞

SITTING IN SILENCE, I pop a Paxil into my mouth as Dad drives us to Vallejo to pick up Bianca at her foster home. It will be the first time I've seen

her since she's been placed in foster care.

At the foster home Bianca gets into the car and we continue to drive in silence toward Concord. The three of us act as if it is another ordinary day. No one mentions anything about Eduardo, or Bianca's foster care family, or what it's like for me to live alone with just Dad in the house.

After picking up Alexander, we drive to a nearby park.

While Alexander and Dad play in the distance, I turn to Bianca and ask her what her new family is like.

"They're okay," she says, smiling. Her hand flutters to her hair and she twirls a strand in her fingers. "I've been going to school and getting straight B's."

"Wow, that's awesome, Bianca! I believe that you can do it. Before you know it, we'll all be back together again."

"Hopefully." Her smile breaks as she looks off to Dad and Alexander. "Dad told me Mom's pregnant, Fredy. He says that she's been pregnant for over three months now…before Eduardo raped her."

I sigh.

"Yeah, no one knows who the father is."

It's funny how before the separation we all lived in our own bubbles at home, pretending Mom wasn't crazy. Here we are now, after the separation, and I realize I had this mistaken belief that, if anything, it would bring us closer, but instead, it makes us play house. Is there such a thing as a functional family without dark secrets burning at the foundation? Why is it that none of us can communicate to one another the irrevocable harm and sadness that has befallen all of us? Why is it that we masquerade behind fake smiles when, in truth, we have a burning desire to find solace in one another's arms?

No, none of us will ever be the same again.

Forever, now, our family is fractured.

The day comes to an end.

As we drop Alexander off at his foster care home, he breaks down in sobs. Bianca and I refrain from losing emotional control as our nine-year-old brother holds tightly onto Dad. At the door, Alexander's foster mother calls out for him and gives us a pained expression. Dad picks Alexander up in a bear hug, walks him to his foster care mother, and puts him in her arms.

"It's okay, Alexander, we'll be back soon—before you know it," Bianca assuages him.

"Don't cry, Alexander. Be a good boy, okay?" I tell him, getting into the car. Bianca follows, closes the door, and rolls down the window. Dad kisses Alexander on the cheek before joining us.

"Daddy! Daddy! Please, I want to go with you! I want to go with you!" He struggles from his foster mother's grip and runs to the car, tears streaking down his baby face. "Daddy! Don't leave me here! Take me with you! Daddy! Take me with you!"

As we drive away, I wonder if Alexander understands that we are all in our own form of prison. Maybe in time, he will forget that any of this happened. Maybe it is a blessing in disguise that he is so young.

∞

BRICKS OF AIR consume the space between Dad and me in his black Ford truck as Linkin Park plays angrily in the background. Occasionally, I avert my cold eyes toward passing cars on the freeway.

I can't believe Dad is forcing me to see Eduardo at Santa Rita jail. Dad says that Eduardo has been asking about me and needing to see me. I want nothing to do with him. Is the pain Mom has caused me not enough—now this? What am I supposed to do when I see him? How can I look him in the eye when all I am thinking about is his darkest sin? And after all the physical abuse I endured because of him, now Eduardo has the audacity to ask me to see him? Now?! I guess karma does exist. I hope he rots in the cell he landed

himself in. It's his ticket to Hell and I'm glad he's in there; as crude as it sounds, he deserves to rot in jail for the rest of his life. That's his penance for all the hurt he's caused me.

"We're here," Dad says cheerfully, as if we're attending a sporting event.

"Great," I say, pasting a smile on my face.

Opening the door, I take a deep breath, step onto the pavement, and pray that I don't lose it. My stomach lurches and dives as we approach the entrance to the facility. A seed of hope germinates in my head. Where is this possibility of hope for Eduardo coming from? A memory hits me of Eduardo at five years old...

"Sit here," I say, helping him up on the washing machine. Blood spills onto the cement floor as I tie a sock around the gash on his foot. "I promise to come back for you, okay?" I stammer.

He looks at me with teary eyes. "You promise?"

"I promise."

I left him there and forgot about him.

Oh, that was years ago.

Two officers open the door and check us in.

"Put anything metallic in the bin," a heavyset officer says sternly.

I take off my belt and shoes, place them in the bin, and pass through the metal detector, continuing onto a waiting room. There, Dad and I sit down at an empty table as if we're attending a tea party.

Then I see him.

Eduardo Jose Espinoza.

He slowly staggers over to us.

A huge smile tries to mask the pain hidden in his eyes. Stringy black hair mats his face and neck. Stocky and muscular, he pulls me into a tight embrace. At first, I flinch and tighten up as he holds me. I don't think we've ever hugged this long. Finally, I release the tension and fiercely hug him back.

Funny how one second you can hate your vilest enemy and the next love him with tremendous respect.

"I'm glad you came, Fredy," Eduardo says into my ear. "Every time Dad comes, I tell him to bring you, but you never come."

"I've been busy with school, responsibilities, work," I reply quietly.

"Can you forgive me, bro?" he whispers.

His eyes search mine as a look of sorrow I have never witnessed before emanates from his eyes.

I stare at him, not answering.

He places his hand over mine and his eyes darken with shadows as he whispers more fervently, "Can you forgive me?"

I shift my eyes from Eduardo to Dad, whose eyes implore me, begging, *Forgive him, Fredy. He's your brother, please forgive him.*

"I don't know if I can forgive you, right now, Eduardo."

The words smack him across the face.

"There must be a way you can forgive me, bro! Please, forgive me, Fredy! I didn't mean for it to happen."

"Tell me how it went down," I ask him.

Eduardo looks at Dad and asks him, "Do you mind if Fredy and I walk outside?"

"I don't mind," Dad says softly. A faraway look haunts his eyes as if recalling a horror he wishes to forget.

I follow Eduardo outside.

It's a beautiful gorgeous sunny day. The sun is sweltering on my skin. Many young men dressed in white-and-blue uniforms stroll around the guarded vicinity.

"What happened that night?" I ask more fiercely.

"You guys left me. I couldn't believe you guys left me behind and didn't take me with you to Disneyland. It was totally fucked up that y'all left without

me. I wanted to go to Disneyland too, bro. I told you guys to wait. I told Victoria how fucked up it was that you guys left without me. I called Rudy up. He had some KJ on him. I never had that shit before, and I thought, what the fuck, I'll hit some up.

"I went over to his apartment. His mom was cool as fuck. We smoked some KJ. Do you know what KJ is?"

I shake my head no.

"It's a horse tranquilizer. You just shoot it up. It feels damn good. I didn't give a fuck anymore about you guys leaving me behind. That night, I went home. Mom's asleep in your bed, Fredy. I love Mom! I love her so much! I wanted to let her know how much I love her. I wanted to show her that I could never hurt her. She had to know that I was the only one in the family who truly loved her. No one else loves her but me!

"So, I walked over to her. I can still see her lying there in bed, like an angel. So beautiful in her blue shirt. I slipped underneath the covers. 'Mom.' She woke up and looked at me. 'I love you, Mom.' 'Eduardo, I love you too, mijo. You know I love you, right? I'd never hurt you,' she whispered, smiling at me. 'Mom, I love you,' I said over and over again looking at her, 'I love you, Mom. I'm sorry everyone left you here by yourself. I love you. I want to show you how much I love you.'

"I took my belt off, and then my pants, and her eyes widened in surprise as she looked at me with questioning eyes. She asked me what I'm doing and all I could say was, 'I want you to know how much I love you.' I threw myself on her. Fredy!" Eduardo's eyes darken with a pain I can't identify.

I look away from his pain.

"Please, understand it was the drug that made me do it. I just wanted Mom to know how much I loved her! And she screamed, 'Eduardo! Please! Stop! Mijo! Stop! Eduardo! No!' and I didn't know why she's yelling when all I wanted was for her to get that I love her. And while I forced myself into

her, I screamed at the top of my lungs, 'I love you, Mom! I love you! No one loves you like I do!' I don't know for how long I made love to her, Fredy. When I stopped, she was sobbing. I didn't understand why she was crying at first. And then it hit me.

"I raped her, Fredy," he says, looking at me with terror. "I raped her. I didn't know what to do. I was scared. I cried and asked for her forgiveness. She just stared at me through her sobs. I got off her, threw my pants on, and ran. I ran off to Victoria's house."

"So, it isn't true that Mom asked you to have sex with her," I say quietly as we walk around the enclosed courtyard.

"No, she told that to the police in order to protect me."

I stare at the sky.

It's so blue and enchantingly endless.

A hatred inside me boils, a rage that wants to be unleashed onto him, but just as it overcomes me, I hear a pain far worse than my own emanate from his voice. And it touches me. It makes me feel empathy for him. Glancing away from the sky, I make eye contact with Eduardo. His tears glisten beneath the fiery sun. I think I know what pain is, but the pain I see chained in his eyes is darker, more powerful, more frightening than my own.

"I forgive you," I whisper.

I don't know whether I mean it, but I feel obliged to say it. Who am I not to forgive? Something tells me I need to forgive him. That it is for the best.

He throws his bulky arms around me and sobs, simultaneously laughing and crying, "Thank you! Thank you, bro! I never meant for it to happen! Thank you so much!"

"It's okay, I forgive you," I say a final time.

∞

HOW MANY MORE skeletons must there be buried deep in my family's closet? Skeletons poisoned with venomous blood, drenched in deep-rooted hatred and misery, screaming and berating as they beat against our psyche's.

Back on campus, I set myself on an inquisition. I seek answers to why life is constructed as it is. Around me the world gradually collapses as I question my teachers and mentors, asking all of them a crucial question: What is your definition of happiness?

None of them are able to give me a definitive answer.

After a whole morning of inquiry, I settle down in English class.

Mr. Wallach sits behind his desk, his white hair disheveled in an outrageous style, his huge spectacles giving him a childish aspect, and his smile taking up most of his face (which only turns into a frown when any of us take a subject matter too seriously).

It slowly dawns on me that maybe all of life is a twisted joke. All the teachers who taught me, all the pastors who preached that the only truth in life is through Jesus Christ, all the social pretensions I inherited send me into a downward spiral of fixation on understanding the true essence of life. And yet, I quickly sniff out that no one has any idea about the true meaning of life. When prodded, people hold onto whatever paradigmatic belief system was passed down to them. I see immediately that people die for a truth that does not even exist.

All my peers are being fed shit and none of them can see it because they are too worried about questioning the very shit that's being fed to them.

I come to the conclusion that there is no God, that there is no meaning to life, and that everyone supports each other in this delusion of life, believing they have power over everything that happens to them. Who are we as human beings to believe we have the truth, when in reality, there is no truth?

As this realization hits me during a discussion of Thoreau, the world I

know of shatters. The towers I have maintained over the years to protect me in a bubble of illusion from the dark secrets that threatened to destroy me come crashing down. All the padlocked doors burst open and I'm overpowered with tidal waves of blood, screams, paralyzing fear.

"In *Civil Disobedience*, Thoreau tries to get across a crucial point," Mr. Wallach is saying. His words fade into an empty void as I become unconscious to my surroundings. Sitting there, I float out of my body as I lose touch with reality.

There is no meaning to life, I think. All my thoughts fall, disappear, become silent whispers in the wind.

"Mr. Wallach! Something is wrong with Fredy," Deauna Doremus cries out, pointing at me. She sits directly across from me on the opposite side of the classroom.

From far away, I hear Mr. Wallach's voice urgently calling my name. "Fredy! Fredy! Fredy!"

His voice cuts through the void, making me highly aware of everyone's attention focused intensely on me. Why is everyone staring at me so fixedly? I don't understand. Did I do something wrong? And why is Mr. Wallach getting up from his desk and approaching me?

"Is there something wrong?" I whisper as my throat constricts and I force a smile onto my face.

"Are you okay, Fredy?" Mr. Wallach asks me.

"Of course, everything is fine," I say despondently, then try to feign happiness as I repeat it again, "Yes, everything is just fine!"

"You're crying, Fredy," Deauna says meekly.

"No, I'm not." In shock, I look down at my notes and see tears spattering my notepad, smearing the ink into meaningless words. I touch my fingers to my face and trace the rivulets of tears that at first flow slowly, then hasten as I feel a dam breaking loose.

Getting up, I manage to mumble, "Excuse me" before dashing out of the classroom.

Running down the hallway, I disappear into the boy's restroom. I find a stall and close the door. I fall onto the floor, clutch my stomach, and break into wretched agonizing sobs.

My illusion of living the perfect life with the perfect world with the perfect grades shatters before my eyes. Every blemish, every imperfection, every lie springs forth, overwhelming me with a shrieking noise of soiled ugliness, of humiliating shame, and of perverse repulsion as it dawns on me I am no longer perfect.

Everything is a complete heinous lie.

There is no such thing as a happy family, of a picture-perfect life.

Sobbing, I pound my fists on the floor as thoughts of Bianca, Eduardo, and Alexander race through my head. I'm so sorry, Bianca. I'm sorry, Eduardo and Alexander. It's my entire fault that this has come down upon us. If I could have prevented it, we'd be a perfect family. We would have been the popular kids who would grow up to have it all; but I failed all of us. If only I had been a better brother, a better son, more perfect at being the best role model, everything would have turned out fine. If I had prayed more to God and if I had kept my promise of entering the monastery we would all have been saved from Satan's grasp.

But then, there is no God.

Like a tumultuous tidal wave slamming me into the lowest depths of my despair, it hits me that I will never be the same. Nothing will ever be the same now that Mom has been locked away for good in a mental institution, Eduardo had raped our mother, and Bianca and Alexander no longer live with me. I should be punished for all this. It's my entire fault somehow. I just know it.

I have never felt so alone in my life.

I place my tear-stricken face against the tiled floor.

There is a huge void in my life and I don't know how to make it go away. I can no longer maintain this lie of being perfect when the premise of it—that I come from an ordinary household—is so far from the truth.

And no one can be here for me in this time of need; I have no one to lean on because no one knows the real Fredy Espinoza. I feel so utterly alone. No one can share my agony, nor understand the horrible dark secrets that eat away at my heart.

∞ CHAPTER VI: DESCENT INTO MADNESS ∞

I CONSIDER DROPPING out of school and stop attending classes. Those few months fly by as summer quickly approaches. I am given the chance to travel to Australia; it is in Sydney that I quit taking Paxil and realize I am a homosexual.

And a joy I have not felt in a long time lifts me out of my depression as I return to my hometown.

I sit in Barnes and Noble, glancing through pictures of New York's twin towers. Wasn't it about a year ago that these two towers fell?

Suddenly, my attention is diverted by the most handsome twenty-two-year-old guy I have ever seen. His brown puppy eyes send waves of electricity in my direction as he passes me. He is masculine looking, with a fit body, and he stands five feet seven inches tall. His nose gives him away as being of Greek descent. His friend follows behind him. Putting down the before-and-after pictures of the fallen twin towers, I perk myself up in the chair and smile as wide as I can.

It works.

"Hey there, my name's Melancton Vassiliadis and this is my best friend, Roger Haryana. What's your name?" he asks me.

"Fredy Espinoza," I say, smiling seductively at Melancton.

"So, how old are you?"

"Eighteen."

I hold his gaze for what seems like eternity.

"I'm sorry, but you're too young, mister." Melancton turns and walks away.

"I think you're hot!" I quickly shout out after him.

That stops him in his tracks.

Turning around, he comes back and says, "You're a bold one. That turns me on a lot. What are you doing later tonight, mister?"

"Nothing," I smirk.

"Here." He writes his number on a piece of paper and hands it to me. "Call me later this evening. I'd like to take you out on a date."

Just like that, he leaves me begging for more.

And I know right there and then that Melancton Vassiliadis will be the first love of my life.

∞

MELANCTON PICKS ME up in a green jeep. He clasps my hand in his and asks if he can kiss me. I lean over and quickly kiss him, then look around to make sure no one notices. He pulls out of my driveway and the wind whips through my hair. Yes, Melancton Vassiliadis is the one. I know it. I feel it. I sense it.

"So, where are we going?"

"To Outback Steak House on Mowry Boulevard," he chuckles. "So, tell me more about you."

"What do you want to know?"

"Everything." He winks at me and squeezes my hand.

"But then where will the mystery be?" I laugh as he whips through traffic, maneuvers quickly through small gaps, and speeds down the roads.

"I feel like you will always be a mystery to me," Melancton chuckles.

"Well, I'm a senior at Washington High School. I just came back from Australia a few weeks ago and I accepted the fact that I am gay." I look away and my eyes become distant for a second as I fight back memories of my recent past.

"Wow! I graduated from Washington High School several years ago. What were you doing in Australia? And how did you accept your sexuality? Are you out to your family?"

"Oh, I was chosen to be a student ambassador for the People to People Student Ambassador Program. A group of students across the states get chosen for this program. We traveled around the country for three weeks: Sidney, Alice Springs, Uluru, Cairns, Great Barrier Reef, and the outback. It was definitely a transformative event. In Sidney I walked down Oxford Street, entered my first gay store, and felt an intense moment of joy as it dawned on me I no longer need to be in denial about my sexuality. And no, I'm not out to my family—not out to anyone except Jacob Lee."

"Who's Jacob Lee?" He asks, glancing over at me.

"He's the first person I knew to be like me, gay. He's a junior now. I can introduce you to him one of these days if our date goes well tonight," I curl my lips into a smile as I wonder what our first date will be like. "So, tell me how old you are, Melancton."

"Twenty-two years old, mister. I have a feeling it will be an amazing date, Fredy," he squeezes my hand again, more gently.

"If you say so, Melancton," I whisper, squeezing his hand back.

Later that night, Melancton fucks me six times. After we eat a delicious dinner at the Outback, he drives us into San Francisco and rents a room at

the Travelodge on the corner of Market and Valencia. He pounds my ass on the bed, then on the floor, then against the wall, then on top of the bathroom counter, and finally in the shower. Like rabbits, I lose myself in Melancton.

He makes me forget about the recent events of my life.

∞

THE REASON WHY I choose to come out to my senior class is due to Melancton. I worked tediously on my first English project: a paper bag plastered with magazine photos expressing who I am supposed to be. But since I am an overachiever, I cut the paper bag down to its parts, then sewed it back together along the edges and plastered a projection of myself onto others on the outside, with my authentic self on the inside of the bag.

"As you can see, the outside of the paper expresses an illusion of who I am. But the truth is, I am none of that," I nervously explain to my class as I undo the strings along the edges of the paper bag, "In fact, the truth of who I am lies within the hidden space of this bag. As you can see, these cartoon figures of the Simpsons from a Halloween episode represent my family." I carefully unveil one side of the paper bag, plastered with doors opening on Bart, Homer, Marge, Maggie, and Lisa all covered in blood with Marge holding onto a butcher knife.

"I don't come from a perfect family; in fact, my mother is paranoid schizophrenic and the reason why I stopped attending the remainder of my junior year is because I had a breakdown. I am still dealing with the ramifications of my mother's mental illness.

"And for those of you who have always questioned my sexuality and have called me gay behind my back, well, it's true." I unveil the opposite side of the bag, plastered with pictures of hot Abercrombie & Fitch men dressed in nothing but underwear. "In the middle of these hot men is my boyfriend, Melancton Vassiliadis. I met him over the summer after returning from Australia."

The room is enveloped in silence until suddenly a classmate raises her hand and chirps out, "I need to use the restroom." As she exits, all my classmates slowly stand up and clap. One by one, my classmates approach me and shake my hand. A few of the guys say, "I never thought you were gay."

And for the first time in my life I feel free, as my classmates accept me for who I am. The worst of my fears never materialized; none of them made me feel horrible for coming to terms with my sexuality. The teacher breaks into a quiet sob and hugs me fiercely as she whispers, "I feel so blessed that you chose to come out in my class, Fredy Espinoza!"

Exiting her class, it dawns on me that the news has spread like wildfire within a single class period. Suddenly I am bombarded with students asking me if it's true that I came out of the closet.

One freshmen girl in particular grabs me and demands, "Fredy, it can't be true! It can't be! I'm the president of the Fredy Espinoza Club! What am I supposed to tell our members about you? You have to go back into the closet for us!" Her eyes brim with tears.

I stare at her in shock.

Who is this girl? There's a club about me? I had no idea.

I stare at her in silence.

Letting out a shriek of frustration, she dashes off into the crowd of students.

<div align="center">∞</div>

THREE MONTHS AFTER coming out to my friends, Melancton breaks up with me. He expresses to me that I have a communication problem, that it's hard for him to consistently force feelings out of me, and that it feels awkward for him to date someone who's still in high school. But the truth comes out when I confront Jacob Lee at his going-away party.

"Tell me the truth, Jacob," I glare into his eyes as we both sit outside his patio. Inside, pop music shakes the foundation as people chatter left and

right, laugh giddily, and drink strong alcoholic beverages.

"I don't know what it is you want from me, Fredy," Jacob pleads, diverting his attention toward the sky.

"I know about you and Melancton Vassiliadis," I whisper.

Jacob lets out a huge sigh.

"Who told you?"

"It doesn't matter who told me. Just admit it, Jacob." My voice thickens as Jacob hesitates and then looks directly into my glistening eyes.

"It's true, Fredy. Melancton cheated on you with me, but I only did it because I love you, Fredy! He used both of us, can't you see that?!" Jacob chugs a huge gulp of alcohol from his cup.

"I want to hear it from your own mouth how it happened."

"The first time it happened, I stopped by his house to see if I could borrow a porn video. Melancton invited me in. I asked him where you were, and he said you were at Starbucks, working. He puts in a porn video and we both watch it. That's when he makes a move on me and we both end up having sex. And we continued to have sex many more times behind your back. He told me never to say anything to you. I'm sorry, Fredy. I'm so sorry." He leans over and kisses me on the lips.

Pushing him back, I burst into sobs.

"Damn you, Jacob Lee!"

Dashing into the house, I search for Tyrone Botelho. Tyrone is a good-looking Native American-African-Brazilian guy whom I befriended through the musical *Footloose*. Whereas I never went into foster care, he spent his whole life in it. After having met him, I knew he was interested in men and it was only a matter of time before he entrusted me with his secret.

Now I consider him like a brother.

"Tyrone, it's true! Jacob just admitted it me! Get me out of here, now!"

Tyrone exits with me from the party.

Calling Melancton, I confront him with the truth.

"He told me with his own mouth, Melancton!" I cry.

"He's lying to you, Fredy! I would never cheat on you," Melancton tells me.

"I don't know who to believe any longer," I moan as his words sink in.

Maybe Jacob lied to me; maybe the rumors are all lies. Melancton would never lie to me. He's the love of my life. Jacob is in love with me, so of course it makes sense that he would create a lie to destroy my relationship with the love of my life. I so desperately want to believe Melancton.

"Fredy, after all that you've been through, do you think I'd go behind your back and do this to you?" Melancton whispers into the phone.

"No, I don't think so." I hiccup.

"Then don't believe anything Jacob has told you."

"Melancton Vassiliadis, I love you. God, I love you so much. If you say you didn't cheat on me, then I believe you. I choose to believe you," I whisper in resignation.

<p style="text-align:center">∞</p>

A FEW WEEKS later, I attend a dinner party at Melancton's.

Driving into Newark, I pull over to the house he's watching over for the weekend. Not having Melancton in my life feels like half of me is missing. Maybe tonight at this dinner party we will get back together.

"Melancton!" I laugh as he pulls me into a tight bear hug at his doorstep. His brown eyes sparkle with excitement and his muscles bulge out of his fitted tee. It feels good to be back in his powerful arms.

"How have you been doing, mister?" Melancton asks, undoing his arms and stepping aside.

"Very good! I'm excited for tonight," I reply with a sheepish smile.

From behind, voices carry over to us.

"Roger! You just made it in time," Melancton calls out as he steps out

and gives him a bear hug, "Look who I invited!"

Roger notices me at the doorstep. His facial expression turns into surprise and shock as he gives Melancton an inquisitive look. Behind Roger, a handsome guy in his mid-twenties appears, briefly says hello to me, and jumps into Melancton's arms.

"Roger, will you keep Fredy company? My boy and I got some stuff to do together," Melancton says, giggling. He gives me a twisted smile, rushes past me, and disappears into the bathroom with the guy.

"I'm so confused, Roger." I look at him, at a loss. "I thought we were going on a double date."

"I'm confused too, Fredy. I swear I had no idea Melancton invited you," Roger replies, his eyes widening as loud laughter suddenly emanates from the bathroom.

I can't believe Melancton would do this to me. Why would he do this to me? What have I ever done to him to deserve this? Why do I choose to keep getting hurt by the man I consider to be my soul mate?

"I need to sit down for a second, Roger," I whisper.

Walking past the bathroom, I hear moans. Entering a dark bedroom, I lie down on a bed as knots of acid incinerate my heart. Fighting back tears, I look at Roger as he lies down next to me.

"I'm so sorry about this, Fredy. Melancton met this guy at Great America and they've been seeing each other since then."

Roger wipes my tears away, leans in, and kisses me.

His lips barely brush mine before I gasp and shove him off the bed.

"What the hell, Roger? What did you do that for?"

"To see if you were truly over Melancton." Roger gets up and steps into the hallway, "I'm sorry. I shouldn't have done that. Crap. I shouldn't have pulled that on you, Fredy."

"I'm so confused and hurt, Roger. I... I have to go. I can't stay here.

Tell Melancton that I left and tell him to be safe. I still care deeply about him and no matter what he does, I will always love him."

∞

THAT NIGHT IS the first of many when I fall asleep sobbing into my pillow. And every morning, I force myself to wake up and make it another day. I have never felt so used in my life. All the times that Melancton told me he loved me, was that a lie? And Jacob, how could he do this to me?

Staring at myself in the mirror, I whisper, "If all I am is a piece of meat to men, then so be it."

Getting dressed, I make my way into the bedroom and blankly stare around me.

Today, at nineteen years old, on June 13th, 2003, I graduate from Washington High School. And yet I feel no joy. If anything, an emptiness eats away at my soul.

Four years of my life gone.

And all I desire is to disappear.

Inside, a rancid coal of self-hatred catches fire as I find myself hating being Fredy Espinoza. There is no point to being alive. Yet I can't commit suicide. I don't have the courage to do that.

No, there must be a way of eradicating my being without physically killing myself.

∞

BECOMING THE ROLE only gets easier as time passes.

As Mark Anthony in the hit musical *A Chorus Line*, I am the youngest dancer in the show and I have to recount to my priest the time I thought I had gonorrhea. It is a role I live for and I easily lose myself in as acting becomes easier for me now that I am twenty years old. Tonight's opening night, spring 2004. I will step onto that stage and forget who I am, taking on a different persona, a different way of being, a new life altogether. Indeed, there

is nothing like going on stage, becoming one with the character, and reawakening to the adoration of the audience. I feel at my most alive on stage. I don't just pretend; I become the character. Through Mark Anthony and the various roles I have played onstage, I am able to dive into my emotions and set loose what keeps me up late at night. The stage is my therapy. I find myself in shock when I return to the life that I call my own.

With Mom out of the picture, Dad falls in love with another woman, Edith, whisks her away to Las Vegas, and marries her in a chapel. Now I have a stepmother, a stepbrother, and two stepsisters. I barely notice they are ever around.

"Is it okay if I drive the truck to the theater?" I ask Dad as I step onto the patio.

"Yeah, sounds okay with me." He smiles.

Edith strolls beside him. She is smaller than me and pudgy with very distinctive facial features. Her brown eyes are round like a doll's and her dark red hair falls to her shoulders. Edith tries hard to be my mother, but my own pain and loneliness stops me from creating a deeper bond with her.

With the three of us in the truck, I put the key in the ignition and take deep breaths to calm my anxiety.

"Are you okay, Fredy?" Edith's voice is laced with concern.

Dad looks over at me.

I nod and force a smile. "Just excited about tonight. Will you guys be there?"

"We're not sure yet," Dad replies, leans forward to turn on Spanish music.

The drive to the theater feels longer than usual.

"Remember that one night when you walked in on me watching a gay show on television?" I prod him.

"Yes," he answers.

"Well, I'm one of *los otros*," I confess.

He laughs. "You're kidding, right? You almost had me there, my first son being *un otro*. I forget how good an actor you are." He glances at me.

Steering the truck along the lane, I frown and repeat, "I'm one of *los otros*."

Edith looks over at my father and then at me and asks, "What do you mean by *los otros*?"

"Yes, tell her what you define as *los otros*," I say coolly.

"Fredy's saying he's a homosexual. Isn't my son an extremely talented actor?"

"And even though I am no longer with him, I'm still in love with Melancton Vassiliadis. You've met him before. He'd come over and pick me up. And you thought he was just my friend all along."

"Ambrocio, I don't think Fredy is acting," Edith says, placing her hand on his knee. She looks up at me. "Right, Fredy?"

"Edith is right, Dad. I'm gay. I've always known I was gay and I can no longer live a lie."

For the rest of the drive to the theater at Irvington High School, no one moves. I am glad to be driving because it keeps me distracted from seeing Dad's face. Who knows how he would have reacted if he had been the one behind the steering wheel. Would he have crashed? Had a heart attack? Kicked me out of the truck onto the curb?

"I hope to see you both at the show tonight," I glance over at Dad and Edith as I pull into the parking lot, park the truck, and open the door.

His face hardens and tears roll down his scruffy cheeks.

Edith merely looks away while massaging his knee with her palm.

He doesn't even glance at me as I step out of the truck and close the door.

∞

LATER THAT NIGHT, I scamper down the driveway, slip past my car, and briskly walk through the warm air toward the entrance of the house. I keep thinking about Dad. He didn't react the way I thought he would have. To be honest, I expected a spectacle, the kind where you hear the news anchorman on NBC reporting a car crash due to a father-and-son dispute. Instead, Dad remained quiet. I don't know which reaction would have been worse.

"What the…?"

I come upon all my belongings stacked on the porch. Ringing the doorbell, I can see my journals poking out of my backpack. My heart races as I tell myself this is a cruel joke from my stepbrother. I pound on the door, frantically pressing the doorbell, hearing it chime throughout the house manically.

Suddenly, the door opens a crack and through the slit of the doorway I make out Dad's glaring brown eyes. He spits out in disgust, "No son of mine is gay! Burn in Hell for all eternity!"

Slam.

Taken aback, I pound at the door.

"Dad! Open the door! Please! I have nowhere to go!" I shout as the porch light flickers out and darkness envelops me. "Dad! You can't do this! You can't do this to me! All that I have done for you! For the family! I chose you in court! I chose you over a future that the Richardson's could have offered me!"

Holding back tears of frustration and anger, I pick up my backpack stacked with journals, the bags of clothes, and slowly take them to the car. Passing the window, I peer into the house and only see the absence of light.

To hell with you, Dad! Of all your children, I was the perfect one! I attained straight A's, I made sure Eduardo, Bianca, and Alexander were taken care of when Mom was sick, I accomplished graduating on time, and I never

got seduced into the world of gangs and drugs! After all I have done for you, this is your choice. And this is how you repay me.

I will never forget this moment.

I slam the door shut and sit in the car, numbed.

What am I going to do?

Think of something... Think of something... Think of something.

I start the engine, pull out of the driveway, and drive aimlessly. I drive in silence as it slowly sinks in that I have just been disowned. A huge black hole of agonizing pain rips open inside my chest.

I find myself driving through my old neighborhood in Newark. I drive down Newark Boulevard and glance tearfully at the apartment complex with all its memories. Turning onto Ardenwood Boulevard, I finally break into gut-wrenching sobs as this black hole consumes me.

Blasting Linkin Park, I recklessly press the accelerator to the floor and speed down the boulevard.

"WHY?! WHY?! WHY?! WHY?! WHY?! WHY?!" I scream at the top of my lungs, pounding the steering wheel. I should just end my life here right now! I should have ended it a long time ago when I had the chance!

"I DON'T CARE! I JUST DON'T CARE ANYMORE!" I cry over the music.

I feel my heart explode in my chest and bright lights flood my vision. Startled, I slow down and shut the radio off. For a brief second, I think it's lightning, but I crane my head to look into the dark sky and only see a vast blanket of stars.

Settling into quiet sobs, I shake my head and focus on driving.

Pulling into Union City Landing, an outside shopping center and local hangout spot for many teenagers, I park in a spot as far away as I can find from the entrance of Walmart.

"I can't fucking believe this," I whisper, dropping the seat and stretching

myself out.

For the first time in my life, I am homeless.

An orphan.

∞

THREE WEEKS LATER, Tyrone says, "Okay, Fredy. Something is going on, or else you wouldn't have all your clothes in your car."

"My dad kicked me out of the house and disowned me."

"What?! Why?! How?! Why didn't you tell me?!" His jaw drops.

"I don't want to be a nuisance or a hindrance to anyone. These are my problems and I am used to dealing with them on my own, Tyrone. I came out to him the night of our opening performance of *A Chorus Line*. That night, he kicked me out and I've been sleeping in my car since then. It's actually nice," I smile, trying to think of a joke.

Tyrone looks at me aghast.

"You should have told me, Fredy!"

"Seriously, it's not bad, and I'm saving money on rent, and I just take my showers at the gym before I head into work at Starbucks."

"Does anyone else know about this?"

"No."

"I can't believe your dad kicked you out." Tyrone sits down on his bed.

"Yeah, I can't believe it either," I look down, searching for a distraction as tears well up in my eyes.

"How about this? I will ask Trudy if you can be my roommate. You can stay here until you find your own place?"

Tyrone always has answers to everything. It's a quality I admire in my new best friend. Whenever there is a problem, he always knows how to jump on top of it and get it solved. How many times has he been there for me now? I must be a horrible friend, always coming to him with my problems.

"No, it's okay, Tyrone. I'm fine living on my own. I just have to save up

a few more paychecks and see if I can somehow manage to get my own studio."

"Wait right here," he says, getting up from the bed and exiting the room.

Looking around his room, I see that it is quite small. Trudy was Tyrone's foster mom when he was growing up; now she's his landlady. Trudy and her husband converted the garage into a bedroom. The walls are bare and the door connects to a small hallway that stores a washer and dryer. It also connects to the kitchen which leads into the main house. On Tyrone's dresser a television is playing *Cats, The Musical.*

I walk over to the television and turn up the volume.

"Daylight, I must wait for the sunrise, I must think of a new life, and I mustn't give in. When the dawn comes, tonight will be a memory too, and a new day will begin..."

"Hey, Fredy, I just asked Trudy if you can move in and she said she's cool with it." Tyrone pounces into the room with a huge smile on his face.

"Tyrone! I just told you I can fend on my own." I step back, upset.

"Fredy, you don't always have to pretend that you're strong. I'm here for you."

"Thank you," I say. Just then, Trudy rushes into the room, looks me up and down, and throws her arms around me. Her gray hair bounces in ringlets of curls and her gigantic glasses slant over her nose.

"You poor—poor child! Tyrone just told me everything that happened to you! Here, come here, now. I am going to give you a tour of the house. Now, come along, come!" She pulls me through the small hallway into the kitchen, Tyrone following behind. Embarrassed, I nod my head as she points out the kitchen, the living room, the bathroom, and her bedroom. She introduces me to her cats and to her foster son, Marcus.

"Now, remember, if you need to use the bathroom at night, you have to be quiet. I'm very sensitive to sounds, so please don't take any showers late at night. If you need anything else, just ask me, or ask Tyrone and he can relay

your needs to me. Oh, I think we have an extra bed somewhere, so we'll put in another bed for you inside Tyrone's room."

∞

"SO IS IT true that you can communicate with the dead?" Tyrone asks me as I lie in my bed and close my eyes.

"Yes, I've done a few séances and dabbled in magic," I reveal nonchalantly, turning to face the window. A sliver of moonlight pierces the dark bedroom.

"I've always been interested in accessing the part of myself that has a direct line to the other side," Tyrone confesses.

"It's quite simple, really," I say, smiling to myself. "In fact, we can do a séance tomorrow evening. I can teach you how to open yourself up and harness your psychic abilities."

"How did you find out you had these abilities?"

"Well, as a little boy strange things always happened to me."

"Like what?"

"This one time, when I was, like, ten years old, I was living in Mountain View. One night, something very horrible happened, but I can't remember it. I knew it had to do with the spiritual side. I just remember trembling in the living room, praying to the brightest star in the sky, and begging for my parents to arrive soon. And in my hand, I was clutching a knife."

"Why were you holding a knife?"

"Something happened in my bedroom, something unfathomable, and I just remember that *it* wanted me. Something wanted me." With a sigh, I roll over and glance toward Tyrone, who is lying on his back on his bed. "That's when I started having recurring nightmares of the playground in my apartment complex. I am swinging high into the sky, swinging higher and higher, when suddenly from behind me dark thundering clouds creep up on me. And I hear this awful devilish voice behind my ear, saying, 'You can't

hide from me forever. Wherever you run, your soul will be mine.' Then I met Joe. I remember the first time I met him; I was swimming in the pool. Getting out, I made eye contact with this handsome older Caucasian guy. And he stared at me, stared right through me, as if knowing something I didn't."

"Wait, how old were you again?"

"About ten years old. He introduced me to his stepdaughter, Rachel. She was only two years older than me. Rachel became my first girlfriend and a few weeks later Joe surprised us with a ceremony. He had purchased a beautiful white gown for Rachel and a tuxedo for me. Before I know it, we're both walking down the hallway toward him and he married us."

"He what?" Tyrone asks incredulously.

"Yeah, he married us. That night, Rachel told me everything, how Joe was a witch and she was a changeling. She told me how on nights of the full moon she would lock herself in the bathroom because she would change into a hawk. A few nights after the ceremony, Joe invited me over to stay the night. He said it was a very special night. I don't really remember much of that night, but I do recall Joe saying, 'You're a very special boy, Fredy. I knew the minute I saw you that you have very powerful gifts. After tonight, you will be part of our family—you will be initiated into a long succession of witches. But you have to promise me, promise me that you will never tell anyone.' I promised. I drank something and passed out. I recall hearing faraway chanting, drums beating, the sound of a hawk, and cold skin against mine as I opened my eyes and saw Joe lying there next to me, naked. I... I don't think anything happened between us because I didn't feel any pain or anything like that."

"Then what happened?" Tyrone inquires.

"Well, a few weeks later, I confided to Rachel how much it had excited me to have Joe sleep next to me naked. Rachel told Joe, and I was never allowed near them anymore. And since then, I have always found myself able

to access that part of me that to most humans is shut off."

"Do you think that maybe the reason your mom is crazy is that she, too, has powerful gifts, but maybe for her, she didn't understand how to control them?" Tyrone whispers, inhaling sharply as if he can't believe he has just asked me that.

"I wonder about that sometimes. Is my mother truly crazy? Or did her gifts become a curse? I don't know. But I do know that she dabbled in magic too. She always seemed to know something before it happened. Something frightened her, obviously, but what, I do not know. I just remember out of nowhere she started taking us to see psychics for answers. When the psychics couldn't give her the answers she wanted, she found God. And just like that, we were forced to attend church every day. The Bible was rammed into us at a young age. Maybe, maybe I have her gifts, but if I do, I hope they don't destroy me as they have destroyed her."

"Do you visit your mother at the mental institution?"

"No, I don't have the strength to see her. I am still reeling from what she did, Tyrone. I don't know if I will ever find it in myself to see her again."

"Bianca and Alexander?"

"I don't want to talk about them, Tyrone," I whisper thickly as I resist being pulled into the arms of sorrow.

<p style="text-align:center">∞</p>

SITTING QUIETLY OUTSIDE Starbucks at the Fremont Shopping Center, I sip coffee and relax as soothing music wafts onto the patio. Warm air caresses my tanned golden-bronzed skin.

Tyrone appears with a guy and they sit down at my table.

"Fredy! This is Cliff, my new boyfriend," Tyrone gushes.

"Nice to meet you, Cliff," I say, shaking his hand.

Chills crawl up my neck as I look piercingly into his eyes.

The three of us decide to move inside the coffee shop.

Tyrone takes a seat next to me and Cliff sits directly across from me.

I can't help but notice a shift of energy around us. Having accumulated enough awareness of knowing when I am in danger, I sit straight up and prick my ears.

"Cliff, stop it. It's useless what you're doing," I say.

"And what is it that I am doing, Fredy?" Cliff replies nonchalantly.

"You can't *read* me, and you will never be able to," I say icily.

"What do you mean he's reading you, Fredy?" Tyrone flusters in confusion.

"Yes, Cliff, why don't you explain to him what you're doing?"

"I'm looking into Fredy's soul to see if he has any gifts and what those gifts signify," Cliff answers unabashedly.

"Oh." Tyrone looks away from Cliff and toward me.

Suddenly, Cliff gives me a piercing look and whispers, "I challenge you."

"I accept."

Our eyes lock.

Exhaling, I quickly fall into a trance state, a state of nothingness in which I allow myself to channel in other spirits. Right now, I only feel one other energy in my domain: Cliff's. The atmosphere of Starbucks disappears around us and a mist envelops Cliff and me. Like a white stallion, I charge my energy at his crown chakra. It explodes against his black energy that dives at me. This continues fiercely until my energy hooks onto his and pulls at his essence to come out of his body.

Cliff pulls back from the table with a gasp and sounds of the environment come crashing back into reality.

"Wow, where did you learn to be so strong?" Cliff says with excitement.

"I am stronger than anyone can ever imagine," I reply.

"What just happened between you guys? I kept trying to break off your locked stare, but neither of you budged," Tyrone says. "And what do you

mean by what you just said, Fredy?"

"Let Cliff explain everything. It's time for me to leave." And with that, I exit.

Retreating to our bedroom at home, I fall into a deep, impenetrable sleep.

I awake with a startled gasp as the sensation of a bucket of ice water splashing over me causes me to fly off the bed, dash across the room, and grab my cell-phone. Quickly jumping back into bed, I let out a moan; how can it be that my body thinks it just awakened from a deep coma?

The phone vibrates incessantly. Dialing my voice mail, I hear Tyrone's excited voice. "Fredy! I hope you're awake! It's urgent I speak to you! See you soon."

Letting out an exasperated sigh, I sink into the bed and close my eyes.

The door slams wide open and Tyrone lunges in.

Screaming, I cry, "Oh my God! Are you trying to give me a heart attack?"

"You're up! I need to talk to you." He closes the door and races to my bedside.

"I know, I just got your message."

"Really? I sent that message two hours ago," Tyrone says with bewilderment.

"Hmm, I just got it."

"I need you to do a séance for me tonight. It's urgent. Cliff said that the only way I can attain my gifts is for you to contact the other side. He told me there is a spirit on the other side who needs to speak to me and who will tell me what to do."

Dark tremors crawl down my spine as shadowy forebodings flutter across my heart.

"I can't," I whisper.

"What? Why?" Tyrone demands as he moves closer to me.

"I won't do a séance, Tyrone. Only evil will come out of this." I shrink away from him.

"Please! I beg you. Nothing evil will happen! Just communicate with the spirit so I can find out how to do what you do," he pleads, getting on his knees.

"No, I'm sorry."

"Fredy, please."

"No."

"Fredy, I'm like your brother. I would do it for you."

"Fine." I cave in to his appeal to family.

Getting up from the bed, I sit down on the floor and cross my legs. I beckon Tyrone to sit across from me in the same position.

"When I exhale, you inhale. Imagine yourself becoming one with me. It can occur within seconds, and it can last up to several minutes. Got it?"

"Got it," he says with excitement.

"From the East to the West, the North to the South, may a circle of protection shield us from any dark intentions. I open myself up to you," I whisper as I exhale and slowly descend into a meditative trance. In my third eye chakra, I see a beautiful woman dressed in white. I communicate to Tyrone what she expresses to me to tell him. "Your mother is the key to your gifts, Tyrone. She knows the way for you to attain them. This is all I can tell you. I must go. And please, do not continue with this séance. There is too much dark energy closing in. Be careful."

I snap out of it and look into Tyrone's eyes.

"That can't be it. I need to continue talking to her," Tyrone persists. "What does she mean by my mother is the key to my gifts? Fredy, let's keep doing the séance. Get in touch with her again—I have many more questions for her."

"I don't know if any good will come of this, but here goes. This time, let's keep our eyes open. And once again, imagine that you are becoming one with me."

I exhale.

In and out.

In and out.

I let go of my mind completely and feel my energy propelled toward Tyrone's. For a split second, I sense us becoming one being as suddenly my third eye opens to let forth a spirit into my space.

An inexplicable horror consumes my mind as a shadow blacker than night, blacker than coal, blacker than death, appears from the left side of my vision. It slowly descends into the room. Out of nowhere, a fly buzzes around us in a circular motion. It buzzes faster and faster as the shadow creeps closer and closer, bigger and bigger.

Snap.

The fly shoots into my ear, the shadow disintegrates completely, and a malevolent force of energy knocks us apart.

"What the hell was that?" Tyrone cries out. "Why did you push me?"

"I didn't push you, Tyrone."

"What just happened?"

"I don't know, but whatever happened, it's not good. It's not good at all." I look around the room for the fly, but it has disappeared.

"Did you hear the fly buzzing around us?"

"I heard something buzzing, but I don't see it anywhere," Tyrone replies. Giving me a weird look, he grabs his duffel bag, throws in a few clothes, and says, "I'm staying over at my friend's house tonight."

Tyrone exits, leaving me alone.

I descend onto the bed and fall into a lethargic sleep.

∞

DAZED AND CONFUSED, I awaken to sweat damp on my skin.

In the shower, I stand for several minutes letting the hot water splash on me. Finishing, I pat my face dry and then drop the towel as an unsettling fear grips my heart. I'm sweating profusely, questioning my reality, trying to ascertain whether I just blacked out. Panicking, I glance into the mirror and am instantly filled with terror as I see another man's face. It is my face and it is not. If I stand very still, I can make out someone else staring right at me through my very own eyes.

His eyes are pitch black and soulless.

Splashing cold water onto my face, I shake my head and find myself swimming in menacing thoughts of murder and death. In the crevices of my mind I listen to echoes of shattering screams and strangling shrieks as blood drenches me. Trembling, I look down to see if there is blood anywhere, but see none. And yet, in my mind, my landlord's family is screaming for help as blood splatters across white porcelain walls. I squeeze my eyes shut with a shudder and open the door to the hallway.

A sigh of relief escapes my lips as the sound of laughter penetrates my thoughts.

Stepping into the hallway, I quickly make my way to the bedroom.

∞

RETURNING HOME FROM a long exhausting day at work, I close the door behind me and stand erect as I see my tarot cards, neatly assembled within a silver cloth, placed directly in the middle of the bed. Something is amiss. The tarot cards are wrapped so carefully.

Picking up the cards, I gasp as a negative energy ricochets out of the cards and into my fingers. I toss them, and a fury galvanizes my body. Tyrone messed with my cards. And someone has deliberately placed a curse on them. I feel it. I know it. How dare anyone tamper with my energy work?

Tyrone walks in.

"Did you by any chance fool around with my tarot cards?"

"They've been lying there all along, Fredy," he replies, glancing away from my penetrating gaze.

"Hmmm… That's funny. It just seems… Out of place."

"I don't know what you're talking about. Talk to you later. Heading out with Cliff," Tyrone excuses himself and hastily leaves.

A surge of anger bursts out of me as I throw the tarot cards against the wall, and then sigh a relief as I feel any energy that was captured in the cards is released. I have never felt such intense anger in my life. Where is it coming from? Looking around the room, I feel as if the world is closing in on me. Disoriented, I collapse onto the bed and take several deep breaths. Clutching my chest, I tell myself that everything will be okay. Sweat breaks across my face as I open my eyes and wonder how much time has passed. Glancing at my phone, I notice that two hours have disappeared. How can this be? I just sat down a minute ago.

Feeling nauseous, I squeeze my eyes shut as wings of terror flutter up my spine.

∞

DISAPPEARING INTO NOTHINGNESS, I suffocate as a damning descent into madness consumes me and strips me of everything I ever knew.

Thoughts race and slip simultaneously. I forget who I am. I find myself moving through an ethereal realm of fog and haze. A state of iniquity beckons my soul as I feel myself surrendering and dying. I once considered myself to be Fredy Espinoza, but now I question the very fabric of who I am. Who is Fredy Espinoza? Who is this being? Whose body is this I possess? And why do I feel like I no longer have any control over my body?

Across the room, Tyrone and Cliff giggle as they close the door behind them, undress, and slip into Tyrone's bed. Their giggling subsides into lip

smacking. Moans, passionate kissing, and a squeaking bed pierce the thick still air. Intense, suffocating sexual energy permeates the claustrophobic room. A feverish sigh escapes Tyrone's mouth, and Cliff makes slurping sounds as a wet noise of penetration quickens into vehement pounding.

"If only Fredy would join us," Cliff moans loudly in my direction. Their breathing gets heavier and heavier.

"I know," Tyrone says, thrusting in heat.

Unable to control myself, I let out evocative moans from the bed as my body writhes, twists, and tangles itself within the bedspread. I command myself to stop this ridiculous behavior, only to find myself a helpless dog as another force takes over and manipulates every mechanism of my being to its will.

Tyrone and Cliff stop and listen to me mimic their sexual exhortations.

I feel Tyrone's palm on my forehead.

"I demand you to leave his body! Whatever you are, I demand you to leave his body once and for all!" Tyrone castigates the spirit.

A quiet peace overcomes my body and I lie still.

"I need to use the restroom," Tyrone tells Cliff. "I'll be right back."

Cliff sits down next to me, prods me with his hand, and softly whispers, "Who's in there?"

Snapping my head to him, I hiss, "The walls-s-s-s-s are shut! The walls-s-s-s-s are shut! The walls-s-s-s-s are shut! The walls-s-s-s-s are shut! It is-s-s-s-s too late!"

Cliff leaps from the bed and cries out, "Holy fuck, Mother Mary of God," staring at me in disbelief.

I roll my eyes into the back of my head, smack my head against the pillow, and feign unconsciousness.

Tyrone enters the bedroom.

Neither of them say a word as I hear them get back into Tyrone's bed.

Cliff implores Tyrone to turn the lights off. Tyrone resists, but finally complies, rises from his mattress, turns the lights off, and slips back into his covers.

And for the first time in my life, I hear a voice as real as lightning split through the thoughts inside my head.

"*Wait, do nothing.*"

Obediently, I slip into a heavy trance state.

A cat's loud shrill screeching eviscerates the placid night.

Then, deafening silence, the kind that sucks any sound into a vacuous abyss.

The hair on my body feels electrified as the thunderous sound of a falling jet engine intensifies. There is a crashing high-pitched sound as the walls of the room ripple and a massive dark energy force flashes into the room, hovers over Tyrone and Cliff, and swiftly swoops into every molecule of my essence and being. As I slump like a rag doll, I feel the energy shoot up from my root chakra to my crown chakra, coil my arms around my torso and spiral my legs together. For a few seconds I have the sensation of levitating.

Tyrone lets out a bloodcurdling scream.

A cold voice counts down in my head, "*Three…two…one…*"

A snap of electricity cuts across my ear.

A force pulls me off the bed and hurls me across the room toward Tyrone and Cliff; their screams echo and ricochet across the walls; my body smacks onto the hard floor a few feet away from Tyrone, who sits upright with his arms crossed and his eyes transfixed in horror.

Sanity grips my mind and I feel reality rush back in.

I realize that I am shrouded in darkness and that within this darkness there is a malevolent force that desires complete possession of my mind.

Screaming, I lunge toward the only light I see and find myself clawing like a caged animal at the window. The moonlight sparkles against my hands

as I shudder and pound at the window. Tears streak down my face as I yearn for the light. Panting, gasping, and shrieking, I fling my body to the opposite side of the room, hoping I don't become possessed again, and in frenzy I flip the light switch repeatedly. Hysteria settles in as the room remains in pitch blackness. I break into frantic sobs and terrifying screams as I feel the dark energy crack against my skin.

Our screams become one.

Suddenly, light illuminates the bedroom.

Crumpling to the floor, I feel my soul die in its wake.

Tyrone jumps out of his paralyzed state, grabs me, and holds me in his warm embrace.

"Why is this happening to us?" I ask fearfully.

Around us, the dark presence radiates its energy; it vibrates a silent hum and our ears prickle as the hum slowly gains momentum, causing reality to bend. It locks down time into a nonexistent flow as the space around us morphs into a supernatural realm.

"We need to get out, Tyrone! We need to leave now!" I croak as I feel a sweeping madness descend on me. Without hesitation, Tyrone and Cliff throw their clothes on and we race out of the bedroom into the cold night air.

It is three in the morning.

We jump into Cliff's car and race to Denny's restaurant.

Tyrone's cell-phone rings.

Answering it, he puts the caller on speaker.

"Tyrone?!" his sister cries out.

"Monica?"

Alarm rises in her voice. "Is everything okay?"

"How did you know?" Tyrone inquires as our eyes widen in shock.

"I'll tell you that later. Where are you guys heading?"

"Denny's."

"I'll meet you there," Monica says.

Tyrone ends the call and drops the phone in his lap.

"How the hell does your sister know?" Cliff cries out in disbelief.

"I don't know! This whole night is just fucking insane!"

Driving into the parking lot, we immediately take account of the deserted complex; the streetlamps in the vicinity are dark and a few empty cars loom hauntingly in their slots with lifelike bestial qualities. Glancing at one another, we gulp, park directly in front of the restaurant, and race inside. The place reeks of isolation and dark foreboding.

Standing in putrid silence, Cliff leans over the counter and rings the bell. "Hello?"

"I've never seen this place so dead," Tyrone says under his breath.

A waiter approaches us.

We break into nervous laughter as he points to the farthest section of the establishment and, without a single word of acknowledgement, motions us to the table, puts down menus, and stalks away.

The three of us squeeze into the cramped table. "Creepy," Cliff whispers.

"Was it just me, or were his eyes devoid of any color?" I ask.

"Oh yeah, his eyes were pitch black, Fredy. I noticed that too," Cliff confirms, shivering with chills.

We make small talk until Monica arrives; she scoots into the seat facing the three of us. Her long wavy brown hair is pulled into a tight ponytail, accentuating her beautiful tanned face and rich brown quizzical eyes.

"How did you know about tonight?" I ask her.

"I had a horrible nightmare. In it, Tyrone was murdered. I woke up feeling death descend on me and I just knew something horrible must have happened. I couldn't fall back asleep without calling to make sure he was okay." She shakes her head. "So, tell me what happened!"

"It all started when I met Cliff," Tyrone begins. "And he told me that the only way I can access my gifts is by having direct contact with a spirit who needed to tell me the way. But to do that, Fredy had to hold a séance…"

One by one, we recount the events leading up to our hallucinatory evening.

An hour later, having heard it all, Monica clasps her palms over our hands, stares into our eyes, and pleads, "Promise me, promise me, none of you will ever mess around with séances or voodoo again! Promise me, right now!"

We all promise.

Getting up, she asks Tyrone to walk her to the car.

Cliff and I sit in silence as we nibble on our food.

On the other side of the restaurant, the waiter stares at us as if he was in on everything that occurred tonight.

Outside, we see Monica and Tyrone walking back to the restaurant.

"I thought you were leaving." Cliff says when they return to the table.

"Hmm, that's funny—my car won't start. The engine is dead," Monica says. "I guess I'm joining you guys for breakfast. I'll just wait until the sun comes up and see if it works; if it doesn't, then I'll call a mechanic."

∞

SCARRED FROM THE horrid events of the previous night, Tyrone and I leave for home in silence. Once we arrive, Tyrone quickly packs his bags and notifies Trudy that he's moving out for the time being.

"Did you hear anything last night?" Tyrone asks her.

"No, slept like a buttercup," Trudy says, with a smile.

As Tyrone stuffs a shirt into his duffel bag, he says, "It's strange that Trudy didn't hear anything at all last night. Usually she can hear me on my phone through the vents. And when she does, she gets upset."

"Let's just add it as proof of this freakish anomaly."

After Tyrone leaves, I debate what to do.

I am not a believer.

However, at this moment I leave home, enter a Catholic church, sprinkle holy water over myself, and sit in a pew.

Lowering my head, I pray for the first time in a long time.

"I know I haven't prayed to you since I was fourteen years old. I refrain from believing in you, but after recent events, I feel obliged to. If you do exist, please watch over me because I don't know what will become of me. I feel that at any moment, I will cease to exist."

I get a bottle of holy water, return to Trudy's place, and splash it around the room. Later in the day, a package of green contact lenses that I ordered the previous week arrives. Excited, I dash to the store and buy a bleach kit for my hair.

That night, I collapse into a demented sleep. I dream of a little boy with brown eyes stabbing his twin self as blood drips across a desolate playground. The Devil whispers to me, "Your soul will be mine!" while I swing higher and higher into the arms of a fallen statuesque angel. I come upon myself dead, buried, and withering away like a whisper in the wind. A requiem plays solemnly and hauntingly throughout the deep dark hours of the night.

<p style="text-align:center">∞</p>

SEDUCTIVE LAUGH ESCAPES my cherry-red lips as I wipe the mist from the mirror and stare at my transformation. My bleached hair accentuates the green contact lenses and gives a glow to my bronzed skin. Leaning over the sink, I plant a kiss on the mirror and smirk.

I am no longer Fredy Espinoza.

"Forrester Kessington," I exhale my name as if baptizing myself.

The process of destroying Fredy Espinoza is complete. He will not suffer as long as I reign over his mind, his thoughts, his body. *I am everything you never could be, Fredy Espinoza.*

"You have nothing to fear, Fredy Espinoza," I whisper. "I will take you to the height of fame. I will make your dreams come true. And when the time is right, you can have your body back, but as for your soul, well, you know how the deal works." I feel the memory of Fredy Espinoza ceasing to exist.

That day, I go to work at Starbucks and quickly enroll everyone in the possibility of who I have become. Whenever I hear the name Fredy Espinoza, I immediately eradicate it and insert my own, Forrester Kessington. At first, my coworkers react with confusion, but they go along with my demands. As Forrester Kessington, I am bold, confrontational, assertive, and a sexual beast. As Forrester, I will get what I want, and what I want is a new life.

I am suffocating in this horrible town.

No, Fremont will not suffice.

<center>∞</center>

WITH THE TICKET in my hand, I feel a rush of anticipating hunger course through my body as I bump along the jetway in a slow queue of disgruntled passengers onto the airplane. *Everything I am doing, I do for you, Fredy Espinoza.*

I settle into my seat and smile charmingly at my neighbor. She's in her late thirties, with dirty-blonde hair and soft blue eyes. She looks frazzled.

"Gosh, I have never been to New York City! Have you?" she inquires.

"Once. I fell in love with the city and now I'm moving to it," I reply charismatically.

"Oh, my dear! Congratulations! We have to celebrate all the way to New York City! Allow me to buy you cocktails." She smiles ecstatically.

"Thank you, you are too gracious. My name is Forrester… Forrester Kessington." I smile, secretly thinking, *I always get what I want.*

And just like that, the plane shoots off to New York City.

Goodbye, Fremont, and good riddance to every single trace of Fredy Espinoza's life.

New York City, here I come.

∞ PART TWO: LUCIFER'S PROPOSAL ∞

"The black moment is the moment when the real message of transformation is going to come. At the darkest moment comes the light."—Joseph Campbell

∞ CHAPTER VII: AVENUE OF SHATTERED DREAMS ∞

CHELSEA INTERNATIONAL HOSTEL looms before my eyes as I dart in with my luggage and ask for a room. It is smack in the middle of Chelsea, one of New York's gayest districts. After dropping off my luggage, I race over to West 15th Street and 9th Avenue. Entering the Starbucks I transferred to, I meet my new manager and introduce myself as Forrester Kessington. After I explain how I have undergone a transformation, the manager becomes enrolled in my new way of being.

That night, I make love to the German Devil.

Stepping into his bedroom, I close the door behind me and seductively walk over to him. He pours me a glass of wine. I take it and quickly drink it.

"Here, have another," he says, refilling my glass.

Batting my eyes, I down that glass as well.

"You sure are thirsty, aren't you, Forrester?" he laughs wickedly, pouring more velvety red wine into my glass.

"I love your crystal-blue eyes," I say, laughing as the wine hits me.

Specks of jade glimmer within the blue hues of his hypnotizing eyes. His black pupils cast a bewitching spell on me and I imagine plunging into the depths of his soul and swimming within his spiritual material. His blonde hair sweeps to the side of his face. His tall frame hovers menacingly over me.

"Ich will ficken," I moan, parting my mouth and licking my cherry-red lips.

"I can't wait to fuck you too, Forrester Kessington," he breathes heavily, mimicking my facial expression as his tongue darts out and moves over his lips quickly.

His pupils enlarge, pinning me down like prey.

Oh, my German Devil, be my predator tonight.

I push the empty glass of wine aside and wait breathlessly.

Suddenly, like a wolf, he sprints and attacks.

He picks me up, throws me onto the bed, rips my shirt off, bites my skin, jostles my pants off, tears apart my boxers, pulls my legs into the air, and stuffs his tongue deep into my parting ass. Like a beast in heat, he snarls as his face thrashes like a hurricane against my smooth buttocks.

"Your ass tastes fucking delicious!" he croons as he holds me down fiercely with his huge palms. His scruffy face pulls away, only to ravishingly plant a trail of kisses along my starving body until his tongue shoots into my mouth. I accidentally bite his lips in my hunger for him. His nostrils flare wide as his eyes widen in surprise, but instead of pulling away, he opens his mouth wide and takes in the lower half of my face. As if by suction, my tongue is forced deep into his mouth.

Then he effortlessly picks me up and knocks me against the wall.

The thud of pain feels good against my cold skin. I cry, "Oh God, it is true that Germans are fucking good in bed!"

"You've experienced nothing yet," he pants, throwing me across the room onto the bed. With a lunge, he slides himself into me. He shreds me

apart as I cry out simultaneously in pain and joy.

"You like this?"

"Yes!" I yell. Lacing his fingers through my hair, he yanks my head to him and bites my cheek. His other bulging arm wraps beneath my stomach as he pulls my upper body against him. And for those few gasping seconds I feel him deep inside me.

"Oh, fuck yes!" I explode as I feel a heat of energy strike at my very core.

Like a puppet, I lose control in his domination as his strength lifts me up and down, up and down, until he pushes my upper body to arch into the bed. Grabbing ahold of the headboard, I pant in pleasure as he pounds into me. The intensity of him banging me sends me into a spiral of dizziness. I feel his breath on my back, then his teeth biting my flesh, and the jolt of exquisite pain as he leaves his marks on me.

"Yes, bite me! Bite me, you German Devil!" Devour my whole body, take me, rape me, abuse me, do whatever you please, just as long as I continue to feel this pain! Make me forget! Make me forget my existence in this moment!

Obligingly, he rips himself out of me, forces my body onto his, and plants me on top of him as I ride him like a wild stallion. Smacking me, he bites my lips and slurps my tongue down his throat. He sucks so hard that for a second I wonder if he will bite it off.

"Oh, fuck me! Yes, just fuck my brains out! Yes! Yes! Oh, fuck yes!" I shout as I ejaculate all over his chest, face, hair, and onto the headboard.

∞

A CATHOLIC PASTOR stays at the hostel. His hazel eyes, smooth opaque skin, and waves of brown hair give off an aura of innocence. An Argentinean jawline defines his profile and his cheekbones sink slightly into his face. He's been here for a week now; something about dealing with a divorce and how

he needs to take care of business in the city. How ironic—just two weeks ago I slept with a German Devil, and now before me, I am tempted into sleeping with a man of the cloth.

"So, you prefer the arms of a man as opposed to a woman?" he asks me from across the room in the wee hours past midnight.

"It's better than copulating with a woman," I whisper, longing to get off my twin bed and slip into his.

"But what of God's wrath? Don't you fear God?"

"Didn't He make us all in His image?" I reply seductively.

"What is it like to be with another man?"

"I can show you," I whisper. I slip out of my bed and approach him in darkness. His breath becomes jagged as his silence gives me the answer I need. Caressing his skin, I wonder if there is such a thing as sin.

No, Forrester Kessington doesn't believe in sin.

"I-I don't know if—" he stammers.

"Shhh," I interrupt, lowering my hand to his crotch.

He becomes hard in my hand.

I slip it into my mouth. His moans penetrate the night as I hungrily bob up and down, seeking his gratification.

"Oh Jesus Christ, Saint Mary Mother of God—"

He comes in my mouth and I swallow.

And then I hear him heaving quietly into the pillow.

"Why are you crying?" I ask.

"Because I don't know why I let you do this to me," he says.

"Tell me what it felt like for a man to go down on you?"

"You were very good, if that is what you are fishing for," he says. His voice quivering, he turns away from me and prays, "Christ, Our Lord, You suffered and were tempted. You are powerful to come to the aid of those who are assailed by the Devil, for You are the support of Christian people. O

Lord, protect with Your right hand those who trust in Your name. Deliver them from the Evil One, and grant them everlasting joy. Amen."

Sighing, I shrug my shoulders, return to my bed, and fall asleep.

∞

"FORRESTER KESSINGTON," FREDY whispers to me. Fredy lies on his bed, covered in purple satin sheets. His hand reaches out to me as I mimic and reach down to him from within this ivory mirror above his bed.

"Forrester Kessington, save me from myself. Save me, Forrester. Save me from myself," he whimpers.

Suddenly, the mirror shatters and I free-fall. Below me, Fredy levitates into the air toward me, brushes my body, and enters me. Lightning cracks and I'm flung backward, only to see Fredy gazing back down at me. His hand desperately holds onto mine, afraid to let go. Around us, shards of glass glitter like raindrops…

Waking up, I gasp as I look around the room. I feel myself for damage.

I think about the Catholic pastor and see him nowhere in sight.

Fredy, I think to myself as I get up and quickly take a shower. Shaking my head, I force myself not to think of him. Fredy Espinoza doesn't exist. He doesn't exist and he can't stop me from living this life.

I promised you, Fredy, so let me just be.

I pack my suitcase and roll out of the Chelsea International Hostel, get into a cab, and ask to be taken to the Manhattan Inn. I've yet to find a studio to call my own. It's amazing how fast time flies in New York. I settle my things in the hostel, grab my application, and head over to Banana Republic on 8th Avenue between 15th and 16th. The lifestyle I desire is too expensive and Starbucks can barely pay for my two-week stays at these hostels.

I long for more sex. No matter how much sex I have with random strangers, my thirst begs for more. There is a black hole inside me that propels me to fill it with the consumption of feverish pleasure. Love doesn't interest me, but the illusion of it does. Whenever I lie down with these

anonymous strangers, I pretend for a few hours that we are star-crossed lovers, only allowed to love intensely for one night of debauchery. In every man I imagine a whole history as we fulfill our needs and pass out in each other's arms. In a stranger's arms, I am taken care of, wanted, loved, admired, desired, and cherished. In the act of copulation, I am whisked away to a land of divine nocturnal pleasure.

I drop off the application, dash into the subway, hop onto the L-train, and get off at Union Square. Slipping into the Starbucks across the street from Barnes and Noble, I buy an ice-cold tea and take it over to the park to linger among native New Yorkers. Now, this is what life is meant to be. Tonight, I need to find information about getting into the Actor Training Program in Juilliard's drama division. I promised Fredy I'd fulfill his dreams and Juilliard is one of them.

Yes, I promised myself.

I choke on my iced tea, beads of sweat caressing my forehead as my thoughts become Fredy's thoughts. *I don't need you, Forrester Kessington. I can do this without you.* No! You do need me! Gulping down my iced tea, I veer toward Barnes and Noble and contemplate my next move.

I'm not you, Forrester Kessington; I'm Fredy Espinoza.

"Shut up!" I say loudly, scaring a couple near me.

Turning beet red, I feign an apologetic smile and dash into Barnes and Noble. It dawns on me that maybe I've been playing a role this whole time and I am not Forrester Kessington, but myself, Fredy Espinoza.

No, it is a role I believe to be my reality and Forrester does exist! I must be Forrester Kessington! I am Forrester Kessington.

In the bathroom, I splash cold water onto my face and look into the mirror. My green eyes are still there, *hiding my brown eyes.* Shaking my head, I convince myself I am Forrester Kessington.

I killed Fredy Espinoza back in Fremont.

This is my new life.

I need no one but myself.

∞

IGOR STRAVINSKY'S *Le Sacre du printemps* plays at Carnegie Hall tonight, December 12th, 2004. Holding onto the ticket, I get off work from Banana Republic, hail a cab, and ask to be taken to West 57th Street and 7th Avenue. The conductor Michael Tilson Thomas will be giving his perspective on Stravinsky.

By luck, yesterday, I came across an ad on Craigslist by a person giving away his ticket to the performance. I jumped at it right away and now I am brimming with excitement as I get to hear my first symphony performance. I'm wearing my best: pleated dress pants, dress shoes, a pink long-sleeve button-down shirt, and a dress coat.

In a way, New York is my rite of passage to becoming a man. I am three weeks shy of turning twenty-one years old. And when I do, I intend to party every night. But for tonight, this is my now. I never got the courage to audition at Juilliard. My life has been consumed with trying to make it paycheck to paycheck. I have now lived in four different hostels: Chelsea International Hostel, Manhattan Inn, Chelsea Star Hotel, and Bowery's Whitehouse Hotel.

As time passes, the more I become Fredy Espinoza again. I try in vain to banish Forrester Kessington from my being. I don't understand who he is and why he took over me, and yet I am lying to myself, because I know I am the one who created him. I created him in a time of need. Now, whenever I feel a crisis, I call upon him and within seconds I manifest his energy and revert to being Forrester Kessington.

Forrester Kessington, I muse. *Who are you?* At times, I catch myself glancing into the mirror expecting myself to become Forrester. Sometimes I see his apparition, but then I remind myself that I no longer need him. Did I really

believe I could destroy myself and have Forrester take complete control? Possibly, but in time I realized I was playing a role; indeed, becoming Forrester Kessington was the greatest role I achieved as an aspiring actor. I fully lost myself in the role—believed myself to be him. I created him from nothingness to protect myself from the pain of being tossed out in the street like a rag doll.

Being on my own in New York is difficult.

I must focus all my energy on ensuring that I do not lose myself again.

How comfortable it is to slip back into my alter ego's role and surrender into someone other than myself. How long can I keep Forrester at bay? Forever, right? After all, he is my creation.

Taking my seat in Carnegie Hall, I find myself in a sea of couples in black tie and gowns.

All around me, couples chat gaily, waiting for the concert to begin. Sitting there alone, as the lights dim and the orchestra begins to play, tears fall from my eyes. A loneliness deeper than pain engulfs me. One day, when I have the money to pay my own way, I will have a man escorting me to the symphony. Wiping the tears from my eyes, I listen in awe and remind myself that I am in Carnegie Hall.

After the show, I call Mom.

"Mom?"

"Mijo? Mijo! Fredy, where are you? Why don't you come visit me? Your father has me locked away in this half-way house in Hayward and won't let me see any of my children!" Her voice sounds frail.

"I'm in New York, Mom," I tell her.

"Come back to me, Fredy. Come back and tell everyone to come visit me. I'm so alone at this place," she pleads.

"I can't, Mom. I live here now."

"The Devil took you there! Fredy, listen to me! I know the witches

turned you gay and the Devil wants your soul! Return to California and let me out of here so I can protect you, mijo!"

Closing my eyes, I hold back tears of anger and frustration and curse at myself for having called her. I knew it would end up like this.

"There is no such thing as the Devil, Mom! And no, for your information, you gave birth to a homosexual son! No one made me gay! You got it? I need to go! Bye!" I end the call without allowing her to say goodbye.

I can do it on my own.

I don't need Mom or Dad.

Shivering, I put on my gloves and make my way back to Union Square. I marvel at the glistening snow and all the shops full of Christmas decorations. Around me families are walking together through the city lights. It will be my second Christmas on my own.

Releasing my tears, I look to the sky and whisper, "What did I get myself into?"

∞

ANOTHER DEAD NIGHT as midnight nears and I've yet to find a man to go to bed with. Sipping a Screwdriver anxiously, I glance around the dark interior of Splash Bar, hoping to make eye contact with a handsome stranger. Only a few gay couples mingle on the dance floor.

Sighing, I finish the last drops of the drink, get up from the bar, and walk out into the cool crisp air. In the distance, a girl screams at a cabdriver, "Fuck you, asshole! I ain't paying you shit!"

It's now February and I am getting desperate. I keep finding myself homeless over and over again. I have been in a vicious cycle where a few days prior the arrival of my paycheck I wind up homeless, being unable to pay for my whole stay at a hostel. Usually, I manage to seduce a man and accompany him to his apartment. There, we have wild sex, I shower, and then fall into a deep sleep, making sure his arms are wrapped around me, cradling me like a

baby. None of these men ever find out my true intention. I consider it a win-win situation: they get a night of passionate lovemaking, and I get a comfortable bed to sleep in.

Sex is sex, is it not?

Sometimes the sex isn't so great; I lie there and take it like a man. Better to take it than to walk mindlessly around the cruel streets of Manhattan.

How fast my dreams of making it big transform into a hideous nightmare!

And right now, I don't know what to do.

Shivering, I amble down West 15th Street to the Hudson River.

A draft of icy air smacks my face as I cross 8th Avenue.

The alcohol wears off and my teeth clatter as the temperature drops. A wave of despair hits me. I fight back tears. I'm not supposed to be homeless! I'm intelligent, God damn it! I was an overachieving student with straight-A's, and I'll be damned if I don't think of something smart!

I finger the keys to the Starbucks store in my pocket, thinking hard about what I should do. A little thought sneaks into the corner of my mind. At first, I shake my head at the thought. Then, caressing the store keys, I feel a glimmer of hope and fear as I persuade myself I have nothing to lose. For a second, anxiety lifts off my chest as I make my decision.

Quickening my pace, I turn onto 9th Avenue and slip into the store. I hastily sprint to the alarm box and enter the code, trembling. In shadows, I creep to the men's restroom, set the alarm on my phone to half an hour before the arrival of my first coworkers, snuggle into a tight ball on the cement floor, and pass out into a restless sleep.

<div align="center">∞</div>

FORRESTER KESSINGTON GRINS psychotically at me as I scrub my face repeatedly. His green eyes flash with luminosity and a sardonic chortle escapes his mouth. His lips part and several tongues fling at me. His voice penetrates the space around me.

"You will never get rid of me, Fredy! You can't destroy that which has a hold over you! I am you, and you are I. As Forrester Kessington, I will take you to the heights of fame and give you everything you have ever desired. I will fulfill your destiny!"

"I don't need you any longer! I never needed you! I can do it on my own! Go back where you came from!"

Pivoting, I lunge and strangle him as his tongues sexually pleasure me. His voice amplifies and vibrates in the mist as I feel him penetrate me and possess me once again. "You will never be rid of me! Fredy Espinoza is dead! Dead! Dead! You will never exist again! Never exist again! Never exist again!"

"No! NO! NOOOOOOO!"

"NO!" I wake up screaming as my alarm goes off.

Shaking myself out of my nightmare, I let out a quiet moan, shuffle to my feet, and slip out of the restroom. Heading into the office, my fingers dash rapidly across the pad entering the code to turn the store alarm back on, and then I hurry out through the coffee shop.

Walking down West 15th Street toward Union Square, I bite my lip in trepidation as I wonder what my next move should be. If only I had a father I could call to help me with my living situation, everything would be fine. But I don't; I'm an orphan without parents to support me or help me in my time of need. I am desperate. I don't know how much longer I can go on being homeless.

I need more income, but how do I go about it? I can't expect to sleep inside Starbucks every time I can't pay for my stay at a hostel. And I'm starving. I haven't eaten a meal in three days. It's embarrassing to circle around Whole Foods in Union Square for samples, but it must be done if I am to nourish my body. Is this how homeless people feel? Shame overcomes as I look at my clothes and pretend to pass for someone who has money when in fact I am on the brink of perpetual homelessness. The thought strikes dread in me. I tell myself I will not allow it to happen. I will not end up

in rags, smelling like urine, and left behind to rot.

What is a commodity that people need right now that I can offer?

Glancing at my reflection in a store window, I look at my handsome face and lean body.

And I consider exactly what it is that I need to do to survive.

∞

THE TOWNHOUSE BAR on East 58th Street bustles with activity in the deep hours of the night as I stand anxiously in front of it. Men dressed in suits smile at me as they step up to the patio and disappear through the doors.

"Pull yourself together," I whisper, strolling onto the patio and casually sticking my head in the door. An old man in his seventies approaches me and for a second I think he is going to introduce himself, but instead he slips past me and heads out, followed by a young guy who looks suspiciously younger than me.

Entering a hallway adjacent to the piano bar, I see a couch and sit down, unsure of what to do. How does one pick up on an older man and ask for money? Damn, I knew I should have paid attention to Julia Roberts in *Pretty Woman*. Maybe I'll just sit pretty and wait for someone to approach me.

Suddenly, a good-looking man in his late twenties sits down next to me. He looks like a young George Clooney. Leaning over to me, his eyes sparkle as he asks, "So, how much are you going for?"

"I don't know," I say, laughing nervously. "One hundred?"

He shakes his head and replies, "Your first time? Let me tell you how much you should ask for. You see all these old men dressed in their finest couture? They're bachelors tied down to no one, with tons of money to give away. Some of them are only looking for a one-night stand, but the majority are looking for a boy to call their own. You see that guy in the corner?"

I glance over to an old man in his early seventies. His thinning gray hair reveals freckles on his scalp. Caucasian, with fading blue eyes, tall at five foot

eleven, and big boned, he catches my stare and winks at me.

"That's John. He's one of the wealthiest men here. In fact, not many people know this, but he's connected to the DuPont family—you know, one of the richest families in the East Coast. His last boyfriend was about your age when they got together; now he has his own apartment in one of the highest towers in Gramercy Park, his own car, and had his education paid for."

"How do you know all this?" I ask, longing for an ice-cold Sapphire tonic.

"Let's just say I know the clientele in this place. You're a hot boy, you know. You're selling yourself short for a hundred dollars. I say shoot higher—ask for a few grand. Most of these men would die to get into your pants. Oh, and remember, his name is John."

And just like that, he gets up and disappears out of the bar.

John is still standing by the doorway adjacent into the piano bar. He catches my eye again and this time he casually strolls over to me.

"You don't have a drink in your hand. Would you like me to get you one?" His voice sounds like my late grandfather's, endearing, caring, and gentle.

"Yeah, Sapphire tonic, please." I force a smile on my face.

"Now don't go anywhere, um…?"

"Fredy Espinoza," I say. "No middle name," I throw in.

"Fredy no middle name Espinoza, got it," he chuckles as he winks and exits the hallway to fetch me a drink.

Well, that was easy. I sigh, gazing around me. Several older men walk around holding martinis. Here and there I can make out a young guy my age also lingering about trying to capture someone's attention. How silly of me to sell my body for a hundred dollars; the more I see how these old men carry themselves, the more I can smell the wealth on their coats.

"I recognize that look in your eyes, Fredy no middle name Espinoza," John says, surprising me. I let out a small gasp.

"Oh, I didn't realize you were watching me," I reply, graciously taking the drink.

"I've befriended many young men your age who all aspire to get to the top, and frankly, my dear, you're one of them. Your eyes give away too easily that you will do whatever it takes to get to the top, am I not correct?"

"I didn't realize I was so easy to read, John." I sip my drink in embarrassment.

"Funny, I never told you my name," he looks at me with amusement.

"Oh, a guy sat down next to me and told me your name," I reveal.

"Ah, yes, well, that figures," he says sourly. "So what brings you into the Townhouse?"

"Boredom, experiencing something new, an adventure, you know, basically anything to keep me distracted," I reply, glancing away from his peering eyes.

"Would you like another drink?" John asks softly as I gaze down and see in shock that I've gulped down the drink.

"Oh my, I must be thirsty." I wince in pain as more embarrassment cascades across my face.

"Many boys are thirsty in this town," he says, chuckling. He gets up and buys me another cocktail.

Suddenly, around me I notice several young guys staring at me. My thoughts begin to race as it dawns on me that they are judging me. This is all so embarrassing and humiliating. What am I doing here? It doesn't matter to me if John is filthy rich! I just can't go through with this. I can wait two more days until my paycheck arrives.

Getting up, I bump into John and the drink almost slips out of his hand.

"I'm sorry, John, I just can't do this." My eyes well up with tears as I

dash out of the establishment.

I careen into a passing couple and mumble an apology as I quickly walk down the street toward 3rd Avenue. The drink hits me strongly and I break down. Lowering my head into my hands, I heave with sobs as I blindly make my way onto 3rd Avenue. Not caring anymore where I am going, I fall to the curb and cuddle myself as I sink into my solitude.

What will people think of me back home? How can I return, having promised to accomplish all I ever desired? My dreams of becoming famous, of becoming someone, of changing people's lives with my presence on this earth are shattered. I'm going to amount to nothing, become homeless, and live on this avenue of shattered dreams.

"What did I do to deserve this, God?! What did I do to deserve any of this?! Please, I beg of you, help me! I just don't know what to do anymore! I know I stopped believing in you, but right now I have no one and I want to believe! Just send me an angel, please! Oh, God, please!" I sob, seeking a star in the sky far above the towering skyscrapers.

From behind, I feel a hand on my shoulder.

Startled, I wipe my face and glance up to see John standing over me.

"Please, say you'll come to my place tonight. I promise I won't ask anything of you," John kindly assuages me as he gently squeezes my shoulder.

Stumbling to my feet, I throw my arms around him and break down in humiliating sobs.

"It's okay, Fredy, you can depend on me," he whispers into my ear.

∞

WITH JOHN'S HELP, I move into a three-bedroom apartment near Columbia University on West 116th Street and Broadway. I share the apartment with a nice Cuban family. My bedroom is located right next to the doorway, so I can enter and leave without ever needing to see anyone. The walls of the room are painted green (my favorite color) and every night I sleep

on a huge queen-sized bed. A small closet faces a barred window that faces other apartments. I am rarely home, since every evening John takes me out to fancy dinners, to the symphony, and to plays in the theater district.

For the first time in New York, I feel a sense of security. John confides in me that he indeed is connected to the DuPont family and has close connections to the city's elite. He is wealthy beyond my dreams, and yet the proposal he made to me on our first date haunts me.

"I will help you, Fredy," he said that night. "I have many connections, I know many influential people, I can make your dreams come true. I will help you enroll in the university, pay for your education, and if need be, help you make a deposit on your own studio in any neighborhood you prefer. I will make all your dreams come true as long as you promise you'll remain faithful to me and only me. I do not tolerate you sleeping with other guys, nor do I tolerate disobedience. If I call you, you answer. If I tell you to drop whatever you're doing, you drop it and immediately do my bidding. And just because I am helping you doesn't mean you can just goof off. No, I have very high expectations, Fredy. If you meet them, the world I offer can be all yours."

It seems too good to be true.

A month into our relationship, I find myself enslaved to John. Although he purchases me a new wardrobe, entertains me with stories of his life, and keeps me distracted from a past I desperately yearn to forget, the glances from my gay peers remind me that all I am to John is his kept boy.

And I desire the flesh of a guy my age.

Above all, I desire a life where I make the shots.

<p style="text-align:center">∞</p>

CROSSING MY ARMS, I stand stiffly near the entrance to John's spacious apartment and repeat, "I can't do this anymore, John. I'm sorry, but I just can't do this anymore."

"What do you mean you can't do this anymore?" John asks

incredulously, raising his eyebrows. He shuffles into the kitchen and I follow him. He opens the refrigerator and pulls out a melon.

"I think what I'm trying to say is that I no longer want to be with you."

John pulls a china plate from his cabinet.

"You no longer want to be with me?" he turns around and faces me.

"Correct, John," I hold my stance.

"Do you have any idea what you are losing out on? Do you not have the faintest clue that any boy out there would wish to be in your situation right now?! I can give you *everything*, Fredy! *Everything*! That's how it works here in this world!" His lips curl into a sneer and his faded blue eyes narrow into slits of anger.

"Don't patronize me, John! I do know what I'm losing out on, but I can't. I won't use you like this," I reply.

"Use me? Of course you're using me, Fredy! I'm not stupid! You use me and I use you! I thought you understood the proposition between us."

"I'm sorry, John," I say, backing away.

John turns his back on me and smashes the plate on the counter.

"You just made the stupidest mistake of your life," he growls, lowering his head. "Just get out, Fredy. GET OUT!"

"I'm sorry," I cry before jolting out of his apartment. A terror consumes me over the intensity of anger that spilled from John.

Entering the elevator, I press Lobby and ruminate about the consequences of ending my relationship with John. Am I making the right decision? I know I'm throwing away a life any boy would die for, but at what cost? Maybe John is right to call me stupid. Who wouldn't want all that John can offer? Yet I can't continue to live this kind of life. I hate being someone's trophy. I can't stand the look on my peers' faces as I walk into a bar and it dawns on them that I'm someone's property. Maybe I'm not a gold-digger after all; maybe it's true that money can't buy you happiness.

I don't need you, John.

I can make it on my own.

And I will get to the top, one way or another—you'll see.

∞ CHAPTER VIII: THE ESPINOZA CURSE ∞

HOT JUNE AIR sticks to my skin. I glance to the window whose black bars trap me inside as Alison Moyet's "Windmills of Your Mind" plays softly in the background. Her voice wilts and droops as I gaze around the barren bedroom.

"I can't do this," I whisper to myself as I slip onto the floor.

I've come so far, and if I keep at it, I can still audition at Juilliard as I promised myself. My eyes dart to Uta Hagen's *A Challenge for the Actor*. After all, if I succeeded in believing I was Forrester Kessington, then I sure as hell can make anyone believe I can be someone other than myself.

Hesitating for a moment, I grab my cell-phone and call Daniel Hansen.

"Are you excited?! In a few hours, you'll be in Memphis!" Daniel says, laughing.

"I don't know if I can leave New York," I reply.

I close my eyes and hold my breath.

"Fredy," he sighs, "I love you. I promise you'll love it here. I already

made plenty of space in the closet for your stuff and all my friends are excited about meeting you. After everything you told me, I want to take care of you."

"I just don't know, Daniel. I love you too, it's just…" I bite my lip as a ball of anxiety rises in my stomach.

"Fredy, you can do this! I'm listening to our song." I make out DHT's "Listen to Your Heart" playing in the background. *Listen to your heart, when he's calling for you, listen to your heart, there's nothing else you can do, I don't know where you're going and I don't know why, but listen to your heart before you tell him goodbye…*

But I don't know what my heart wants.

"Fredy…" Daniel pleads, "Fredy, I love you."

"I love you too, Daniel. I… I'll go, for you, I'll go."

"Is there anything you want me to get you?" his voice rises in anticipation as I note relief in his words.

"No, I won't need anything."

In the depths of my being, I sense that our serendipitous encounter at Splash Bar a few weeks ago occurred for a reason. Maybe a higher purpose is at work and I'm meant to move to the South.

"Okay, honey. I can't wait to see you. Love you."

"Love you too," I end the call and drop the phone onto the floor.

Grabbing my duffel bag, I glance around the barren room one more time, say my final goodbye, and quietly exit the apartment.

I hail a cab. "La Guardia Airport, please."

<p style="text-align:center">∞</p>

DANIEL HANSEN STARES in shock as I appear at the Memphis International Airport baggage claim with only a duffel bag swung around my shoulder. His brown eyes are masked behind blue contact lenses and his dirty-blondish hair is perfectly styled. Daniel is twenty-three years old and five feet seven inches tall; he hunches over slightly as I throw my arms around him and kiss him. His skin smells of Fierce, by Abercrombie & Fitch. Taking in

his face, I find myself thrown back to my high school years: Daniel reminds me of Jacob Lee. If I didn't know better, they could pass for brothers.

"This is all you brought with you, honey?"

"I always pack light."

"It doesn't matter. I'm just glad to have you in my arms. You're going to love Memphis, Tennessee." He squeezes me tightly before releasing me.

"I can't believe I'm in Memphis."

"Well, you better believe it, Fredy!" Daniel grabs my bag, "Misty's in the car. She's going to love you, I just know it. We're going to be a happy family, the three of us. I took a few days off so I can show you around Memphis. Did you know Graceland Mansion is located here?"

"Graceland Mansion?"

"Oh, Lord, have mercy on my soul! Tell me you're kidding." His eyes bulge in shock as I look at him in confusion.

"I don't know what Graceland Mansion is," I say, smiling sheepishly.

"One of the most famous sites in Memphis. Elvis Presley used to live there. Oh, Lord, help me." He bursts into laughter.

"Hmmm, I am not a fan of Elvis Presley," I confess.

"We don't have to go there if you don't want to."

As we approach his car, a beautiful Norwegian Lundehund barks wildly. She has the most gorgeous reddish-orange coat and her tongue rolls out as Daniel opens the door and grabs her.

"Misty, say hi to Fredy. He's family now, okay?" He motions for me to approach her. "Here, let her smell you. That's right, Misty. This is Fredy. He's the newest addition to our family."

"Hi, Misty, you have a beautiful coat," I whisper in awe, "She looks like a fox."

"Yeah, that's the reason why I had to have her. Before you know it, she'll love you to death. How are you feeling?"



"Excited, scared, sad, and well, all sorts of emotions," I reply as I get into his car.

"Why are you sad?" Daniel inquires, pulling out of the parking lot and driving onto the freeway.

"Over leaving New York." I stare out the window into the darkness.

"Are you not happy to be here?"

"Oh, no, it's not that at all! I'm happy to be here with you and I can't wait to sleep in your safe arms. It's just that I moved to New York in pursuit of my dreams and I can't believe I'm no longer there. Even when times were tough and I thought I couldn't survive another day, it was the possibility of fulfilling my dreams that kept pushing me through. But it's for the best."

"Well, I'll see if I can get a teaching position in New York, Fredy. You never know, maybe the three of us will wind up in New York."

∞

THREE MONTHS LATER, Daniel surprises me with the exciting news that he has accepted a teaching position in Pensacola, Florida. Not only am I happy for him, but I am ecstatic over the prospect of moving out of Memphis, Tennessee.

"If you moved for me, honey, then I sure as hell can move for you. Let's start a new chapter, you and I, together," Daniel leans over and kisses me. His eyes twinkle with enthusiasm as we load the last of the dishes into a box.

"God, how much I love you, Daniel Hansen," I whisper. "Nothing will ever separate us."

"Daniel?" a woman's soft voice floats into the kitchen.

I jump several feet back, but Daniel looks at me with assurance. "Oh, Lord, my parents are finally here. Remember, they're very nice Southern folk and they don't know we're together."

"Daniel? Where are you?"

"We're in the kitchen, Mom!"

"Oh, there you are!" Daniel's mother enters the kitchen. She's slightly taller than me and she has the softest expression on her face. Her red hair falls past her ears and her brown eyes look me up and down impassively. She's thin, and she looks nothing like Daniel. Extending her hand, she warmly introduces herself in a Southern accent. "Hi there, I'm Daniel's mother, Leslie Hansen. It's a pleasure to finally meet you, Fredy. Daniel has told me so much about you."

I smile without speaking, afraid my voice will give me away as gay.

"I'm so happy you're moving down to Florida, Daniel," she says, bending down to pat Misty. "It means you'll be much closer to us. I just don't know why you didn't accept a teaching position in Tampa."

"Oh, Lord, Mom! I'd be living too close to you and Dad," Daniel says with a laugh.

"Don't be mean to your mother, Daniel," she replies, laughing along with him.

My eyes darken as I watch their interaction. Will I ever know what it's like to have a mother I can joke around with? What does it feel like to know the meaning of being loved, supported, and taken care of by your parents? If Dad had accepted me, would I be here now?

"So, what brought you to Memphis, Fredy?" Leslie asks me timidly.

"I took time after graduating from high school so that I could travel and experience the world firsthand before enrolling in college. I do intend to pursue my education once I get the chance," I say in a slightly deeper voice, forcing myself back into the closet.

"Where's Dad?" Daniel interrupts.

"Oh, he's outside, dear." Leslie looks away from me and follows Daniel to the yard.

Daniel's father breaks the ice by cracking one joke after another.

Laughing, my mood brightens as I tag along and help move boxes to the

rental truck. In Daniel's parents' presence I feel completely at ease. Neither of them questions who I am or stares me down with skepticism. Whenever I meet someone's parents, I revert to how I used to be with my own parents: needing their unconditional approval, acceptance, and love. Maybe Daniel's parents can offer me this.

"Oh, Lord, here we go! You must get tired of constantly moving," Daniel says, his face brightening into a huge smile as he puts on his shades, lights a cigarette, and pulls out of the driveway. Ahead of us, his parents lead the way in their own car.

"I'm used to it," I reply, returning his smile. I grab his hand, squeeze it tightly, and take a cigarette out of the pack.

"Pensacola is a beautiful beach town. You can work, go to school, and on the weekends we can head out to the beach and walk Misty along the shore. You can tan all you want and write in your journals."

"You know me too well," I say, laughing.

"I just want you to be happy," he says, looking over at me.

"I am happy. I'm very happy."

<div align="center">∞</div>

THE PERFECT HOUSEWIFE is a role that suits me very well; I take pleasure in washing dishes, taking Misty out for leisurely walks around the neighborhood, ironing the bedsheets and clothes, doing the laundry, and being a great host whenever we wine and dine guests. And when his parents come over, it doesn't bother me to sleep in the guest bedroom while maintaining the fabrication that Daniel and I are just roommates.

The two-bedroom apartment on the second floor is spacious and huge, with a patio that overlooks the swimming pool. It is a few blocks from the airport and only costs us six hundred dollars a month to rent. When Daniel informed me of the rent, my jaw dropped, considering that I spent that much for a little boxy room on the Upper West Side of Manhattan. Whereas I never

fully adjusted to the Memphis lifestyle, in Pensacola I find myself capriciously alive again.

But how much longer can this good life last?

It seems too good to be true.

<div align="center">∞</div>

ANXIETY SILENTLY FURROWS my gut as I head into work. Entering the Gap at Cordova Mall, I halt in front of a table stacked with neatly compressed jeans and inhale deep belly breaths. Ms. Cunningham told me to just breathe deeply whenever I become anxious.

Sale signs come down as the third weekend of August rolls in.

"Is everything okay, Fredy?" Jen, my coworker, asks me.

"Yes, I'm just catching my breath," I lie as I unsuccessfully try to shake off a foreboding feeling.

Daniel has been acting rather strange lately. I haven't been able to place my finger on it, but I feel that he's hiding something from me. Not a romantic getaway surprise, more like a deception of some kind. I just can't shake it off.

Jen, like most people, wound up in Pensacola because her partner is in the military. It wasn't until she told me the story of how she followed her fiancé to Pensacola that I realized Daniel and I have moved to a Navy-based town. Many men in uniform infiltrate the town. Some stay for years, while other move on to other postings.

After clocking in, I attend to a customer, then focus on carefully folding a pile of disheveled shirts into perfect replicas of one another and placing them on a shelf fixture along the wall. Humming, I feel gratitude for how effortlessly time flows here in Pensacola. In Manhattan, Banana Republic was abuzz with a high volume of customers and frenetic energy.

"Fredy, you have a phone call," Jen informs me, "It's Daniel."

As anxiety grips my throat and I begin to perspire, I make my way to the

phone. Time elapses; actually, it comes to a deafening halt. Reminding myself to breathe, I clutch the phone, hold it for a few seconds, and then bring it to my ear.

"Hey, honey," he says quietly, "I'm calling to see if it's okay with you if I hang out with a few friends in Biloxi. It's been years since I've seen them and we put together a reunion."

Between the lines, I register a subtle note of tension at his end, which only further fuels my anxiety. My knuckles turn deathly white from strangling the phone. Voices chirp and flutter in the back of my head, warning me that something is terribly wrong. But I choose to ignore them because I trust Daniel, right? After all, what could possibly go wrong with Daniel leaving Pensacola for a few hours? Nothing.

I softly whisper, "Of course you can, love."

"I'm not sure what time I'll be back home today, so don't worry if it gets a bit late," he says, holding his breath.

"I have Misty with me, Daniel. Have fun, love. I'll be fine," I reply as the back of my throat constricts and tightens disconcertingly.

He hangs up without saying "I love you."

Swallowing, I wince as my mouth goes dry.

Jen approaches me with a look of concern on her face.

"You look so pale, Fredy. Are you coming down with something?"

"Daniel's going out of town. Maybe I'm being overly dramatic, but my gut tells me something awful is coming my way, Jen," I confide to her as I follow her into the dressing room, "I'm afraid the Espinoza curse will strike again."

"The Espinoza curse? You never told me your family was cursed, Fredy." Jen searches my face to see if I'm being serious.

"I've noticed a pattern in my life where every time something good happens to me, something horrible, twice as horrible, occurs right after. And I

have a feeling in the pit of my stomach that I recognize too well from previous traumatic events in my life."

"Fredy, now you're being melodramatic. Nothing will possibly happen to you or to Daniel. You're feeling insecurity. You trust Daniel, don't you?"

"I do trust him."

"Then don't worry about it. Just brush off those feelings and take good care of yourself. Remember, in any relationship, you come first. Daniel will return this evening and everything will be fine and dandy. All you have is the present moment, Fredy." Jen smiles.

Yet how can I focus on the present moment when, with every step back to my delegated duties, black snakes slither across my spine, twisting and strangling my heart, injecting insidious poison? Daniel Hansen isn't Melancton Vassiliadis, Fredy! What you're feeling right now is misplaced feelings of betrayal from Melancton. Daniel would never cheat on me. No, he isn't that type. Daniel is loyal and caring. I will not allow Melancton to interrupt my present moment with his past; history will not repeat itself.

After work, I dash home and make myself a Sapphire tonic. Sitting down at the desktop, I turn on the computer, click on the Google address tab, and gasp as a gay chat room website appears on-screen. A sinking heaviness settles in my lower abdomen as I click on the history tab and a list of chat rooms appears before me.

I call Tyrone and ask for his advice.

"Don't assume anything, Fredy," he tells me. "You're only setting yourself up for making an ass of yourself. If I were you, I'd just ask him about the chat rooms when he returns. Don't do anything silly."

"You're right. I'm just overreacting. Thank you, Tyrone."

Taking a cool shower, I hop onto the bed, open my journal, and write. Misty curls into a ball beside me and stares at the entryway of the hallway.

"Don't worry, Misty. Daddy will be home soon," I whisper into her ears

as I nuzzle my face in her fiery red fur. Glancing at the clock, I finally decide to call Daniel.

I get his voicemail. "Hey Daniel, it's me, Fredy. It's eleven o'clock and I haven't heard from you. Just wanted to let you know I'm thinking of you and I can't wait to see you. Hope you're having fun with your friends. Please call me when you get this. Love you bunches."

An hour later, I call him again. I'm sent straight to his voicemail again.

Finally, around two in the morning, I pass out into a restless sleep.

<div align="center">∞</div>

A CRACK OF THUNDER as the door slams shut.

Gasping, I jolt awake.

Screams and sobs pierce the house. In the doorway, Daniel stands in disarray, drenched in tears, stained with traces of black mud and crimson blood, his mouth gaping open in a fixed expression of terror.

"FREDY!" Daniel sobs hysterically, rushes in, and collapses in my arms.

"What happened?!" I inhale sharply.

"FREDY! THEY RAPED ME! OH, GOD, THEY RAPED ME!" He breaks down in shuddering sobs.

My mouth drops open, only to find myself speechless.

I sit there, frozen in disbelief and shock, holding the love of my life as his anguished sobs yank at my heart.

My nostrils flare wide. A stench of putrid sex and rancid alcohol smacks my face cold. Daniel sinks onto the floor and covers his face in shame as his sobs are muffled into quiet despair. His hands are streaked with dried patches of dirt and blood.

"Daniel, tell me what happened." My voice thickens in trepidation.

"I went to Emerald City in downtown Pensacola for a few drinks after returning from Biloxi. As I got ready to leave, two guys approached me and forced me into the car." He clenches his eyes shut as if trying to forget the

incident. "I pleaded with them, told them they could have whatever they wanted, but they laughed and mocked me. They had a bottle of vodka and forced most of it down my throat."

He lets out another heartrending sob.

I stare at him, not sure what to do.

Did I bring this upon him? If he hadn't met me, would he have escaped this fate? It's as I told Jen earlier today: I am cursed; my family is cursed. And this is only further proof that anyone who enters my life will be consumed by fire.

"Oh, God! Oh, God!" he wails. "They took me to a house where they forced my clothes off and they... And they... Oh, God! They kicked me, Fredy! They kicked me, punched me, forced me to give them blow jobs, and then dragged me into their house and tied me up on their bed, and then... Oh, God! Fredy!" He looks at his hands in terror as if seeing them for the first time.

I sit with him until his wails subside.

Moaning, Daniel slides his crusted shirt off to reveal his broad upper back bruised, scratched, and blood-spattered.

"Then what?" I tremble as Daniel's revelation finally sinks in.

"They raped me, Fredy," he whispers.

"How did you escape?"

"They just let me go after threatening to kill me for several hours."

"You need to call the police!" I jump out of bed and reach for the phone.

"NO!" He gets up and yanks it out of my hand. "No, these guys are in the Army. They told me they know where I live and if I told the police they'd kill us!"

"You can't let them win, Daniel! You need to call the police and report this!"

He stares at me blankly with bloodshot eyes.

Sitting back on the edge of the bed, I slip into a state of denial. I don't want to believe any of his words. A part of me accuses him, reasoning he brought this unto himself. Is it selfish of me to think this? How am I supposed to respond when I can't even access my own feelings, let alone my emotions? Who is this man in front of me? You're supposed to be the strong one, Daniel, not me! I didn't move to Pensacola to be dealt another traumatic event.

Stirring from my position, I sink to the floor and wrap my arms around Daniel.

I sit in his grief as his moans lace the thick air with misery.

I sit in denial and make up my mind that somehow he is responsible for this.

When the sun comes up, Daniel undresses himself completely, takes a long steaming hot shower, and then attends to his usual morning ritual. He dabs his neck with Fierce, by Abercrombie & Fitch, picks out his jeans and polo shirt, and neatly styles his hair with gel.

"You shouldn't go into work after what happened to you, Daniel."

"I have to, for the children," he whispers.

<div align="center">∞</div>

A STIFFENING SILENCE blankets us. Each time I open my mouth to mention the rape, his eyes glaze over with a menacing coldness and he quickly slips away to another room. I relapse into a depression—I no longer know whom to turn to. I yearn for the intimacy, connection, and open communication we shared before this befell us.

And the nights are the worst.

I lie in bed next to him and wonder if he is staring into the darkness like me. Shivering, I consider reaching out to touch him, caress his back, wrap my arms around him, and make love—planting a thousand kisses over his body

like the first night we consummated our love, in this very bedroom.

But the idea of Daniel snapping keeps me at bay.

And every night, I fall asleep with tears in my eyes.

I no longer know what it is that Daniel wants from me.

<p style="text-align:center">∞</p>

DANIEL'S RAPE UNLEASHES a monster in him.

"You didn't take Misty out for a walk?" Daniel growls in anger. His face turns a dark shade of red and the veins pop out over his arms as he flexes his knuckles.

"I didn't think you'd get so easily upset over this. I'll walk her right now," I reply, putting aside a magazine I was reading on the couch.

"Don't worry about it, okay? I'll walk Misty." Daniel's eyes furiously widen.

"Please, don't get upset over this, Daniel. I don't mind walking her. Misty!" I call out as I walk to the closet door and grab Misty's leash.

"Don't, Fredy. Just go back and sit down on the couch," he says, yanking the leash out of my hand.

"No, I said I'd walk her, so, I'm going to walk her." I assert myself.

"Just don't!"

The door slams shut as Daniel disappears with Misty into the cool night.

I stand there, dumbstruck and in shock.

For how long I don't know. Then Daniel returns and embraces me in his arms.

"I'm so sorry, honey. I didn't mean to hit you," he whispers, searching my face for bruises.

"You hit me?" I ask, not understanding.

"I didn't mean to, I'm so sorry. I'm extremely stressed out over everything. Please, forgive me," he says.

"You hit me," I whisper quietly as I bury my face into his chest, and for

the first time since his rape, he holds me in his arms. "Don't apologize, Daniel. I don't remember you hitting me."

As if in a dream, I sit down with him and we fix a normal dinner.

He asks me how work is going for me at both the Gap and Starbucks, and if I've made any new friends. I tell him about how I befriended a beautiful model, Albana Ferizi. How she immediately took me beneath her wings and adopted me as her younger brother.

"She's from New York? What's she doing here?" He sips down a vodka cranberry.

"She has her reasons," I reply.

<p style="text-align:center">∞</p>

CHANGING INTO PAJAMAS, I pull the blanket down and slide beneath the covers. Misty jumps onto the bed, licks my face, and curls up next to me. Daniel steps out of the bathroom, applies lip-gloss to his soft pink lips, and powders his face with cover-up. I raise my eyebrows inquisitively as he dresses himself in skin-tight fitted clothing.

"I didn't know we were going out, Daniel."

"Oh, I didn't tell you? I'm going out with my coworker Annette tonight. She thinks it's a good idea for me to go out and have fun after all that I've been through. She should be here any second now." He grabs his cologne and sprays copious amounts onto his neck, chest, and arms.

"That sounds like fun! Look at me, I'm not even dressed," I say with a laugh. "Should only take me a—"

"No, don't get dressed. It's just me and Annette tonight," he cuts me off as he grabs his keys, turns around, and glares at me with a look that sends chills down my body. Revolted, he harshly hisses, "To be honest with you, Fredy, I can't sleep in the same bed with you any longer. Just seeing *you* reminds me of that *night*."

Cringing, I look away as my eyes sting with tears.

"By the time I return later this evening, I want all your things out of my bedroom. Since you have nowhere to go, you can stay in the guest bedroom. If I had it my way, I'd throw you out, but I know you have no place to go. I...I do love you, but I just can't sleep in the same bed with you. You're a constant reminder of that painful night."

His phone rings.

He answers. "Be right out, Annette."

The door slams behind him as he dashes into the night.

A silent sob escapes my lips as his words impale me.

I clutch my chest, grimace, and choke out, "Oh, Misty, how did I get myself into this?" Pulling the covers aside, I make my way into the kitchen. As I rummage through cabinets, pain ricochets and slashes across my body. I find a bottle of gin. Twisting the cap open, I pour pure gin down my throat.

It burns.

Fuck my life.

Slamming the cabinet doors shut, I return to our bedroom—his bedroom. Coming across several pictures I saved from New York, I pick them up and slip into the living room. I take several swigs of gin before collapsing into sobs of anger.

"Damn you, Fredy Espinoza! How foolish of me to think I can escape the Espinoza curse by starting a new life as Forrester Kessington! I knew the Espinoza curse would follow me! I hate you, Fredy Espinoza! I hate you with every molecule of my fucking existence! You don't deserve to live! You don't deserve to be! How can I destroy the very essence of you if I don't even have the fucking balls to commit suicide?! DAMN YOU TO HELL!!!"

I scream at my face in those portraits of me posing in Union Square on blankets of snow. Anger consumes me and I shred the pictures apart. I shred and shred and shred every single picture that captures any essence of who I used to be.

"I FUCKING HATE YOU, FREDY ESPINOZA! WHY DON'T YOU JUST FUCKING DIE! DIE, DAMN IT! DIE!"

Chugging more gin down my throat, I force myself up, enter Daniel's bedroom, and find the fourth journal of my life, chronicling my adventures and misfits in New York up to encountering Daniel serendipitously at Splash Bar. Letting out a scream of angst, I toss the journal into the hall. Gazing around his bedroom, I come face to face with my image in the mirror. Snarling at what I see, I dash into the hallway like a rabid animal, snatch up the journal, and claw and lacerate every page in it.

"WHY?! WHY?! WHY?! YOU FUCKING BASTARD, I HATE YOU, FREDY! I HATE YOU!" I spin uncontrollably amid maimed memories and slashed pictures.

Sinking to the floor, I knock the bottle of gin over and pass out.

∞

THE NEXT MORNING, I wake up in the guest bedroom, or should I say my bedroom. Rubbing my temples, I grimace as a throbbing headache consumes me. Pulling the covers off, I see I'm naked.

Pulling on a pair of gym shorts, I go into the living room.

"So you finally wake up," Daniel grumbles.

"I don't remember a thing from last night," I say, frowning as I see the mess I created.

"I don't know what to do, Fredy," he sighs. "I came home and you were passed out in vomit. I had no choice but to bathe you and help you into bed. Seriously, what the hell is your problem?"

"I got upset. What else am I supposed to do? Everything that I believe no longer exists, Daniel! I moved all the way from New York to be with you. I left everything behind to be with you, and now we're just roommates. I'm sorry about what happened to you, Daniel! I am, truly! It just hurts me that you think I am the cause of all this… And maybe it is. Maybe this is my entire

fault! If you had never met me, none of this would have happened! And if I had it my way, I would move out, but I have nowhere to go, Daniel. What am I supposed to do? If you want, I can leave today, but I don't know where I will go. I don't want to cause you any more pain."

"Please, just clean this up. I'm taking Misty for a walk."

It is true that I had no idea where to move to.

I promised myself I would never return to California. That place holds too many skeletons, too many buried secrets, too many dangerous memories of a past I resist remembering. Then there is the possibility of returning to New York. I could easily transfer back to the city. Although I still have my dreams about making it in New York, I feel in my heart that right now is not the time for me to reconsider returning to the city I love.

<div align="center">∞</div>

DANIEL'S PROMISCUITY KILLS me softly as each night he consumes another stranger in his bedroom.

Horrified, I confront him after witnessing the umpteenth guy leave his bed.

"Why do you bring men into our house when I'm still here? I don't bring any guys over, Daniel! I know we're no longer together, and I don't care if you date other men, but can't you do this when I'm not around?"

"I need to forget I was raped, Fredy," he answers nonchalantly, reaching for his crotch and rubbing it. "People who are raped deal with it by sleeping around."

The doorbell rings.

An attractive nineteen-year-old boy saunters in and walks straight into Daniel's bedroom.

Daniel smirks as he slips into his bedroom, jumps onto his bed, and giggles.

In the background, they continue to whisper and giggle as I enter the

kitchen and pretend to make myself something. Peering into Daniel's bedroom, I catch the boy kissing his neck.

He catches me and mutters something to Daniel.

"Don't worry about him. He's my ex-wife," Daniel states blatantly, loud enough for me to hear.

Frustrated, I make myself a Sapphire tonic and storm off into my bedroom.

Turning on DHT's "Listen to Your Heart," I hold myself tightly, sinking into my twin bed. I place the drink on the nightstand, plant my face in the pillow, and let out stifled sobs. *I know there's something in the wake of your smile. I get a notion from the look in your eyes. Yeah, you've built a love but that love falls apart, your little piece of heaven turns to dark. Listen to your heart when he's calling for you... Listen to your heart before you tell him goodbye...*

<div align="center">∞</div>

ROXIE, DANIEL'S GORGEOUS redheaded coworker, has a dark revelation to share as she and I sit down at a booth in a Mexican restaurant and order a round of delicious margaritas.

"So tell me, what is this revelation that you need to tell me?" I ask her as the waiter drops off our margaritas.

"So, at first, I thought you were the crazy one, Fredy. Daniel makes you out to be an asshole, but every time I hang out with you, you seem the exact opposite. Whenever you stop by the store, you are always so nice, caring, and gentle. But it wasn't until I hung with him and Annette that the truth came out." She looks away. "God, just thinking of it makes me sick."

"Tell me," I say, looking at her with big dewy eyes.

"Last night, the three of us went out to Emerald City, you know, the gay club. I generally don't care at all about going out, but Daniel and Annette have been acting rather strange around work lately. After paying careful attention to their interactions, I wanted to include myself in their night of

clubbing." Roxie's brown eyes darken and she hesitates. "I think your ex is sick, Fredy."

"He hasn't been the same since the rape," I reply, defending him.

"We're on the dance floor, and I notice how Daniel and Annette grope each other as they dance. I thought nothing of it at first because, let's face it, Daniel is gay. They down several shots; unbeknown to them, I only had a few drinks. But they just keep drinking up. Concerned, I offer driving them back to your apartment. And since I was exhausted, I decided to stay the night."

"Oh, so that was you who slammed the door hard early this morning." I gulp down my margarita and order another.

"Would you like another margarita, miss?" the waiter asks.

"Please," she says, smiling briefly. Her face turns sour and she forces herself to gulp down her margarita. "I swear Fredy, thinking about this is making me nauseous. I could just throw up right now." She shakes her head and continues, "Late last night, I think Daniel and Annette forgot I had passed out in the living room because I awoke to the sound of giggling and smacking inside Daniel's bedroom. At first I was confused, but it became clear what was happening when their giggles became moans. Once the headboard started smacking against the wall I realized they were having sex. I wanted to vomit on your carpet, Fredy. It was so fucking disgusting that I grabbed my purse and slammed the door hard, making sure they heard me."

"Wait! Whoa! Daniel and Annette had sex? So, what you're telling me is that Annette is having an affair on her husband?" The waiter drops off the second round of margaritas.

"I'm still sick over it all, Fredy. And the horrible thing is that she has children! I just don't know what to do. I thought about writing a letter to her husband and revealing this affair. God, Daniel is a monster. How do you stand him?"

"I don't know, Roxie. I love him, and I think a part of why I haven't lost

it is because I still hope that I can help Daniel with this whole situation, but now that you've revealed their affair, I find myself at a loss for what to do."

"Why don't you just move out?"

"I can't. I have nowhere to go. And I don't want to be a nuisance to anyone."

"I don't know how I'm going to face them at work tomorrow," Roxie whispers, taking a huge swig from her second margarita and looking at me with pity.

We sip the remainder of our margaritas in silence.

<p style="text-align:center">∞</p>

THAT NIGHT, I take a cab to Emerald City. I can't face returning to the apartment and seeing Annette's face, or Daniel's.

As I lose myself to the beat of the music, I happen to make eye contact with the most gorgeous man in the club. He catches me dancing and twirling to my heart's content on the dance floor. His striking blue eyes hypnotize me as I take in his smooth tanned skin, bulging muscles, and black hair.

"I know your secret," he says, winking at me as he pulls up beside me at the bar.

"What secret?" I laugh. I order another Sapphire tonic.

"You do energy work," he says, smiling and showing his pearly-white movie-star teeth.

"I'm sorry? If this is your way of hitting on me, it's working because no one has ever come onto me like that before," I laugh again.

"When you dance, you move the energy about in this room. I'm gifted and can see energy work in colors. Yours are the brightest in this room; you stir the energy all about. I haven't met anyone so...gifted. Like me." He leans over and widens his smile.

"Fascinating reading," I reply. I sit back and swallow his words.

He steps back from the bar and motions to the dance floor. "Come on,

join me on the dance floor. I want to feel how you harness your energy."

Forgetting about Daniel, Annette, and all that's transpired, I slip back onto the dance floor and make love to the music. I go along with his hypothesis as I imagine vibrant bold blues and incessant spiraling jades being called forth from my being; imagine these energies consuming us as I bask within the light of a vibrating force.

"That's it!" He laughs, hypnotically mimicking me.

We dance until the club closes.

I decide to return to his place when he offers.

His apartment is beautifully decorated with earthy colors. On the counter, a book of witchcraft and spells lingers open. I sit down on the couch and nervously look about the room as he picks up the remote control and turns on his flat-screen television.

"Want to see *Donnie Darko*?" He asks me.

"Yes, it's one of my favorite movies." I smile as he lies down on the couch and beckons me to sink into his arms.

"You're trembling." He kisses my head and his arms tighten around me. "You don't have to be afraid of me. I promise, I have no intention of sleeping with you tonight."

"I'm sorry… It's just that I don't know how I got myself into all this," I confess.

How can I confide in him that it's not him I'm afraid of, but of returning to Daniel's apartment—to the maddening memories of him rushing in screaming after being raped, me waking up on the opposite side of our apartment alone in the guest bedroom, and the denial of believing that Daniel and I can return to our lives before they were destroyed.

A calming wave of energy radiates from the guy's body and it calms me.

I stop shivering and lie in the arms of another man.

It's time I got over Daniel Hansen.

Will I ever fall in love again?

"What are you thinking up there in that head of yours? You look so intense," he says, kissing my forehead. His piercing blue eyes penetrate me.

"Oh, nothing. Nothing."

"I promise not to harm you, handsome. I will protect you," he whispers.

Isn't that what they all say?

Can I ever trust again?

"I believe you," I whisper back as I fight away ghosts lingering in my head.

He doesn't make a move on me the whole time my body is pressed against his on the couch. A part of me desires him to just take me right there and make love to me. And yet the thought consumes me with guilt; the last time I had sex was with Daniel, before his rape.

When the movie is over, I ask, "Can I sleep here tonight?"

"Of course." He smiles as he nudges his nose into my hair.

In his bedroom, I put on a pair of his pajamas and get into his bed. Turning the lights off, he pushes a button on his remote control and a song by Radiohead plays softly in the background.

"What song is this?"

"'How To Disappear Completely,'" he says, pressing me into his strong arms.

"I like it," I reply as I allow this beautiful stranger to hold me.

Thom Yorke's anguished voice lulls me into a deep sleep.

In a little while, I'll be gone. The moment's already passed, yeah it's gone. And I'm not here, this isn't happening; I'm not here... I'm not here...

∞ CHAPTER IX: LUCIFER'S PROPOSAL ∞

REVELATION AFTER REVELATION flings me into the arms of Lucifer. And he goes by the name of Morgan Medeford. It is not until the end of October that I end up crossing his path at Emerald City; when I do, he torches my life into crimson fires and catapults me into the lowest depths of Hell.

Leaving the dance floor that night, I step outside onto the patio and make my way upstairs to the roof. As I clear the landing, I immediately make eye contact with the most bewitchingly handsome man who could possibly exist in my world. His luminous and magnificent green eyes leave me speechless and I am paralyzed within his enchanted stare; my knees buckle as his overpowering masculine energy consumes me in a frenzy of peaking sexual desire; and his dark-blonde hair casts a glowing halo over his translucent alabaster skin.

Above us, a new moon hangs a tapestry of finely woven silver and gold stardust. Below us, electronic dub step music pulses profusely throughout the

building, sending shockwaves to course through my body. I hold my ground, give him a Mona Lisa smile, and wait for him to approach me.

His voluptuous cherry-stained lips curl into a playful smile as I throw myself on him and whisper into his ear, "I need to know you." Stepping back, I let a glint of total submission escape from my eyes, thinking, *Take me, I'm all yours. Do whatever you please with me; ravish me; steal me far away from here, use me, and destroy me.*

In his presence, thoughts of self-destruction amplify.

"Morgan Medeford," he says, winking at me.

He is slightly taken back by my boldness as I lean in and passionately kiss him.

"Wow, aren't you something." Morgan's eyes sparkle with mischief.

Smirking, I grab his hand and beckon him to follow me down the staircase onto the patio. Heading to the bar, I order us two cocktails. Maybe the fact that I haven't had sex in over two months causes me to act blatantly assertive. What I desire is for him to become my first cadaver. Indeed, Morgan Medeford will be the first of many men who for now on will be my victims. Of course, I have no intention of actually killing these men. It is the possibility of love I kill as I choose to lose myself in sex.

Whatever it takes to forget I ever loved Daniel Hansen; to forget I ever loved Melancton Vassiliadis.

After a few more drinks, some shallow conversation, and more forceful passionate kisses, Morgan and I ditch the nightclub and get into his car. His hand slips under my shirt, caresses my back, slides down into my underwear. He presses his middle finger into the base of my asshole.

"Fuck, you're hot," Morgan pants. He takes his hand out, smells his finger, and licks it, "You taste good."

"I taste better in bed," I whisper heavily as I crave him deep inside me.

Driving to his house, I tell Morgan how I wound up in Pensacola.

"And you're still with this guy?"

"No, we're no longer together." I say, shaking my head. As we turn onto Spanish Trail Road, I show him the apartment complex I live in. Suddenly, Morgan's bewitching green eyes flash with shame and he whispers, "In that apartment complex, you don't happen to live with a guy named Daniel?"

"Yes," I inhale sharply.

"And he drives a red Sentra?"

"How do you know?"

I clutch the door handle, expecting him to tell me what I already suspect.

"I hate to tell you this, but we slept together."

"When?"

"I don't really remember, but I'm certain it was around the second or third weekend of August. Why do you care? You told me you guys aren't together any more."

It matters to me because that's the time period when Daniel was raped.

And just like that, I snap full force into Forrester Kessington.

Letting go of the door handle, I lean over with a cunning smile on my face, place my hand on his thick crotch, and whisper seductively, "Tonight is a night neither of us will ever forget, Morgan. As for Daniel, let's not speak of him any longer. In *my world*, Daniel doesn't exist."

Forrester Kessington always knows when to take over when I need him.

He's my blessing.

And my curse.

<div align="center">∞</div>

THE PRINCE OF DARKNESS galvanizes my heart. I step into his house and am enveloped in a scent of death. It is a very distinct, sharp, bitter odor. Morgan rushes me into his bedroom. Dropping my coat on the floor, I alluringly sit at the edge of his bed before lunging at him, and like a vampire, bite his neck and leave behind purple bruises.

Header: FREDY ESPINOZA
Footer: ∞ 168 ∞

"I want you badly," I moan in heat as I kick my shoes off.

"You want a good fuck, then let me give you the best fuck you will ever have." Morgan's nostrils flare as he inhales my scent.

Pushing himself off me, Morgan opens a small cabinet door.

He reaches in, pulls out a couple of small white crystal rocks, and smoothly places them on the glass counter in the middle of the room. Bemused, I stare with a perplexed look on my face as he gently crushes them into dust, compiles them into several tiny bumps, and produces an elongated glass stem from out of nowhere.

"What is that?" I ask, my eyes flickering to him.

"You've never seen this before?"

"No, never in my life. Cocaine?"

Morgan smiles wickedly in my direction. "Tina."

"Tina?"

"Crystal meth," he says with a laugh, lighting the bottom of the glass stem with a fluid lighter.

Morgan places the end of the stem over a bump; the red-hot heat vaporizes it instantly. He quickly leans down and inhales the vapor into his nose.

"It's called a hard rail. Go ahead—it won't harm you, if you can handle it."

Whether it is the revelation of Morgan having had sex with Daniel, or my habit of needing to escape from the ghosts of my past, I smile wickedly and tell myself it doesn't hurt to experiment.

Morgan heats the bottom of the stem and passes it to me; I place it over another bump on the nightstand, and as the white powder vaporizes, I quickly inhale the Tina into my nostril.

Within seconds, a rush of bliss cascades across every hair follicle on my body. Laughing, I grab Morgan and fling him onto his bed. I feverishly

undress us—belt buckles come undone, shirts get tossed wildly across the room, and pants and underwear twist into a pile of discarded remnants of our erotic lust on the floor.

"Fuck me, Morgan," I whisper, forcing him into me. "Just fuck me as hard as you can!"

A savage thirst for sex possesses me as Morgan thrusts himself powerfully into me. Yes! Fuck me! Like a white horse, I straddle him as he pounds into me. Arching my back, I bounce up and down, up and down. The smell of sweat fills my nostrils and I come onto his face. He opens his mouth and swallows my load. Then we fuck again, Morgan pinning me down and monstrously thrashing his body into mine. I come again all over his black satin sheets. We commence to fuck in frenzy as I get on my knees in a doggy position and cry out in pleasure as Morgan grabs my waist and smacks me into him.

Stopping, Morgan locks his devilish eyes with mine.

"You're an amazing piece of machinery."

"I'm not done just yet," I pant as I push him onto his back, get on top of him, and demand, "Keep fucking me, Morgan." I throw my head back as he slips into me and I devour him like a cannibal.

Yes, let me stay in this vortex of saturated bliss, Morgan, as you fuck my pain away. Fuck it away, Morgan. Fuck the pain away. Harder. Harder. Faster. Faster. Just fuck it all away!

Six visceral hours later, I finally get off Morgan and fling myself into his arms.

Our bodies are soiled with sweat and cum.

"I need water, babe," Morgan pants, squeezing his eyes shut.

"Don't leave me," I whisper. "Tell me about yourself."

I close my eyes and listen to Morgan's dark sensual voice as he exposes his history to me. "I used to live in Manhattan. My parents abandoned me as

a child. I worked my ass off to get into Columbia, and once I graduated I had every intention of becoming a real estate agent. But then I met the love of my life. After he proposed to me a year later, he committed suicide by speeding his car into a metal pole."

"Oh, God, I'm sorry, Morgan," I say, in a state of shock, my eyes watering.

"Yeah." His voice thickens with pain. "It sent me over the edge. His death put me on this path of consuming crystal methamphetamine and down to this shithole town, Pensa-fucking-cola. I don't plan to stay here, baby. I'm moving to Miami in a few weeks. I've never met anyone like you."

"And I've never met anyone like you either, Morgan." I frown as I remember my true self. "You know, sometimes I wonder about myself, Morgan. Most of the time I'm Fredy Espinoza, and other times I go by Forrester Kessington."

"Forrester Kessington?"

"Yeah, the best way to explain is by calling him my alter ego. And to be honest with you, I became Forrester Kessington tonight. Does that frighten you?"

"No, but tell me why you take on your alter ego." Morgan gazes into my eyes as he wipes tears away from his own.

For over an hour I tell him how Eduardo physically abused me for four years, Mom tried to kill me while I was dead asleep, Dad disowned me and discarded me on the street, and how I just woke up one day becoming another persona as Forrester Kessington stole me away to New York, only to find myself on the brink of perpetual homelessness.

"…and all I have ever desired, Morgan, is for the love of my life to find me, recognize me, see right through into the essence of my soul, and accept me unconditionally. I don't know if I will ever find him, Morgan. Just look at me." I weep, "I have nothing to offer."

Morgan leans his face into mine and kisses my tears away.

"From the minute your eyes captured mine, you left me speechless, Fredy Espinoza, and I knew right then that there was something extremely special about you. I love everything about you, your boldness, your kindness, and your history. I will never harm you, Fredy. I will protect you forever, as long as you're by my side. I will buy you the world, and give you whatever you desire. I'm moving into a penthouse on Ocean Avenue in Miami in a few weeks, and I want you to be there with me; to experience life with me the way I am experiencing it with you right now. Will you be forever mine?" Morgan holds my gaze with his electrifying magnetic green eyes.

"Yes, Morgan, I will be yours, forever." I accept Lucifer's proposal and seal my fate with a voracious kiss. Slipping his bulging cock into me, I ride him as I strangle another suffocating kiss out of him. "Yes, forever yours... Forever yours, Morgan. Now just *fuck me*."

<p style="text-align:center">∞</p>

I SLEPT WITH the Devil, and let me tell you, it was the most ravishing, steamy, and liberating night of my life. Now I will never return to my previous state of being.

Scorching sun scathes my skin as I step out of Morgan's house and walk to his car. I watch Morgan as he approaches his side of the car and gets in. Purple bruises adorn the side of his neck.

Morgan looks over at me and smiles.

"I am so in love with you, Fredy. I trust you with my life."

He puts the key into the ignition, starts the car, and we speed off to downtown Pensacola.

"Where are we going?" I ask, basking in the aftermath of our intense copulation.

"You're going to run errands with me," he says, rolling down the windows.

The salty air smells good as it whips into the car.

"Sounds like fun," I say, grinning.

Driving down a secluded street, we arrive at a tacky beat-down house. The windows are secured with bars and the door is ajar. Dead grass is scattered across a shredded lawn.

"Should I wait for you in the car?" I ask, biting my lip nervously.

"No, babe. I want you to come with me. From now on, we do everything together." He leans over and plants a passionate kiss on my lips.

"I love you," I say, clasping his hand, then letting it go and stepping out of the car.

Following him into the house, I hear a dog bark. From deep inside, the owner shouts at it to shut up as Morgan calls out that he's arrived. A few seconds later, a sickly-looking young man appears at the door, stops as he sees me, raises his eyebrows, and asks who I am.

"Oh, don't worry about him. He's my boyfriend," Morgan says, his teeth flashing charismatically.

"Oh, who would have thought that Morgan Medeford would ever get himself a boyfriend?! Let me tell you, he's been single since I've known him, isn't that right, Morgan?" He chuckles.

"Let's not talk about my business. I brought you what you need," Morgan says, reaching into his pocket and handing over a small bag of crystal meth.

"That's a hot man you landed yourself, Morgan. I would love to celebrate your success by doing a line with him, if it doesn't bother you, Morgan?" He looks in my direction.

"No, it doesn't bother me at all," Morgan replies indifferently. The three of us walk into the kitchen.

A heat of anticipation rushes over my body and my eyes glaze over.

Is this the cost of beauty?

Snorting a line, I feel a rush of euphoria. I stare into Morgan's eyes.

Yes, baby, I'm all yours.

Back inside the car, Morgan clasps his fingers in mine.

"I didn't know you were a dealer, Morgan," I say.

"I'm the best in this town, baby. With me, you'll never have to worry about anything. And if anyone hurts you, I promise they will be hunted down."

"You promise?"

"I promise." Morgan's eyes glitter with intense fire as he kisses my hand.

And for the remainder of the day, I find myself tagging along with Morgan as he sells crystal meth to all his clients. At each stop, his clients find me irresistibly attractive and ask to do a line of meth with me. In a strange way, I feel courted: every client I meet wants me. And for Morgan to trust me as I intimately snort meth with these strangers makes me fall deeper in love with him.

As night descends, I realize I have snorted over six hits.

Racing back to Morgan's lair, we continue to do hard rail lines.

Then we commence another night of insatiable sex. An intense fire consumes me in a feverish dream state as Morgan thrusts into me for several hours.

In this frenetic heat, I forget being loathed by my brother, mother, and father.

In this burning fire of sexual consumption, I disappear, exulting in the beauty of the flesh of man as Morgan plants his seed in me many times over through the course of the night; and it is in this obsessive fire that I am unconditionally loved.

∞

"MORGAN MEDEFORD, MY sweet love, I have a flight to catch in five hours," I whisper.

I roll over and caress his arm.

"What?! You never told me you were flying today." Morgan looks at me with suspicion.

"To the Bay Area. It's been in the works for awhile. If I'd known I was going to meet you, Morgan, I wouldn't have bought a ticket to California."

"You're leaving Pensacola?!" Morgan's green eyes flash with anger as he pushes me off him.

"No, silly." I look at him in shock. "I'm vacationing for a week and spending that time with my best friend, Tyrone. I have every intention of returning, and when I do, I promise to be with you again. After all, you proposed to me, and I love you."

"You've got to be kidding me, right? I mean, you told me yourself you're an actor," Morgan glances at me with a playful smile as his anger vanishes into thin air.

"No, I'm not kidding, Morgan. I have a flight that leaves in five hours and I need to be on that flight. Look, these past two days have been amazing and I plan to return for more. I want to follow you to Miami and see what further adventures we create together, babe."

Getting up, I reach over Morgan to get out of bed when suddenly he grabs my arms and fiercely yanks me onto him.

"No, you're not leaving me, Fredy Espinoza," Morgan snaps.

"But Morgan, I already told you I'm coming back to you," I cry in slight trepidation.

"I'm not letting you go anywhere," he says, tightening his hold on me.

"Morgan, I'm serious! I have to leave now! I promise I will return," I plead.

Struggling out of his embrace, I lunge toward my clothes, slip into them, and hover over him.

"If you leave me, Fredy, you'll never come back. I love you—can't you see that? Please, just get back into bed and we can both fly out to California later this month if it means so much to you. Don't I mean a lot to you, babe?" Morgan's eyes flash with sorrow.

"Oh, Morgan, don't do this to me. How many times do I have to tell you that I love you. You're the only one for me, and if you trust me, you'd let me go and see my friends, whom I haven't seen in over a year now. Please. I will come back to you, I promise."

"Please don't leave me, babe. You'll never come back if you do. I need you so much in my life. Please don't go like this, Fredy," Morgan pleads as he reaches out to me.

His vulnerability overcomes me as he tells me he needs me. How I've always wanted to hear those words from another man: that he needs me. But as I glance around his dark room, a sudden urge to escape clutches my heart. It's as if, for a split second, a veil of truth parts, revealing the danger I have put myself in. If I don't stand up against Morgan and his proposal, if I continue to do as much meth as I have done in the past two days, a shroud of death will descend upon me. Although the idea of committing myself to Lucifer sounds enticing, I decide to step away from that precipice and into the light.

Like a snake awakening from its deep slumber, an instinct of survival overcomes me and I strike. I grab Morgan's cell-phone and dial a number.

"What are you doing!?" Morgan lashes out, snatching the phone from my hands.

"You don't understand, Morgan! I promised my best friends I'd fly out today. I can't let them down. Call a cab for me, please!" I change my strategy, lean into him, wrap my arms around him, and softly plead, "I promise to you

on my mother's grave that I will return to you, Morgan. I'm a man of my word."

"You're going nowhere, Fredy. Not without me, ever."

Terror sweeps through my body. I freak out, drop to my knees, and desperately beg, "Please, Morgan! Please, I promise! Please don't deny me this trip! This one chance to leave and spend time with my closest friends! I've suffered enough and I need to get out of this suffocating town, even if for just a bit! Please, Morgan! MORGAN!"

"You promise on your mother's grave?" Morgan whispers, finally giving in.

"Yes! On all my family's graves!" I nod adamantly, "You're the one for me, Morgan! The second I fly in, I will return to your arms and we can start a new life in Miami."

Morgan holds my gaze for a minute before sighing and calling a cab.

∞

FLEEING MORGAN MEDEFORD'S house, I quickly jump into the cab and ask to be taken to my apartment. Dashing inside, I rush past Daniel on my way to my bedroom.

Daniel's facial expression is priceless. "Where have you been? And what happened to you?" Daniel asks as I throw shirts and jeans into a duffel bag.

"I don't have time to explain anything to you right now, Daniel," I sneer. "My cab's waiting for me downstairs."

Clambering down the stairs, I race back to the cab, jump in, and ask to be taken to Starbucks. Once there, I hardly notice the shocked expressions on my coworkers' faces as I burst in, seize my paycheck, and storm out as quickly as I stormed in. Catching my reflection in the window of the cab, I startle myself with a sight everyone else witnessed but me: a deathly gaunt man clutching for dear life and his soul.

At the airport, I dash through the crowd. My flight leaves in forty

minutes. Passing through security, my face glistens with sweat and I wonder if they will stop me for having consumed drugs in the past forty-eight hours.

I scarcely make it onto the plane as the door to the jetway closes behind me.

Gasping for air, I crash into the last seat toward the back of the plane, clamp my eyes shut, and lose myself within a streak of paranoia. A churning sea of frightening cyclical thoughts consume me. Why is everybody looking at me? Do they all know what I did? Are the police waiting for me at San Francisco? Oh my god, the FBI is following me! That flight attendant is an FBI agent! I can't go to jail! What if I fall asleep and never wake up? I have to stay awake! Stay awake! Just stay awake!

The plane sets off into the endless blue sky.

And that's when the withdrawals take root.

The most horrifying, mind-numbing, excruciating pain wrenches my body. Clenching my arms for support, I rancorously scratch at my perspiring skin to stop the pain from galvanizing me. As an intense demonic craving for crystal meth heightens, I find myself clawing at my arms, drawing blood, and clamping my mouth shut from making any noises as I gnaw the insides of my cheeks, my lips, my tongue. Monstrous cravings come at me in heinous waves; gritting my teeth, I imagine myself howling, screaming, and thrashing about the cabin as the insides of my body purge themselves of this poison. I throw my head against the seat as severe urges to mutilate myself crash over me.

Is this what Hell feels like?

I am burning in crimson fire as my blood boils with demonic thirst for a hard rail. It pains me so much that I am willing to do anything for it. Anything! Hellish fires possess me, flames slash, shred, and shear my soul into a million little pieces. If there is such a place as Hell, the Devil is surely feasting on my soul right now. Is this the price I have to pay for all that will

come to be?

Someone taps me softly on the shoulder. "Excuse me, sir."

Opening my eyes, I see a flight attendant looking at me with concern.

"Yes?" I reply thickly.

"Are you okay?" she inquires. "Would you like something to drink?"

"Oh, yes, thank you. Soda would be fine, and do you have something I can munch on?"

When she returns, I force a painful smile onto my face and exert my hands mechanically to grab a soft drink and a bag of peanuts. As I pull the soda to my mouth, I cringe as a drop of it stings my mouth. Turning my attention to the peanuts, I pop one into my mouth and grimace as I can't find the strength to bite into it; the texture is akin to a block of cement.

I spit the peanut out into the napkin and set it aside. I don't touch the peanuts or the soda for the remainder of the flight.

<div align="center">∞</div>

TYRONE BOTELHO'S JAW drops as I exit the terminal and hug him.

"Oh my God, Fredy! You look sick! Are you okay? What happened to you?" Tyrone badgers me with questions.

"I'll explain in the car," I answer.

"You don't have AIDS, do you?"

"Tyrone! Of course not! I'll explain everything in the car. I just want to go back to your place and sleep. You will not believe what happened to me in these past two days."

"You just… You look so skinny, and your face, where did it go? And why do you have bruises all over your arms and neck? What's going on, Fredy! This isn't you at all," Tyrone insists as we walk to his car.

"Please, I'll explain in the car. Can we go straight back to your place this evening?"

"I can't," Tyrone says with a mischievous glint in his eyes.

"Oh, no, what did you plan, Tyrone?"

"Well, I threw you a surprise welcome-back party at the Cheesecake Factory! Everyone is going to be there!"

"No! You know how much I hate surprise parties! Cancel it! I just can't show up like this, Tyrone!" I cry in shock, afraid to face everyone looking the way I do.

"Don't be silly, Fredy. Everyone's excited to see you and they're all there already." Tyrone laughs.

"Who's there?"

"Everyone," he smiles.

"Great, just great," I mutter beneath my breath as we get into his car.

The evening rushes past me. I sit through an awkward dinner party, everyone wearing matched expressions as they all look at me with concern. Conversation touches on my stay in New York, Daniel Hansen, my life in Pensacola. After it becomes obvious to everyone that I'm not in the right state of mind, we end the dinner party early.

In Tyrone's bathroom, I step on his scale and gasp as it weighs me in at a hundred and twenty-eight pounds. *No, this can't be right! It must be broken!* Before meeting Morgan, I weighed a hundred and fifty-two. If this scale is correct, in the span of two days I have lost over twenty pounds.

Gazing in the mirror, I wince at the sight of my hollow cheekbones, bloodshot eyes with dark circles underneath, deathly malnourished skin. Huge purple bruises cover my neck, giving me the look of having been choked all night long, and dry scratches lace up and down my gaunt, sickly arms.

"This is what happens when all that self-loathing manifests, Fredy," I whisper. "Look upon your self-hatred."

Damn you, Morgan Medeford!

∞

REHABILITATION THROUGH THE moral support of my circle of friends aids me through this crisis as I quickly strip myself of the need for crystal meth. Tyrone takes time off and steals me away in his car to West Hollywood. We run amok through the gay scene, hit up the beach, and make our way back to San Francisco; we let ourselves loose in the bars of the Castro and sunbathe beneath the Golden Gate Bridge. There, I slowly regain my power as I fully accept the consequences of having consumed crystal meth. And the horror of what I experienced during those hours of withdrawal only cements my decision never to touch that drug again.

None of my friends understand when I tell them that my chapter in Pensacola isn't completely over, that I must return for unfinished business, things undone; that for whatever reason, something calls me to return. Maybe I'm propelled back to Florida because I don't have a home in California to call my own.

At the terminal, Tyrone hugs me fiercely and reminds me, "Remember your promise, Fredy! Whatever you do, keep your promise never to get in touch with Morgan Medeford!"

"I promise," I say, returning his hug. "I honestly don't know what I would have done without you, Tyrone. You're like a brother to me—like family—and it means so much to me that you helped me recuperate from that horrifying experience."

"Anything for you, Fredy," he smiles, tears welling up in his eyes.

"Hey, at least I have a nice figure now!" I laugh as I lift my arms into the air and pretend to model my body.

"That's not funny, Fredy," he chastises me. "I just don't get it. Why return to Pensacola? There's nothing for you there."

"Something tells me it's not my time to return to California just yet, Tyrone. I wish I could explain. Goodbye, my dear friend."

∞ CHAPTER X: SEXUAL ESCAPADES ∞

A PROPINQUITY OF SADNESS saturates my being as I return to Pensacola.

I keep my promise and ignore Morgan's messages. I also think a lot about Daniel Hansen. It is so much easier to be in denial and believe he wasn't raped, that he fabricated the whole event to excuse his betrayal. But how can I crucify a man if it's not his fault? And why am I returning to him? It's obvious Daniel loathes me, finds my presence unfathomable, and wishes me gone from his life. And yet I yearn to believe that there is still a chance between us.

Stepping into the apartment, I come upon Daniel half asleep on the couch.

"I thought you weren't returning, Fredy." He smiles and his blue eyes twinkle with joy.

"Why wouldn't I return? You know I don't have a home in California."

"I just figured you have no reason to be here."

"No, there is still a reason, but I don't know what that reason is. I feel that there's one more lesson I need to learn before I embark on my next journey." I plop my duffel bag on the kitchen counter.

"I missed you being here," Daniel confesses, sitting up. His silky blue Sponge Bob pajamas look adorable from this vantage point as he removes the blanket.

"I missed you too," I say, heading over to him and giving him a hug.

"Oh, Lord, I think I'm hard," he says with a laugh. "Do you want to go down on me?"

"Of course, Daniel," I answer.

All I crave is to be close to you, Daniel.

Let me show you that I love you so that you may love me back.

<p style="text-align:center">∞</p>

AN EXCHANGE STUDENT from the Netherlands befriends me at Starbucks. Twenty-four years old, tall, muscular, blue eyes, dark-blonde hair, and with a gorgeous smile, Theo entertains me for the remainder of his stay in Pensacola.

I jump into his blue jeep and we drive off to New Orleans. As we make our way into Louisiana, I am full of shock at the destruction Hurricane Katrina left in its path when it struck in August 2005, just last year. That was the first hurricane I ever experienced.

Theo is saying, "So, there we are, on the beach, getting naked, and I'm thinking, 'Holy shit, they're a fucking couple!' This guy's penis is bigger than mine, Fredy. And I have a huge penis. I could tell the other guy is insecure, but we all end up blowing one another. You know what, Fredy, I can admit to you right here that I'm a slut. And I don't care what anyone thinks."

"I care too much," I reply.

"Who gives a fuck what people think about you, Fredy. Who are these people anyway in this town? One day, you'll be gone, doing your own thing,

and no one will care about what you did in this town. I'm only here for one semester, then it's bye-bye for me. Do you think anyone cares about what I do out here? No."

"Why don't you sleep with me, Theo?" I flirt.

"Because it'll mean a lot more than just sex to you, Fredy. I don't want to hurt you. I have sex for recreational purposes and to fulfill my sexual appetite."

"Oh, please! Stop it! You can't possibly hurt me." I laugh. "I've been told I'm good in bed."

"I don't doubt that one bit, Fredy." He laughs as he reaches over and pats my thigh.

"Then let me go down on you," I say boldly.

The comment lingers in the air for several awkward seconds before he turns to me and says, "You're a real good friend and I know you're going through a lot with Daniel. I just don't want to ruin our friendship, so let's keep it that way."

As I sit there, I think to myself, *No wonder I'm falling for him. I'm used to men sleeping with me for my looks, but here's a guy who genuinely cares about my well-being.*

Theo cracks a joke and I burst into laughter as the awkwardness dissipates.

The weekend passes in a blur.

I get second place in a strip contest at Oz, a gay bar in New Orleans.

I go to my very first sex club; I inhale poppers and fool around with five different men. Theo disappears on me, and when I find him the following morning he tells me that he had sex with six different men.

The following weekend, Theo and I leave for Atlanta.

Once again, I find myself at a sex club. This time, I play nice; I survey the grounds, hang out in the sauna, and take a dip in the cool pool. Theo runs about doing his own thing. For the remainder of the stay, we hit up every

nightclub. Wet Bar is my favorite.

And because of these recent escapades', I get fired from Starbucks.

If I hadn't quit the Gap back in January, I'd be fine with this predicament, but now it seems that my life is barely hanging by a thread. I wonder what will become of me. It will only be a matter of time before Daniel finds out. And then what?

I can't imagine myself living on the streets of Pensacola.

Just as I lived on the streets of Manhattan.

<p align="center">∞</p>

ALBANA FERIZI TAKES me beneath her wing as my older sister. A regular customer of mine at Starbucks, she befriended me the day after I found out Daniel was raped. She consoled me in my hour of need and promised to be there for me whenever I needed her. At twenty-four years old, she is strikingly gorgeous and has modeled for many fashion designers. From her long silky legs to her long sleek blonde hair, her presence is luminous—people cannot help but notice her when she enters a room. Her rare and yet exquisite eyes are different colors: a lush hazel brown and a sapphire blue. And whenever she speaks, not only does a beautiful accent magnify her essence, but her voice sounds sophisticated and mature for someone her age.

"Why are you so sad, my little brother?" Albana kisses my cheek as I step into her car.

"I feel cheated of a life I could have had, Albana. It's already May and I feel like I'm doing nothing with my life. I don't know if I should return to New York, or move to Miami, or leave for San Francisco. I'm so depressed in this town." I pout and help myself to a cigarette.

"Cheer up, little brother! I've got a surprise for you!"

"Surprise?"

"I'm going to show you my world. Buckle up—we're driving to Miami."

"Miami? But Albana, I have no money!" I gasp.

"Don't worry one bit about that, little brother. I promise to take care of you. I'm your older sister now, your family, and don't you ever forget that." She smiles a dazzling smile.

"But I'm not even dressed for that part."

"We'll buy you something in Miami."

And just like that, Albana kidnaps me to Miami.

Upon arrival, we sleep in a suite at one of the most expensive and lavish hotels on Ocean Avenue. Albana finds me an outfit and dresses me up so that I can pass as one of the rich. As I stand there before the mirror and see Albana beside me, a burning yearning for this life consumes me and I think that I would sell my soul to live this life every waking second.

Music blaring, Albana hops around the room, laughs and giggles, and showers me with compliments as she tries on several outfits.

"Which outfit, darling?" She puckers her cherry-red lips and stares into the mirror.

"I love the Armani miniskirt, but that Dolce & Gabbana outfit is to die for, and your Gucci couture makes you look drop-dead gorgeous. God, I don't know which outfit you should wear, Albana! You look too gorgeous and perfect in all of them!"

"To hell with it, I'll put on the black miniskirt." She races into the bathroom and puts it on.

An hour later, I meet Lei Marco, one of Miami's well-known Italian designers. He introduces himself with such ease and sophistication. His penthouse is astonishing; he shows me the various pieces of work he's been laboring over.

"So, you're Albana's brother? You never told me you had a brother, Albana," Lei Marco questions her.

"There are so many things you don't know about me, Lei Marco," Albana replies with a quiet laugh as she places her hand on my arm to put me

at ease. "I'm your favorite model, am I not, Lei Marco?"

"Yes, my beautiful, gorgeous, and stunning angel. Everyone else pales next to you," Lei Marco answers, his lips curling into a smile.

As Lei Marco disappears into his bathroom, Albana leans over and whispers, "Remember everything about tonight. Just watch and learn, my little brother. One day you will have all this."

Nodding my head, I relax and follow her tutelage.

To think that one day I can have this life; it's all I've ever wanted.

As the night descends, we leave Lei Marco's penthouse and schmooze with wealthy socialites and social climbers. Lei Marco gets us into VIP rooms in many exclusive night clubs. Among these socialites, it dawns on me there is no difference between me and them except for one obvious detail: money. But no one here knows my story; I can easily pick up the essence of their style and pretend to be one of them.

Albana, Lei Marco, and I sit behind a rope in the VIP section of Mansion Nightclub as bottle service flows freely. Albana warned me not to get drunk, but I haven't been able to help myself, pouring drink after drink.

"Will you attend me to the restroom, Albana?" Lei Marco asks.

"Of course, my dear." Albana looks over at me. "Stay right here, Fredy. Don't disappear on me, now."

After they leave, I look toward the dance floor and a hot guy winks at me. I glance around to see if he means it for someone else. I make eye contact with him and he winks at me again. Even though I promised I'd wait for Albana, I can't help it. I get up from the seat and descend to the dance floor.

We dance to a few songs. Laughing, I feel his muscles through his shirt. When I notice Albana and Lei Marco returning from the restrooms, I wave my arm to make myself known. Albana whispers something to Lei Marco and then smiles my way. As I dance, I glance at Albana and Lei Marco; they look like demigods separated from the common people as they commune

intimately in the VIP section. Neither of them has the faintest urge to step onto the dance floor; they sit, watching over everyone.

Someone taps my shoulder.

A good-looking girl my age is standing there. "Hi, aren't you that actor in that upcoming film?"

"Oh, yes, I am, how did you know?" I lie.

"I just knew it! I saw you up there in the VIP section just a bit ago as I walked in."

"Yeah, I'm with Lei Marco and Albana Ferizi," I name-drop. Her jaw drops and she begs me to introduce her to Lei Marco.

Shrugging my shoulder, I take her to our booth.

Lei Marco gives me an incredulous look before smiling and introducing himself. Within seconds, he brushes her off and she runs back to the dance floor. Lei Marco shifts his body to me, gazes at me, and then with a biting tone snaps, "You may be Albana's family, but I will not be a made a fool in this city. No one is allowed to talk to me unless I say so, is that understood?!"

Mortified, I nod and sit down beside Albana.

When Lei Marco gets up again, Albana leans over and whispers, "I'm sorry that he yelled at you like that, honey. I will talk to him." Getting up, she disappears into the crowd after Lei Marco.

For the remainder of the night, I stop consuming alcohol and observe the way the rich interact with one another. I watch how they carry themselves, how they speak to one another, and how they keep to themselves. I wonder if they ever think about people like me, who come from nothing, without assets or money, desiring only to get to the top. What does it feel like to be born into money? As I observe and take it all in, I promise myself that one day I will have wealth, financial security, and a position among them, because I am one of them.

I am one of you and nothing will stop me from attaining this.

∞

SOUTH BEACH LOOMS before us as Albana and I stroll down Ocean Drive and onto a pathway leading to a bench. Palm trees sway as a warm breeze envelops us in its embrace. The strip is quiet as the moon casts its light upon the city.

"I don't know what I'm going to do with my life, Albana. But what I do know is that I belong in your world of the wealthy. I just know it! I feel it! But how am I going to get there? Who knows, maybe something good will come out of my life," I say, taking a seat on the bench.

"Fredy, darling, everything will come to you in time. What you need to learn from all these experiences in Pensacola is patience. Believe me, I know where you have been, and it will come. You're a talented writer and you just need to focus all your energy on that. Come here"—she embraces me in her silky arms—"you're my little brother and I promise always to take care of you, okay? Stop worrying and live in the present!"

"Okay, Albana," I smile at her as I glance down and see a small white poodle cuddling near my feet.

"Oh—hello there, beautiful!" Albana laughs, kneeling down to pet the dog.

In the distance, an old man sprints over and apologizes profusely. "I'm so terribly sorry for interrupting your evening! She likes strangers."

"Oh, you're not interrupting anything at all. Your dog is beautiful," Albana tells him.

"Why, thank you. His name is Munchkin and he always knows how to smell out the gorgeous people. I mean, just look at the two of you, underneath this moonlight, along the strip, so stunningly beautiful. Such a handsome couple you make."

Laughing, Albana puts her hand to her chest and confesses, "Oh, we're not together. He's my little brother. Albana, a pleasure to meet you," she says,

extending her hand to him.

"Arthur. The pleasure is all mine," he replies smiling gently as he shakes her hand and then shakes mine firmly.

"Fredy," I say with a shy smile. I turn away from his penetrating stare.

"So, what brings you out on this beautiful evening?"

"Oh, we're on vacation from Pensacola for the weekend. I'm showing my little brother around the city," Albana confides to him.

"What do you do for a living?" he inquires.

"I'm starting my own interior design business," she replies charmingly, "and Fredy, here, is a talented writer. Aren't you, darling?"

God, everything she says is like a line from a movie. So perfect.

"Oh, is that true?" Arthur turns his attention to me, "And when is your birthday, if you don't mind me asking?"

"January second," I reply, baffled by the odd question.

"Funny that you say that. My father's birthday is January second as well, and he recently passed away."

"Bless his soul," Albana murmurs.

Arthur leans in, sizes me up, and with a lighthearted laugh says, "Yes, I can see that you're a talented and gifted writer. I bet you will write just as well as Hemingway. In a few years, your name will be known. Here, do me a favor, take my card and call me tomorrow. Stop by my office. I just want to hear your story. Pleasure to meet you, Albana."

"Pleasure to meet you, Arthur."

"Remember, Fredy, call me, tomorrow," he says again before turning around and walking away. "Come on, Munchkin!"

"Why does he think you'll be famous in a few years?"

"I don't know, Albana. I don't know." I look toward Arthur's direction. His card feels like hot coals in my fingers.

∞

IN ARTHUR'S PAD on Ocean Drive I make myself comfortable in a chair as Arthur pulls his chair up to me and sits directly across.

"You must be wondering why I asked you to drop by," Arthur says, bending down and picking up Munchkin. "And I can assure you right now that I am in no position to make you uncomfortable. So please, relax. You have nothing to worry about."

"It must be nice to live right above the strip with the ocean right downstairs," I say, trying to figure out what he sees in me that I do not.

"I don't mind it," Arthur replies, leaning toward me. "So, tell me your story. Something tells me you have a powerful story and I want to hear it."

I tell him everything.

Sitting back in his chair, Arthur looks at me in shock and sorrow as his eyes mist up.

After a few seconds of silence, Arthur turns to his computer and starts typing away.

"Just to let you know, Fredy, I'm a top player within the entertainment industry. I have connections left and right, and I can lead you to the right person to get your story out. How are you planning to tell it to the masses? Are you thinking of writing a screenplay? Of producing a play? You might even consider doing what MTV is doing lately—turning your story into a reality television series. You can even have Albana help you with it."

"To be honest, Arthur, I'm not sure just yet how I'm going to produce my story. As of right now, I do know that I want to be a screenwriter, so maybe I'll head in that direction."

"Well, how about this. I'm printing out a list of names of key players in the entertainment industry. You have a very promising future ahead of you, and all you have to do now is just believe in yourself. The only person who can stop you is yourself." He smiles, grabs the paper out of the printer, and

hands it to me.

"What do you want from me?"

"Nothing. I know what you're thinking," he says, bursting into laughter, "I'm not gay, and no, I don't want to get into your pants, as handsome as you are, young fellow. I'm happily married with two beautiful daughters. Something about you drew me to you last night and now that I've heard your story, I'm glad I did. Just remember to keep this list of names in your possession, and even if I never hear from you again, use it. And be sure to mention my name when you contact any of these people."

"But there must be something that you want from me," I persist.

"Well, there is one thing," he sits back in his chair and gazes at me for several seconds. "My wife wrote this beautiful children's story about a boy who has always wanted his own little secret. Here, wait a second."

Arthur gets up and disappears into another room. He comes out with a copy of the tale and hands it to me. Skimming through it, I find myself relating to the boy's need to have his own secret, how he runs away and gets lost in the woods, and stumbles upon the realization that he has a secret no one else could ever have. What a sweet contrast: the boy who yearns to have a secret of his own and the boy who has too many to keep hidden. And although my life is indeed full of secrets, I feel like this boy: I yearn to have one more secret, something in my soul that no one could ever grasp.

"I want you to make an adaptation of this tale one day. That is all I ask of you," Arthur says.

"Consider it a deal, Arthur. Thank you, so much. I-I don't know what to say." I look intently at the little boy on the cover of the children's story.

"No, thank you for coming into my life, Fredy. Now, you better run along before Albana worries too much over you. Tell her I say hello and that I hope you both enjoy the remainder of your trip."

And just like that, I leave Arthur's home with a golden treasure.

∞

ALBANA FERIZI AWAITS me at a coffee shop, curiosity and suspicion etched across her angelic face. I order a cappuccino and plop down beside her. She doesn't say anything as I stir two packets of Splenda into the red commie tea cup, gently raise it to my lips, and sip. Albana picks up her Italian *Vogue* magazine and skims through pages, every now and then casting her eyes on me.

"Arthur says hello and hopes that we have a great remainder of our vacation," I say without putting the cup down.

"So, why did he want to see you?"

"To hear my story and to give me a list of contacts so, when the day comes, I can call them to help me sell my story to the masses."

"Fascinating. And he didn't try to touch you in any way, did he?" Albana's eyebrows rise.

"No, the most intriguing part of the whole encounter is that he not once made a move on me. I thought he would surely try to put one over on me and ask to sleep with me."

Albana puts down the magazine and peers over at me. Her eyes become distant as she whispers, "Only God knows."

If there is a God, I muse.

"Look, darling, I've been invited to attend a modeling show at the Versace House tonight. You're more than welcome to come with or you can do your own thing. What would you like to do?" She smiles and looks at me.

"I think I'd rather check out the gay nightlife here," I say. "I'm pretty sure it'll just be the same as last night, you know, schmoozing and fancy talk." I finish my cappuccino and set the cup down. After what happened with Lei Marco last night, I don't want to jeopardize her friendship with him, so it seems best for me to remain low key.

"If that's what you desire, my little brother, then you can check out the

gay nightlife. But keep your phone on. I don't want to hunt you down tonight. And I don't want you leaving to any man's house, you hear me?"

"Yes, Albana. I'll do my best to behave tonight."

<div align="center">∞</div>

UPON MY RETURN to Pensacola, Daniel and I get into another heated argument. I plead with him that I have no place to go and I haven't been able to find a job. He informs me that he has the intention of moving to Tampa to be closer to his family.

Desperate, I call an acquaintance and ask him if we can hang out. Larry picks me up in his truck and I ask him if we can drive to Jack and Ron's Piano Bar downtown. At the age of forty, Larry has the demeanor of a college professor with a hick attitude from Alabama. His glasses dangle on the tip of his nose, conveying a paternal quality. He lives in East Hill, a gorgeous neighborhood near downtown. He has a breathtaking three-bedroom, two-bathroom, two-story Victorian house.

Entering Jack and Ron's, I immediately notice the piano to the right of the doorway. Exposed brick interior walls surround wooden floors, and a walkaround balcony overlooks the first floor. Larry and I make our way to the rectangular central bar. I notice a few regulars playing at the pool table. Numerous wall-mounted televisions hang throughout the bar, displaying the lyrics to the karaoke songs people come to sing.

Larry gets me a Sapphire tonic and we make our way to a booth. Sitting across from me, he takes his glasses off and places them on the table.

"So, what's going on, buddy?" he says in cute drawl.

"I need your help. Daniel is moving away, I don't have a job, and I need a place to crash until I can get my shit together," I tell him flat out.

"I'm willing to help you, Fredy, being that you're such a nice kid and all, but only under one condition: you have to promise me you're willing to get your life back together." He chugs down his beer.

"If I stay with you, I don't want you asking to have sex with me," I add.

"You will never need to worry about that," he says, assuaging my concern. "So, they fired you from Starbucks. And you aren't working at the Gap any longer?"

"Right." I bite my lip. "Starbucks fired me because I kept calling out on the weekends to travel all over the South, and after I returned from Atlanta my boss had enough and let me go. As for the Gap, I quit back in January since I figured I was making good money at Starbucks."

"How much were you making?"

"As much as an assistant manager, if not more. So, whenever I get these huge paychecks, I run off to explore the South."

Around me, regulars go up to the front of the bar and sing into the microphone. A lady in charge of the karaoke stand swings by and asks me if I'm going to sing my number. Nodding, I smile at her and thank her as she informs me that I'll be called in a bit. I found out about Jack and Ron's back in February. Whenever I'm not escaping Pensacola on the weekends, I find myself at this bar every Sunday and Thursday night, singing away and drinking Sapphire tonics. Albana enjoys accompanying me and we usually stop here to sing one song, or grab a cocktail, before we hit Pensacola's downtown nightlife. It's a nice escape that has kept me mostly away from Daniel.

"What are you going to do for a job?"

"I don't know." I sigh depressingly, lower my head, and shoot the delicious cocktail down my throat.

"Well, Memorial Day Weekend is right around the corner. This bar will be packed with men from all over the East Coast, most of them Southerners. You should get a job here as a server. I'm certain with your looks you'll make a lot of money."

"But I've never served before." The thought lifts my mood.

"Oh, it's easy. I'm certain Ron will give you a position. That way, you can save up money, spend some on yourself, and then both of us can move down to South Beach, Miami—that is, if you choose to move with me to Miami. I can get us a two bedroom apartment and will help you get back into school."

I think over the proposition.

"I'm in. When are we moving down there?"

"At the end of this month." Larry glances up as we hear my name being called.

"Fredy, I'm counting down to three and if your ass ain't up here, someone's taking your spot," the karaoke lady announces.

Taking one more swig, I jump out of my seat and dash to the stage.

The locals turn their attention to me as I bring the microphone to my mouth and lose myself in the lyrics of Liza Minnelli's "Cabaret."

"*What good is sitting alone in your room, come hear the music play; life is a cabaret old chum, come to the cabaret…*"

After tonight, you will never see my face again, Daniel.

I won't even say goodbye.

<div align="center">∞</div>

A HOT NAVY BOY romances me at Jack and Ron's Piano Bar a few nights after I move into Larry's place. The whole evening he flirts and stares at me as if he's fallen head over heels for me.

I wind up returning to his hotel.

There, we fuck for two hours straight.

He tosses me from one side of the bed to the other, flips me over as I hold onto the headboard for dear life, pushes me up against the wall, and it ends with me coming all over his face and hair.

"This is like that scene from *There's Something About Mary*," he repeats over and over as I fall asleep in his arms.

I think he has no idea what he got himself into.

With my ravenous sexual appetite, I can become a full-fledged monster in bed, unleashing a tigress that attacks and devours every drop of essence of the man I bed. Ever since I met Morgan Medeford, it's as if a sexual explosion erupts in my being and I'm compelled to ravage the male body. For me, it's not about making sweet love; far from it—it's about making his body sweat in profusion until every ounce of energy is tapped.

The following night, I attend a birthday party for one of Larry's friends.

Arriving at the house on Okaloosa Island, I get to know a small crowd of men. Counting bodies, I realize there are only ten of us, all good-looking guys. I didn't realize it would be such a private event. Downing two shots of Jägermeister, I feel smitten and privileged to be among the beautiful people.

Before I know it, I'm boarding a yacht and sailing across Choctawhatchee Bay.

The ten of us drink, laugh, and enjoy the wind whipping across the yacht as pitch darkness surrounds us. Suddenly, I notice one of the guys taking his shirt off and planting a kiss on his neighbor. They start making out heavily as the rest of us watch in unison.

The yacht comes to a complete stop and the water laps against the side gently.

Next to me, a Norwegian guy drops his pants to the floor. He motions me to feel his smooth abdomen. Obliging, I strip down naked and kiss him fiercely. From behind, a good-looking Spanish guy touches my buttocks with his rough palm. Moaning, I close my eyes and feel a heat of sexual tension arise.

Men join one by one, and an orgy ensues as all of us become intoxicated with one another's ripe and hard, smooth bodies. Skin brushes against supple skin, lips tangle with lips, heavy breathing intertwines with wet moans as men interlock with one another in different sexual positions. Before I know it, I

am twisting within these men's arms like a Latin tourniquet. Round and round I go, as up above, stars gaze down upon me, feeling neither shame nor remorse.

Yes, this is what life is meant to be like for a twenty-two year old.

∞

SEXUAL ESCAPADES CONSUME ME throughout the week of Memorial Day.

After getting off work at Jack and Ron's Wednesday night, I go to Emerald City and meet three Navy boys. The four of us dash to a nearby hotel where we unleash our inner animals.

A black guy from Kansas smacks me across the face as he throws me against the wall. Slipping on a condom, he inserts his hard cock into me. I gasp in pleasure as he pounds me furiously. On another bed a Latin boy bobs his head up and down on a white Texan's penis.

"Fuck yeah!" I cry out in pain as the black guy rams himself into me. "Wait, stop. I don't want to come just yet."

I jump onto the bed and stuff my face into the Texan's crotch. The four of us feel one another's bodies before commencing a heavy session of overpowering copulation. Like a train, the four of us bump up against one another, ferociously grinding back and forth.

It doesn't dawn on me to ask their names.

But who needs names when lust is enough.

Thursday night, I meet a flight attendant from Indianapolis; he's a jock, well-defined and built, straight acting, my height, olive skin, with hazel green eyes. He picks me up at Jack and Ron's after I serve him a few cocktails.

We arrive at the Hilton Hotel on Pensacola Beach, step onto the elevator, and get off at the fourth floor. The second the door to the room closes behind us, we strip naked.

I galvanize his body with my hands. It's hard as a rock.

I suck on his cock for half an hour; his penis is six-inches long and smooth and I love every inch of it; it fits perfectly in my mouth. After I suck it, he turns me over, spits on his cock, and enters me slowly.

He fucks me with our legs intertwined.

I've grown used to fucking in feverish animalistic sessions, but this flight attendant is the first guy since Daniel Hansen to take his time. He's sensually slow and tender; we move like the tide, as if we were an ocean on a calm summer night, moving in and out, in and out, in unison, and in rhythm.

In my thirst for sexual fulfillment in all these encounters, I lost myself and forgot the meaning of experiencing lovemaking; I don't even know this man, yet this is exactly what it feels like—lovemaking. The motion of him pulsing in and out of me in such an intimate manner is soothing; he enters all the way, until I feel his scrotum at the base of my quivering butt and his penis deep inside me, pulsating against my prostate.

And for the first time, I think it is possible for me to fall in love again. As this stranger and I make love, I imagine him being my lover. I imagine him making love to me like this every night, caressing my body, kissing my face, smelling my hair, whispering that he loves me before he plants his seed inside me.

We copulate for over an hour.

I come.

He pulls out and shoots his load all over my smooth chest.

Afterward, we fall into an enchanted sleep, my legs enlaced within his, my arm wrapped around his chest, my supple lips kissing the back of his neck, and his hand interlocked with mine.

Too bad it's only a one-night stand.

∞ CHAPTER XI: NIGHTS OF RUMINATION ∞

ERIC MORRISON PERSUADES me to move to Tallahassee after meeting me at Emerald City over Memorial Day Weekend. A twenty-three-year-old computer nerd, a redhead with freckles all over his body, lean, five feet eight inches tall, with grayish-blue eyes, extremely straight acting. After spending the whole weekend together with his friends, we fall head over heels for each other.

"Are you going to tell Larry that you're not leaving with him to Miami?" Eric's eyes fill with concern.

"I'm going to call him right now." I reluctantly pick up my cell-phone and call him.

"Well, if it isn't Fredy Espinoza!" Larry drawls in his Southern accent. "Where have you been hiding this whole weekend?"

"Hey, Larry. You're going to hate this but I can't move to Miami with you. I met a wonderful guy my age who's taking me to Tallahassee with him," I announce quickly.

"What! You're fucking kidding me, right?! I have everything packed and we're supposed to leave today, Fredy! How are you supposed to get your life back together if you're running off with the wind!? I can't fucking believe this!"

"I'm sorry, Larry," I raise my hand to my face and wipe perspiration off my forehead.

"Don't fucking apologize to me, Fredy!" Larry's voice drops to a serious tone. "You know what? It's fine. It's all fine. You're just a twenty-two-year-old without his head put together, so do what you need to do. You can find your stuff at Starbucks."

Click.

He hangs up on me.

"Wow, he went off on you for a second there." Eric looks at me apologetically.

"Yeah, but it's worth it. He said my stuff will be at Starbucks."

Arriving at Starbucks, I am shocked to find all my belongings spread across the lawn. Embarrassed and humiliated, I step out of Eric's green pickup truck and grab my belongings. Many of my regular customers look at me flabbergasted and in astonishment as they watch me load the stuff into Eric's truck. At the picnic table, I notice Albana, upset. She gets up and rushes at me.

"Darling, what's going on? One second you tell me you're leaving to Miami with Larry, and the next second he storms into the parking lot yelling obscenities about you and throwing all your things onto the grass as if it were trash!"

"Oh, you see that guy in the truck? That's Eric Morrison, and I'm moving in with him," I reply.

"Where to, my little brother?"

"Tallahassee," I fight back tears as it dawns on me this may be the last

time I ever see her.

"But what about Larry and Miami?"

"Larry made several sexual moves on me when I stayed at his place, and I was afraid that if I moved to Miami with him, it would only get worse. He confided in me the other day that he could see himself falling in love with me and hoped that I could reciprocate those feelings. Oh, Albana, I just couldn't think of becoming his kept boy."

"Just stay here in Pensacola. Move in with me, Fredy. I will protect you and help you get back into school," she pleads.

"I'm sorry, Albana," I frown as tears well up in her eyes, "Please don't cry. Thank you for being a sister to me and caring about me and for all that you have done. I promise, I will make my way back to visit you, but I feel like my time is up in Pensacola. I need to move forward. If I stay, I will only become your burden."

"Darling, don't say that! Here, give me a hug!" Albana pulls me into an embrace and kisses my forehead.

"Now you're making me cry," I laugh as tears flood forth from my eyes and down my cheeks.

"It's okay to cry, Fredy, you know that. How many times have I told you it's okay to cry," Albana says, smiling through her tears.

"Many times." I burst into tears again as I bury my head in her hair.

Inside the coffee shop, everyone's attention is fixed on the unfolding scene; for a second, it feels as if I am acting a scene in a movie, and the audience behind the windows is actually gazing at a movie screen.

"Don't let him hurt you okay, and if anything goes wrong, don't hesitate to call me," Albana whispers into my ear as she looks over at Eric.

Nodding my head, I pull away, grab the remainder of my things, and throw them into the back of Eric's truck.

I wave goodbye as I enter the car. "Bye, Albana, I love you."

"You take good care of my brother, you hear!" Albana yells to Eric.

"I will," Eric yells back.

And just like that, I leave Pensacola in the dust.

<center>∞</center>

LUSH GREEN SCENERY surrounds me as I gaze into Eric Morrison's backyard. The sound of insects buzzes about me and thunder rumbles in the distance. Funny, there's not a single cloud in the sky yet there's thunder. I think I can get used to this. Whereas Pensacola is cool breezes and salty, misty air, Tallahassee is humidity and luscious trees.

Did I sacrifice my direction in life once again for the false notion of love and security? Is it foolish of me to run away with a boy I've only known for a few hours? If so, to hell with it. I'm still in my early twenties, with plenty of time to figure it out.

Stepping into Eric's bedroom, I look upon the mess of clothes thrown about the room, toiletry items strewn across the floor, empty beer bottles and dirty plates casually placed on bookshelves.

"He lives like a bachelor. This will have to change," I murmur to myself.

Stepping out of his bedroom, I pass the empty guest bedroom across the hallway and descend the staircase to the kitchen.

On the countertop I notice several bottles of Bacardi 151. There are many full ones, but many empty ones are still in sight.

"It looks like you have a party here every night," I say as I look about the kitchen.

"Oh, hey, kiddo. How do you like the place?"

"It's huge! You live all by yourself here?"

"No, my roommate owns this place. He's an anchorman for the weather channel. You know, just your local celebrity." Eric grins as he opens up a bottle of Bacardi 151 and pours himself a strong drink. "Would you like one?"

"Sure, why not! Let's celebrate new beginnings and a new chapter." I laugh as he pours me a strong Bacardi and coke.

He leans over and clinks my glass. "Cheers to that, kiddo."

∞

FORRESTER KESSINGTON STRIKES at me and shards of glass tear my face apart. Sobbing, I frantically find a needle and sew my skin back together as blood rushes forth into the sink. His green eyes flash with fury as a monster is unleashed.

"You can't escape me, Fredy! Wherever you go, I will always be there," Forrester howls around me.

"Please, leave me alone! Leave me alone!" I cry, staring stupefied at my image in the mirror...

"Please, leave me alone!" I accidentally kick Eric as I thrash about under the sheets.

Eric rolls over to me and gently shakes me from my sleep. "Fredy, wake up, kiddo. You're just having a nightmare, wake up, kiddo."

"Oh, God, I'm so sorry, Eric," I moan. "I didn't warn you, but I'm always beset with nightmares." I shudder and curl into a ball and fit myself within the shelter of his smooth body.

"I understand, baby. It's why I drink myself to sleep," Eric whispers, holding me.

"Why do you drink so much?" I ask, squeezing my eyes shut, hoping to push away the remnant of a nightmare.

"My Dad died a few years ago," he says.

"Oh, I'm sorry."

I think to myself that this is probably not the best time to talk about his father's passing, but Eric is already snoring lightly in my ear.

I lie there in the darkness, thinking about Forrester Kessington and whether a day will ever come when I no longer feel him within me. I ruminate about everything that transpired between Daniel and me, and

between Melancton and me, and about my parents' choices that led me onto this path of self-loathing and self-destruction. Will I ever be able to find myself again?

Unable to sleep, I stare into the darkness and feel the hours drag on. Undoing Eric's arms clasped around me, I shift across the bed, let out a sigh, and silently make my way into the bathroom. Closing the door behind me, I flip the light switch on, head over to the sink, turn the faucet on, and splash myself with cold water.

Patting my face dry, I become paralyzed within my own brown eyes.

When was the last time I allowed myself to look intensely into my natural-colored eyes?

Grimacing, I avert my eyes from the mirror but find myself hopelessly drawn back. So many shadows and demons lie at bay behind these eyes. My brown eyes are full of resignation, numbness, and disbelief over everything that has happened to me.

Tears well up in my eyes as I force myself to keep looking at them.

Look at me.

Just look at me.

Could anyone recognize the self-destruction that cinders from within these deceitful eyes? I've hit rock bottom; never have I felt so alone or so utterly worthless as at this moment, right now. How will I ever learn to love myself again? I don't even know if I have the strength to do it even if I wanted to.

I am cursed.

God, where's the bold and courageous Fredy Espinoza I used to know and be? Fredy had his life in the palm of his hands and knew exactly what he wanted from life, until Forrester Kessington consumed him. Forrester Kessington was my greatest achievement in a character role, until I succumbed to becoming Forrester Kessington himself.

I lost everything at that moment: my friends, my life, and my sense of direction.

Maybe I never knew where I was going in life. Be authentic with yourself, Fredy Espinoza. I had no idea what I was doing with my life. All I knew was that I had to escape from my past. All I could do was run and keep running until I found the secret to burying the past for good—a past full of lies, hatred, deceit, betrayal, lunacy, and tears.

"Why do I keep insisting on living another day? Fredy Espinoza, whatever happened to you?" I whisper, reaching out to touch my reflection. "Ugh! Just look at me! I can't stand the sight of my own face!"

Snapping my eyes away from the mirror, I dab my face with the towel and slip back into Eric's bedroom. The light from the bathroom casts a rectangle on the floor. I switch off the light and make my way quietly into bed. I gaze upon Eric as he sleeps peacefully on his side of the bed.

Lying down, I close my eyes and count sheep in my head, but thoughts of self-hatred penetrate my mind as I ruminate about why I continue to wear green contact lenses. Gazing into the mirror is a reminder of what haunts me every waking moment of my life: a decrepit soul shuddering in venomous skin; eyes hidden behind a futile mask that can easily be shattered with the flick of a nail; and a darkness so vile that no man could ever love me unconditionally, for if he were to ever stare into my natural eyes all he would see is a being so disgusting and worthless.

Maybe Eric will help me find myself.

Maybe that's why I was brought into his life.

And in return, I will help him find himself.

I fall asleep and awaken to Eric kissing me goodbye.

"Love you, kiddo. Don't get yourself into trouble. Do whatever you like. I'll be home around four in the evening." At the doorway, he smiles and shakes his butt.

"Why are you doing that?" I giggle.

"Whenever I'm happy, I wag my invisible tail," Eric explains, wagging his tail a final time before closing the door.

<div align="center">∞</div>

CLUB JADE, IRONICALLY, is located on Pensacola Street in downtown Tallahassee. Eric and I step out of the truck and head toward the entrance. As we enter the nightclub, several heads immediately turn in my direction. Eric and I make our way to the main bar and order two Bacardi and cokes. Then we slip through another entrance to the adjacent two-level elevated dance floor.

Chugging down his Bacardi and coke, Eric excuses himself and orders another drink.

It astonishes me the amount of alcohol he drinks without fading.

Eric introduces me to several of his friends, and as the night wears on, it becomes evident that they consider me his trophy. Their facial expressions convey their attitudes; side comments linger in the air about where Eric happened to find this handsome token. Upset, I ask Eric for cash and order myself another Bacardi and coke.

"Make that a double," I shout to the bartender as punk industrial music blares around us.

As the night draws to a close, Eric informs me that one of his friends is throwing an after-party.

"So, do you want to go, or would you rather go home, kiddo?"

"I don't know. Whatever you want, Eric," I answer with a slur.

"It's an easy question, kiddo. Just answer me," Eric helps me into the truck.

"I'm too drunk. I don't know how you can hold your alcohol—I'm ready to pass out." I squint as everything begins to swirl.

"So, that means you want to go home?"

"You make the decision for me," I say, closing my eyes and leaning my head against the seat.

"That's what I hate about you," he says beneath his breath.

"Huh? What is it you hate about me?" I snap my eyes open. His words sting like acid.

"Your indecision," Eric mutters as we drive home in silence.

"I'm sorry, babe," I murmur, falling asleep.

<center>∞</center>

SWEAT GLISTENS ACROSS my face as I wake up from another nightmare a few nights later. Turning to Eric, I wrap my arms around him and hold myself. Will there ever come a night when I don't wake up from nightmares? As I stare at the ceiling, images of the Devil at the door send chills down my spine and I try to resist the rising fear.

I don't believe in the Devil or in God.

Why do I feel so emotional suddenly? I just want to fall asleep, but I'm afraid to; I'm afraid I will lapse into another nightmare. Most of my nightmares have been about the Devil waiting at the door, telling me he's found me again; sometimes a few sneak in that deal with Forrester Kessington. If it's all symbolic, what does it mean?

Eric Morrison is too good to me. Even though I don't have a penny to my name, he takes good care of me. I've placed applications at various jobs, but haven't heard anything from them. My stress rises as I find myself unable to get one interview. I'm beginning to think there are no job prospects for me in Tallahassee. I don't want to become Eric's burden. He's doing enough supporting both of us.

Damn you, Dad, for throwing me out in the street! Damn you for not allowing me to transition into adulthood properly! I don't know how to be a man because of you. Just look at me, I'm nothing. I have nothing. I own nothing. All I have is Eric.

I can't help but feel hopelessly worthless.

Although Eric hasn't done anything to convey it, I feel like a piece of meat to him. Is that what I am? A piece of meat? I notice how all his friends perceive me as a naïve child, how they look upon me as the handsome guy without intelligence. But I need to take responsibility, because I do convey that. If they only knew my story, they'd understand my predicament, and why I need Eric in my life right now.

I need you, Eric.

And then there's Melancton Vassiliadis. He emailed me recently expressing how he's changed since I left and how he still firmly believes I will be a valuable asset to the entertainment industry. How is it possible to fall deeply in love with three different men: Melancton Vassiliadis, Daniel Hansen, and now Eric Morrison? All my life I've been told I only have one soul mate. But as I think about Melancton and how deep and passionate our connection was, I consider that maybe I never truly loved him, only the idea of him. The sex between us was so emotionally addicting from my side that I may not have been in love with Melancton but rather with the sex. After all, I was recovering from Mom's mental illness, Eduardo's incessant physical abuse, and Dad's inability to be emotionally and physically available. In a way, Melancton was the plug to all those vacuums and he gave me the sense of being in love. I was in love, all right—with the sex Melancton gave me.

Is this why I crave so much sex?

And was Morgan Medeford the lynchpin to igniting a sexual demon in me? Now I crave only to lose myself, man after man, to forget I ever existed. I find myself practically raping Eric at times. He'll come home from work and I will jump on him, shower him with compliments and kisses, then take him to bed.

As I look back upon all my relationships, I notice a pattern. I fall in love within hours of meeting someone I feel can take care of me, protect me, and

watch over me. I'm beginning to realize that maybe I'm not in love with Eric but with the idea of him taking care of me. No, of course I love Eric. I must, otherwise, why did I move for him?

<div align="center">∞</div>

A BLANKET OF SADNESS wraps itself around me as I sink into a deeper depression. I finally got an interview at a smoothie shop downtown. Tropical Smoothie offered me a job at a minimum wage, six dollars and forty cents an hour. Mortified, I turned it down.

I never told Eric.

Eric bounces into the room. "InuYasha is about to come on, Fredy," he says, handing me my dinner and settling down next to me at the base of his bed.

"What's InuYasha?"

"Are you kidding me? Like the most awesome cartoon on the planet! It's a Japanese manga series and I just love it!" Eric turns the television onto the Adult Swim network.

As the intro to the cartoon comes on, I smile in amusement and munch on a burrito. Grabbing my Bacardi and coke, I take a sip and allow the drink to wash around my mouth for several seconds before gulping it down.

"How's your job hunting coming along?" Eric asks halfway through the cartoon.

"Same shit, different day, Eric." I look at my drink guiltily as I give him my first lie.

"Don't worry, kiddo. Maybe tomorrow you can stop by the college and inquire about what you need to get enrolled for fall classes."

That sounds like a brilliant idea. "Oh, Eric, all I want to do is return to school," I tell him. "And in a month, I will have lived in Florida for a year, so I will hopefully be considered a resident. I'll work part-time at some coffee shop and spend every evening with you." I finish my plate and snuggle next

to him.

"Sure, kiddo. Things will turn up for you," he says, smiling as he briefly plants a kiss on my head then returns his attention to the show.

Later that night, I wake up trembling in bed.

A sticky cold drench lingers across my body and I move into Eric's arms. His body warmth does nothing to soothe my temperature; it drops even more drastically. A roll of anxiety rumbles through my body. This peculiar sensation is akin to a heavy withdrawal, except this time I do not crave any drugs.

Getting up, I dash into the bathroom and take a piss.

Leaning over the toilet to flush it, I lose my breath.

My body convulses and shakes as I try to hold myself steady.

An unbearable icy draft envelops my skin and dread compresses itself heavily across my chest. I recognize this feeling. Whenever something traumatic happens, this feeling consumes me.

Back in the bedroom, I slip into sweatpants and lie down softly on the bed.

I manage to persuade my upper body to stop trembling, but my thighs continue to shake.

Eric rolls over, throws his arms around me, and snuggles up next to me, putting me at ease. I fall back into a deep sleep.

∞

ENTERING THE PALACE SALOON, I take in the bare-bones décor of beer posters along wood-paneled walls, electronic dart boards, and pool tables.

"I couldn't shake the feeling of something terrible having happened until a few hours ago," I share my frustration to Eric as we head directly to the bar and he orders us a round of Bacardi and cokes.

"And here you are kiddo, without anything bad happening," he relies. "I

think you were just dehydrated. You need to drink more water."

Behind us, a group of girls suddenly gushes, "Oh my God! Guess who's here! It's Jose Tapia from *The Real World*!" Looking past them, I see a handsome young Latin guy make his way to the back of the saloon.

"Well, aren't we lucky," Eric chuckles. His eyes follow Jose and he wags his tail.

"I bet you'd rather be with him than me," I say insecurely, my heart racing with the fear of losing Eric.

"Aww... Don't say that, kiddo. I'm happy with you." Eric's eyes soften as he diverts his attention to me. "Here, let's go play a game of darts."

The first dart I throw hits smack in the middle of the electronic dartboard.

"Look at that! Are you sure you never played darts back at home?" Eric laughs as he positions himself to throw a dart.

"It's plain luck," I laugh. "You'll see, Eric."

Playing a round of darts, I find myself truly liking Eric's company. He's intelligent, computer savvy, logical, and rational, and what further propels me to him is how in tune I feel around him. It's as if Eric is a spiritual companion.

Because of Eric, I feel like a hermit in repose from life.

Even though there are evenings when I feel as if I could sink into depression, a peace I haven't felt in a long time tides me over as I retreat from the chaotic lifestyle I recently led.

"One round down and four more to go." Eric leans in and kisses me.

I wag my tail.

"You're freaking adorable, kiddo."

"I love how you always call me kiddo, Eric."

∞

A TOUGH DECISION lingers in the air as I end the call.

"What is it, kiddo?" Eric looks at me with a look of concern on his face.

"That was Melancton Vassiliadis," I murmur as I pour myself another Bacardi and coke.

"The first love of your life? What are you doing talking to him?" Eric's eyebrows rise as he drops his work bag on the kitchen floor, saunters over to me, and helps himself to his favorite cocktail.

"After telling him about my situation, he agrees with Tyrone that I should return to California. They would both help me get rooted there," I tell him.

"Oh." Eric becomes quiet as he reopens the bottle of Bacardi and splashes more of it into his drink.

"For the past week I've been telling Tyrone and Melancton how difficult it's been for me to find a job. I also conveyed to them my fear of not having the funds to enroll at the university—it's so expensive."

"What's stopping you from returning to California?"

"You are," I admit, chugging down my drink and swiftly making myself another.

Eric sighs, looks up at me with a pained expression on his face, and sets his drink down.

"I love you kiddo, but I think it might be best for you to return to California. I'll even purchase you a one-way ticket."

"Please, Eric, you don't have to do that. Tyrone said he'd pay for the ticket as long as I paid him back. You're already done too much for me. I've been here for two months now without any money. I can't expect you to shelve out a few hundred dollars for me, after all your kind charity."

"Fredy, none of it was a charity. I did it out of love. First thing tomorrow morning I will purchase you a ticket to California. Just promise me

you'll think of me and return after you get all your schooling done." His eyes become misty with tears and he lowers his head like a sad puppy.

I set my drink down and throw my arms around him. "Oh, Eric, I promise I will return to you." Cupping his face, I kiss him passionately, my heart fluttering with anxiety at the prospect of returning home.

∞

ON MY LAST NIGHT in Tallahassee, Eric and I get into a heated argument in the kitchen.

"I can't believe I'm with a man who's addicted to alcohol!" I snap.

"Don't judge me under my own roof! You should be grateful I took you in," Eric retorts, throwing back his sixth Bacardi and coke.

"I am grateful, but I don't feel as if I know you any better! You never express anything to me! It's difficult for me when I feel like I'm yanking your emotions out, Eric! All I want is for you to communicate to me, damn it!"

"You know what? You're right, Fredy! You're always right! I can't win with you. I love my alcohol, I have no emotions, and I'm just a plain fuck-up, kiddo!" Eric slams his glass down on the counter and storms out of the kitchen.

"Fuck," I say beneath my breath as I stand there.

Why do I always have to make things worse!

I go up the staircase and into the bedroom. Eric is passed out on the floor. Staring at the empty bed, I hover over him.

"Eric, don't be ridiculous. You should be sleeping in your bed."

"Leave me alone, Fredy," he moans.

"Doesn't it mean anything to you that I'm leaving for San Francisco tomorrow?! Is this how you want to spend our last night together?"

"Look kiddo, I made the choice for you. Just go to bed. I don't mind sleeping on the floor."

"Eric, I'm not going to sleep in an empty bed that's not even mine. I'm

your guest, so it's only fair that you sleep in your own bed. Eric... Eric, are you listening to me?"

"Damn it, Fredy. What do you want from me? Leave me alone, okay?" He glances at me for a split second before turning his head away.

"Fine." I choke back tears as I storm out of the room.

Stepping across the foyer, I enter the guest bedroom and lie on the floor. Closing my eyes, I weep silently. My heart yearns for Eric to tell me to stay with him, to tell me he loves me, that my choice to leave isn't a smart one. But he never talks about it. The past week has gone by without Eric mentioning anything of it.

"Hey, kiddo," Eric whispers from the doorway. "Please, come to bed. It's your last night and I don't want you sleeping on the floor."

"I just want you to tell me that it's the wrong decision for me to leave you, Eric. I'm terrified of returning to California. I'm so terrified." I weep as Eric kneels beside me and caresses my face.

"Kiddo, we both know how depressed you are here," he whispers. "It hurts me seeing you so sad. Tyrone and your friends will help you get back on your feet; otherwise, I wouldn't think of letting you go." He wipes my tears away. "Now, come back to my room, please."

He helps me to my feet and I follow him to the bedroom.

"Eric, I'm so sorry for lashing out at you and saying those horrible things about you. I don't know what came over me." I break down sobbing.

Eric embraces me in his arms and kisses my face.

"Kiddo, don't be sorry. You know I love you."

"I'm just not ready to face everyone, Eric! I'm not ready!" I tremble.

"Kiddo, don't worry about what people think of you back home."

"You don't understand! Just look at me, Eric! Do you want to know the real truth of who Fredy Espinoza is? I'll tell you who Fredy Espinoza is. The truth is, I left California because I have no family there! I'm an orphan. And

Tyrone became my worst enemy after I decided to become Forrester Kessington. He didn't understand the amount of pain I was dealing with and I didn't have the power in me to commit suicide, so I created a role to give me the strength to escape from the town that suffocated me! I was suffocating in Fremont, Eric, and tomorrow I'll be returning to it! When I left Fremont for New York, everyone believed I was extraordinary. But the truth is, I'm ordinary. I'm just an ordinary human being, lost, without any idea of what I'm supposed to do with my life. And you know what, Eric? I like being ordinary! I love you, Eric. I love you a lot."

He gently pulls me toward the bed and holds me quietly as I continue to weep into his arms.

After a few minutes of silence, he says, "There, now, kiddo, don't cry anymore. I love you a lot too and it pains me to see you leave. It's why I've been drinking myself silly this past week. I don't want to see you leave, but I know you need to."

Kissing, we unclothe each other and pull the sheets back.

"You're beautiful to me, Fredy, so beautiful. Everything about you is beautiful," Eric whispers into my ear, holding me softly in his arms. "Have I ever told you how beautiful your brown eyes are, kiddo? You should really consider showing them more often."

Eric and I make passionate love deep into the hours of the night.

∞ CHAPTER XII: THE PRODIGAL SON ∞

TYRONE DRIVES SLOWLY into Fremont as I anxiously remind myself to breathe.

I can't believe I'm back in this town, I think. This town with its haunting memories. Back in Lucifer's palm as he seals me within his excruciating grip. All I want to do is cave into this dark abyss and never see the light again.

"Everything will work out fine, Fredy," Tyrone chirps reassuringly.

"I can't believe I'm back for good, Tyrone. I promised myself I'd never return to California, but here I am."

"Well, it's for the best! Don't worry about anything. I already spoke to Mom and she said you're more than welcome to crash on her couch until you get your life back together."

"But what if my life doesn't get back together, what do I do then?"

"I think it's about time you enroll in the Landmark Forum, Fredy." Tyrone grins at me as I bite my nails.

Tyrone has been nudging me for the past two years to participate in a

program through Landmark Education, a program based on transformative learning whereby people become conscious of the basic structures by which they know, think, and act in the world. From that consciousness arises a paradigmatic shift that leaves people more fully aware of their own possibilities and those of others. If I were to enroll in the Landmark Forum, I'd come out with the possibility of thinking and acting beyond my existing perspectives on life.

I sigh.

"I wish I could, Tyrone, but that three-day workshop costs seven hundred dollars and I don't have that kind of money."

We drive past Washington High School on Fremont Boulevard.

God, I've returned to square one. I don't know if I have the strength to face all my demons. If I could only run as far away as possible. But I would only be prolonging my perpetual Peter Pan state of being.

"There's a possibility that I could pay for it, Fredy," Tyrone proposes.

"It's too much money, Tyrone," I gasp. "I just can't accept that right now."

"Well, I never said it would be free," Tyrone says with a laugh. "You can always pay me back. Just consider it a loan."

"I'd rather wait, Tyrone." I eye him suspiciously. "Please tell me you didn't put together a welcome-home party."

"I thought you might want to relax this evening and stay in, so to answer your question, no."

I slump in my seat.

"Thank God!"

"Are you going to see your parents?" Tyrone glances over.

"No, I'm not ready to see either of them. I want no one to know I'm back in Fremont, at least, not right now."

∞

MELANCTON PULLS UP in his green jeep.

Stepping into his car, I shyly glance into his brown eyes. It's been so many years now since I last saw him, but he looks the same: fit, dark Grecian features, long hair combed to the side, with a puppy facial expression as his eyes glint with joy.

"How does it feel to be back in Fremont?"

"I'm adjusting slowly," I say, hugging him tightly for several seconds.

"Looking good, as always, Fredy," Melancton compliments me.

"You too, Melancton." I smile, letting go of him and leaning my head against the passenger seat.

"I need to pick up Odin from the vet." Melancton pats my thigh and squeezes it. "He'll be so happy to see you."

"I can't wait to meet Odin, after all that you've told me about him. Is he a very protective dog?"

"He's extremely protective of his daddy," Melancton says with a chuckle.

We pick up Odin at the vet and then drop him off at Melancton's parents' home. Stepping into their house, I am engulfed by memories of all the times I used to come here when Melancton and I were boyfriends. His room is still the same. A mirrored closet lines the wall, reflecting several Disney characters placed around the room; his queen-size bed faces an armoire, on top which sits the same stereo that woke us up every morning with our song, DJ Sammy's "Heaven."

Baby, you're all that I want, when you're lying here in my arms. I'm finding it hard to believe we're in heaven...

"Whenever Trevor and I get into a fight, I crash here," Melancton tells me as he walks in from behind and places his arms around me. "It's good to have you back in Fremont, Fredy."

"It's good to be back in your life again," I murmur, pretending he didn't

mention his boyfriend of several years.

Leaving his bedroom, we exit the house, get into his car, and drive to the Outback Steakhouse.

Déjà vu.

Sitting down at a booth, I order a Sapphire tonic.

"When you were in New York, you told me I was the reason you left," Melancton states matter-of-factly.

"That's true," I reply. The waitress drops off our drinks.

"I felt horrible for the longest time," Melancton says, glancing down.

Taking a swig of the drink, I reply carefully, "You were one of the reasons why I went to New York. But my intention was to start afresh in Manhattan. I was hoping that starting a new life would help me get over you, considering you were one of the most passionate relationships I have ever experienced."

"Why did you move back?"

"I don't know. Something called me back here."

"Fredy, I truly envy how you just pick up and leave without saving anything."

"Oh?"

"Yeah, I'm too nostalgic. I need to keep everything. I don't know how you do it."

"That's funny." I chuckle. "You're just like Tyrone. God, it took me forever to persuade him to throw away his old clothes. That's why I envy both of you."

"Well, when we're both eighty years old in rocking chairs in our cabin, you'll have to make me throw things away in the fireplace." He gives me a playful smile.

"Okay." We both laugh.

His brown puppy eyes darken. "I have to admit to you that my

relationship with Trevor has been rocky lately. It's been over a year since we've had sex."

I shake my head in disbelief. "No."

"Yes, and he treats me like a second-class citizen. He puts his career before me. I just can't deal with it anymore."

"I'm sorry."

"No, I'm the one who should be sorry. I shouldn't be venting to you about Trevor like this," he apologizes.

"Don't go there, Melancton. That's why I'm here." I gently touch his arm. "It's what friends are for."

<div align="center">∞</div>

MELANCTON'S BED FEELS comfortable as I lie down on it.

"That was an amazing dinner," I purr, closing my eyes.

"You're so far away from me, Fredy. Are you afraid of me?" He laughs as I feel the edge of the bed on the opposite side of him.

"I could never be afraid of you, Melancton," I lie, considering the power he has over me.

In the background, vocal house music lightens up the mood as Odin sits on the floor, wags his tail, and gazes at us intently. His huge eyes correspond to Melancton's; no wonder he took Odin in.

"There's this shirt at Banana Republic I want that looks a lot like the one you're wearing," I say. "It's green and it has a design"—I touch his left pec and trace my finger across it—"right here."

"Where?" Melancton giggles.

"Right here," I repeat, tracing my finger across his pec again.

"Can you do that again?" he whispers mischievously.

"Hmmm... maybe the design is more like this," I say, pressing my palm onto his chest.

Suddenly, he grabs my shoulders, pulls me in, plants his lips ferociously

on mine, and kisses me passionately. Heat and electricity consume us—we interlock lips for what seems like eternity. A maddening rush of desire catapults us to fulfill our lust for each other.

We both know that we have just crossed a line, but we don't care. He pushes my head into his crotch, moans of pleasure escaping his mouth. I kiss him feverishly, and whisper, "I want to eat you out."

"No, next time," he whispers back.

Melancton yanks my shirt off, undoes my pants, and gets me naked. Taking his clothes off, Melancton turns me over and presses my body against his.

"God, I want to penetrate you," he breathes into my ear.

"I want you to."

"No, next time."

I turn to face him and we kiss for an hour.

"I don't think I can come," he sighs.

"It's okay, I understand."

He gazes down at my body. "You're about to come."

"No."

"You can if you want to." He reaches down and starts masturbating me.

I grab his hand and pull it away. "No, if you don't come, I don't want to either."

A silence blankets us and we lie there saying nothing.

Then he kisses me gently on the shoulder.

He turns over and faces the mirror. I trace my finger down his smooth back and along his tattoo. I trace over and over, my finger following the Celtic cross within the sun. I count sixteen flames surrounding it.

Looking up, I catch Melancton's stare and realize he has been watching me the whole time.

We get up and quickly get dressed.

"I hope you don't think I'm trashy," he says with a trace of guilt in his voice.

"No, if anything, I'm the one who feels trashy for having tempted you."

Kissing Odin goodbye, I follow Melancton to his jeep.

Arriving at Tyrone's house, I finally break the silence. "Can I hit on you?"

"Yeah, hit on me," Melancton says, smiling.

"When you first meet someone, you feel butterflies in your stomach," I say. "And the more you see this person, the more this feeling begins to rise. And this feeling rises and rises as you realize just how attracted you are to this person, until you can't help it—your face turns red. Just like right now!"

"You're good!" Melancton laughs as his face flushes red.

I lean over and hug him, and he grabs me, pulls me in, and kisses me softly. I can't recall a softer or more endearing kiss.

"I'll see you around, Fredy," he whispers into my ear.

"Yes," I say, hesitating. "I'll see you around, Melancton."

A smile beams on my face as I step away and think that the love of my life has returned to me.

<p style="text-align:center">∞</p>

SAN FRANCISCO SKYSCRAPERS tower above me as I make out Melancton in a crowd of people.

"Melancton! Over here!" I wave and dash giddily toward him and plant myself in his arms.

"How does it feel to have a job?"

"Great! It feels good to be back at Banana Republic," I reply. We stroll through Union Square.

"What about school?" Melancton inquires.

"I took a placement exam at City College of San Francisco. God, Melancton, I almost cried." I look away from his concerned expression.

"Why?"

"It's been three years since I've graduated from high school. And as I tried to recall how to do simple algebra, I almost caved in and ran out of the test. But I pushed myself."

We head toward Zara. Inside, I come across a fitted dark-blue blazer. I try it on and run my hands across the fabric.

"Melancton, you know you want to buy me this, right?" I joke, batting my eyes.

"I'll buy you one if you buy me one."

"Let's do it, then!"

"Awesome! When you aren't here, I'll return it and get my money."

"What?! In that case, I'll make sure not to give you a receipt. If you do return it, you'll have to exchange it for something else."

Sticking my tongue out at him, we leave the department store.

At a hot dog stand, Melancton buys me an Açaí energy drink and a Mountain Dew for himself. Chugging the drink down, he tosses the can into a nearby trashcan. Glancing at me, he frowns.

"You must not like your drink."

"Why do you say that?"

"Because I can tell it's still full."

"Of course I like it! It's delicious!"

"What does it taste like? Berries?"

"Yeah." I take a long sip. "Do you want to taste it?"

"Okay! Okay, I believe you." He laughs as I stick the drink in his face.

Taking it back, I answer, "The reason why I'm drinking it so slow is because I'm making this moment last as long as I can between us, Melancton. I want to prolong this feeling."

"Did I tell you my friend Carrie got married?!" he says, changing the subject. "I spent this past weekend with her and not once did she mention

her marriage. She seemed unhappy."

"Then why is she with him?" I ask, slightly perplexed.

"Just to be with him out of sheer loneliness."

"So, she married him out of loneliness even though she doesn't love him?"

"Yes."

"How sad." I look into his eyes. "I'd rather live a life I desire than settle down just because."

I want to lean in and kiss him softly, but I don't dare. I am not a homewrecker—I don't want to come between Melancton and Trevor. If Trevor knew I was hanging out with Melancton, how would he feel? Would he feel the way I felt when I heard rumors of Melancton sleeping behind my back with Jacob Lee? I remind myself that Melancton told me he never cheated on me; but if he was able to cheat on Trevor with me the other night, how do I know for sure that he never cheated on me?

"Want to get a drink at the Renaissance Hotel?" he asks me.

"Yeah, definitely!"

Strolling to the hotel in Union Square, I find myself falling deeply in love all over again with Melancton. Maybe there is a chance for us; if it's destiny, there will be a way.

Ordering Sapphire tonics, we lounge on chairs beneath a crystal chandelier.

"What's on your mind?" Melancton asks.

"I'm just thinking about how I have no pictures of us."

"Yes, you do. You have the picture of us going to Alcatraz."

"Oh, right. Hmm... I must have lost it. I have a bad memory. I envy you—you always have a good memory," I say, masking my guilt.

"You do too, Fredy. You just choose not to remember, that's all." He stares at me.

I take a swig of my drink. "You're, right."

Melancton changes the subject again. "Fredy, you're the only boyfriend I've ever been so sexually active with."

"I remember," I say, smiling at the memory. "You know what else I remember? The time we fondled at Lake Elizabeth Park. I wanted you to fuck me in the dark beneath the moon and stars."

"I was too nervous!" Melancton laughs. "We were in a public setting. Hmm… When I saw you for the first time after you returned from Florida, I wanted so badly to fuck you."

"When I saw you, I wanted to fuck your brains out as well," I confess, blushing.

I grab my drink and take another huge swig. The cool gin lingers on my tongue before I swallow.

"Why do you want me to fuck you so badly? I'm not hung," Melancton says bluntly.

"You're the only ex who made me feel so sexually fulfilled—and on top of that, you're just fucking hot, Melancton Vassiliadis!"

I think, *And because I love you.*

"Cheers! Here's a toast to having shared a part of our lives," I announce. "To all those hot sex sessions."

"A toast to that!" Melancton laughs as our glasses clink.

I blink back depression as I sip my drink and feel ghosts flutter silently in the pit of my chest.

An hour later, Melancton glances at his watch and informs me that it's time for him to leave. Hugging him goodbye, I watch him leave the hotel. Returning to the bar, I order another drink and return to the chair, thinking about Melancton.

My phone vibrates. I reach into my pocket and get it.

"What the?!" I gasp as a text from Morgan Medeford pops up on the

screen.

"I can't stop thinking of you baby. Move to Miami. I will pay for your ticket. You can do whatever you want. Come move into my penthouse on Ocean Avenue, baby. Just as long as you say you're mine."

For a second, I imagine what life could be like for me if I were to move to Miami. But then the horror of the withdrawal I experienced on the plane constricts my throat and I fight back the demons of that flight.

Shaking my head, I press Delete.

∞

REVELERS IN COSTUME haunt the streets of the Castro as Halloween night commences. Entering Badlands, I walk through the crowd to the rectangular elongated bar along the wall. A few coworkers follow and we all order Sapphire tonics.

A coworker nudges me.

"Fredy, Superman keeps looking your way."

I look over my shoulder and notice a five-foot-nine, chiseled, green-eyed Caucasian man in a Superman suit undressing me with his eyes.

"Fredy, he keeps checking you out! Go talk to him! He's so fucking hot!"

"And? I'm here to have fun with you guys, not here to cruise," I reply.

"Just talk to him!" he yells playfully, pushing me in Superman's direction.

"Fine." I laugh and trot over to Superman.

"Has anyone ever told you you're very handsome?" Superman says, revealing a perfect Crest smile. Gosh, his teeth are so perfect I wonder if they're dentures.

"Yes, I've been told," I answer. Superman catches me by surprise and plants a kiss on my lips.

From behind me, my coworkers cheer.

I play hard to get.

"I'm sorry, but I don't kiss strangers off the bat."

He dives in and kisses me again, more passionately than before.

This time, I allow the kiss to linger a bit longer before pushing him off me.

"Do I have to repeat myself? I don't kiss strangers—even if you are a terrific kisser."

My coworker comes up to me and tells me they're heading over to the Mix down the street and will return.

Superman says, "Please, you should go with your friends. I have to be honest—I have a boyfriend."

"Oh? Then why did you kiss me?"

"Because I wanted to."

"Too bad. I was hoping for more." I wink at him. "I so wanted to be your Superboy and you could have been my Superman."

I playfully give him a sad puppy look.

"My boyfriend and I are into threesomes."

"Oh, it turns out that I enjoy threesomes."

"Let's meet him."

Next thing I know, I'm swept away into a taxi between two handsome men, their hands on my thighs. Superman's erotic whispers burn my ears. Within minutes, the three of us are strolling into a two-bedroom apartment in Diamond Heights. Stepping out onto the patio, I see a breathtaking view of all San Francisco, the Bay Bridge, and the Bay Area.

"Magnificent, huh?" Superman's Brazilian boyfriend comments.

"Yes." My eyes drift over to him. A gentle spirit emanates from his maple-brown eyes, his dimples only accentuate his flawless face, and his chiseled chest amplifies my attraction toward him.

He pulls me in and kisses me.

In their guest bedroom, Superman undresses completely. He gazes at us

patiently as his boyfriend and I make out on the patio. Then he steps out onto the patio, kisses his partner's neck, and beckons us to follow. Beside the king-size bed Superman caresses my face, my throat, my shoulders, undoes the buttons from my shirt, slides it off, and leans in as he devours me with his mouth. His partner whips off my belt and unlatches my crisp black khaki pants; it slides down to reveal that I'm going commando.

The three of us sink onto the goose-feather bed.

Superman grabs my legs and gently lifts my torso off the bed as he pushes himself in; his thick cock blooms in me. It hurts intensely, yet the pleasure overrides it.

Superman takes his time as his partner kisses me. After he ejaculates, his partner takes over. I come twice as the evening progresses.

Superman and I jump into a hot shower as his partner remains behind.

"You're wearing green contact lenses," he says.

"Yes, you noticed."

He takes the shampoo and washes my hair with it; he lathers his palm with soap and bathes me.

After the shower, Superman gives me a tour of their impressive apartment. He fixes me dinner and we talk about our lives. His partner goes to sleep in their bedroom.

In the guest bedroom, I lie down under the covers and whisper, "It's okay. I can sleep by myself. I want you to sleep with your boyfriend."

"He won't mind. I want to sleep with you." He turns the lights off, closes the door, and slips between his pressed Egyptian silk sheets.

"Here, take the pillow," he whispers. I place my head on it, and he slides his arm beneath me and firmly embraces me in the curvature of his firm body.

"You can always be my Superboy," he says, snuggling me.

"And you can always by my Superman," I whisper, falling into a deep

sleep.

∞

THE LANDMARK FORUM shifts every paradigm in my being. In a span of three days in February, I come to the most powerful realization that all my life I have been unconscious to the reality I am constantly creating. Now that I have the tools, I recognize the importance of maintaining integrity in all realms of life—from finances to love—and how my word has the power to get complete with the past so that it never influences my present state of being.

Because of the Landmark Forum, I am standing in front of a gate to the entrance of Hedco House in Hayward, a psychosocial and prevocational rehabilitation program for adults with severe and persistent mental illness, where Mom resides. It's been over five years since I last saw her. Taking a deep breath, I remind myself that it is time for me to get complete with Mom so that both of us can move on from all that has happened in the past—a past that no longer exists when you choose to live only in the present moment.

Entering the gate, I come upon a white cat bathing itself. It lets out a soft and soothing purr as I pass it. Butterflies swarm across my heart as I take another deep breath and tell myself that I am a powerful human being who has the awareness of impacting Mom's life. With this intention in mind, I subside into peace and acknowledge the true purpose of this visit. I come to a blue-and-white one-story wooden house. The door is wide open, the sound of a soap opera blaring from a television within. Going up the steps, I wonder if I will recognize her.

As I step inside, an old woman stares at me in shock and asks, "Can I help you?"

"I'm looking for my mother, Alma Espinoza."

"Alma, yes! Oh, Alma, she's down this hallway. Come, come. Over

here." She smiles as she beckons me deeper into the half-lit hallway. To my left, I pass a common room and notice two women staring vacantly at the television. Suddenly, I recognize the voice emanating from the television and it transports me back to the time when I loved watching *Days of Our Lives*. It is Hope speaking to Marlena.

The caretaker raps at a door and cries out, "Alma! Someone's here to see you! Alma!"

The door opens and I hear Mom's feeble voice quietly ask, "Yes?"

I step through the doorway and see her sitting at the edge of the bed.

Gray streaks slice through her thin unkempt hair, wrinkles crease the corners of her eyes, and dark circles drop beneath them. She has a faraway look in her eyes as she smiles innocently in my direction.

She doesn't notice me at first.

A gray shirt dangles loosely over her black sweatpants; it fails miserably to cover her pudgy body. The smell of cigarette ash permeates the room; she grips a packet of cigarettes. Her nails are long, yellow, brittle, and chipped.

Wasn't it just yesterday she would wake me up at five in the morning to prep for elementary school; how I would stare at her from the doorway as she sat in her boudoir, gazing at herself as she applied red lipstick, makeup, and Chanel perfume; how she would laugh when she caught me gazing intently at her; how I would run in and jump beneath her covers demanding to stay with her.

Her eyes vacantly shift from the caretaker to me.

At first, she seems to stare through me as if I'm not there.

Then recognition dawns on her face. She lights up with a smile and tears spring to her eyes.

"Fredy! Oh, mijo! Is that really you? I can't believe you finally came to see me!"

She gets up from the bed and embraces me.

"Yes, I recently moved back from the East Coast."

"Oh, how I missed you, my son!"

She steps back and holds my gaze for several seconds before capturing my face, my body, and finally my essence.

"I sit here every day wondering when you will come see me, mijo." Her eyes mist up again as she reaches out for my hand.

I smile. "I know, Mom."

She returns the smile briefly, but then her brown eyes become dark, cloudy, and distant. Letting go of my hands, she grabs her cigarettes, steps out onto the patio, and lights one up. I stand at the doorway behind her, and watch her smoke heavily. She inhales deeply with each hit of the cigarette. The sunlight strikes her arm as she pulls another cigarette from the carton; long unshaved hair covers her delicate arms.

I step out into the backyard and sit beside her.

Deep thoughts keep her emotionally distant from me; her eyes are caught up in the past, her face is expressionless, and her lips gape open as smoke escapes into the air. I resist the urge to dwell on the night I awoke to her straddling me with a butcher knife in her hand.

"I came to tell you I am sorry for who I was being."

"Sorry?"

"I want forgiveness for the way I was being toward you growing up," I continue.

"Don't say that, honey. I love you." Mom's eyes remain despondent.

"What I'm trying to say is that I know why you are going through this, Mom! And I need to tell you that I love you. I will always be here for you."

She stops smoking and faces me.

"I also came to tell you that I am very blessed that it was you who gave birth to me. Looking back, I now see clearly that you could only do what you could do with what befell you. Thank you for being an amazing teacher, and

above all, an amazing mother. I am who I am because of you and I would never have it any other way, Mom."

I focus deeply into her eyes, fighting for her soul as I make her see me for who I am in the present moment. I do not focus on what befell her, and thereby befell us; I look at a woman whose life can still be awakened. I search for the innocence of her being without the stories that persist clinging to us all.

Suddenly, her eyes become clear and light up with emotion, and I find who I was looking for: my true mother, who I can only imagine gave me the same look when she first laid eyes upon me after giving birth to me.

I got her.

I grab her fiercely in my arms and hug her tightly.

I resist breaking out into a sob as tears well forth.

We hold each other for many minutes as Mom's silent sobs lace the air, as her body weakens in my arms, and her back heaves slightly. I envision sending her all my love, washing away all her pain, and healing our history through this conversation. There is no need to bring the past into this present moment. No need to bring up anything, for all we have is this present moment.

I whisper into her ear, "I love you, Mom, and I'm blessed to have been born from your womb."

I choose you, Mom, unconditionally.

<div align="center">∞</div>

IN THE TERMINAL AT SFO, I race down an aisle empty of people. I step onto an Up escalator just as a flight attendant steps onto the other one, heading down toward me. Cocking my head, I inspect her as we approach each other.

She looks up from a brochure, reveals her face, and smiles at me.

"Mom!" I gasp.

An aura of joy showers her as she passes me and continues down to the main level.

Her hair is silky brown, crowned in curls, her skin young and smooth, free of wrinkles, and her body is flawless in her uniform.

"Oh, don't worry about me, mijo! Now that I'm free, I'm off to see the world for the first time in a very long time!"

Waking up, I smile as I retrospectively consider my dream. Maybe I set Mom free when I visited her. Yawning, I quickly get ready to meet Dad, whom I have not seen since my departure for New York. I'd think it would only get easier after seeing Mom, but for some reason it's more difficult staying in the present moment with Dad. The past persists in intruding into the present moment.

Arriving at his apartment, I knock on the door.

A look of shock and surprise crosses Dad's face as he opens the door.

"So, the prodigal son returns." He smiles as he hugs me.

"It's been many years," I murmur as I step into his apartment.

Dad has aged considerably since we last saw each other; his face is taut, with sun spots and wrinkles, his body is slightly overweight, and his head is bald. His eyes still carry the same stern disapproving look that cuts my heart every time I see it. But then I remind myself of the purpose of my visit.

"What brings you here?" Dad asks, sitting down directly across from me on the couch.

"To tell you some things that must be said," I reply. I look around the apartment. The living room is full of pictures of Dad's new family; one of Dad happily kissing Edith on the cheek stands out.

Dad's eyebrows go up, expecting words of anger or disappointment.

"I recently took a course through Landmark Education and it left me standing in the possibility of moving forward with my life, Dad. And in order to do that, I need to have a conversation with you. I saw Mom," I add.

He looks at me uncomfortably. "Oh?"

"She told me to tell you hello and that she wants to see Bianca, Eduardo,

and Alexander."

"Bianca's in Utah, Fredy. And Alexander's in Mexico. He started following Eduardo's path so I sent him away."

"I see." I think about the last time I saw him. "And Eduardo?"

Dad diverts his eyes from mine as if hiding something. "He's back in jail."

"Dad, I'm not here to make you wrong for the choices you made regarding our family's affairs. I no longer choose to be upset with you over having been kicked out and disowned for coming out of the closet."

"Fredy—"

"Dad, please, let me finish. I get you for who you are, Dad. And who you are is perfect to me. If I strip away everything between us and choose to see you just for you in this moment, right now, then who I am seeing is not my father, but a man whose lot in life taught him to process life the only way he could. And who am I to judge and crucify this man who has to work daily to put bread on the table?

"And it is from this vantage point that I choose to forgive you for disowning me. It is because of you that life unfolded the way it has for me, leaving me stronger than ever before. Mom taught me to question every aspect of how human beings see reality, and you gave me the gift of taking on the world without fear of it consuming me. You are an incredible teacher, father, role model, and human being.

"All that matters to me is your happiness in this lifetime, Dad, and I wish you the resources you need to be successful in all realms of your life. Lastly, I want to apologize for my way of being toward you growing up. I never understood where you were coming from until now. I love you, Dad. Can you forgive me for making you wrong this whole time?"

Dad's eyes water up as he gets up from the couch, walks over to me, and embraces me. "You've always been the perfect son, Fredy."

"No, I'm not perfect, Dad. I'm just me," I whisper as I blink back tears. I'm just me.

∞ PART THREE: REQUIEM MASS ∞

"Life can only be understood backwards; but it must be lived forwards."—Søren Kierkegaard

∞ CHAPTER XIII: RISEN FROM ASHES ∞

MELANCTON VASSILIADIS PEEKS curiously from behind the menu at the Daily Grill on Geary Street in Union Square. His hair is perfectly parted to the side and his clean-shaven face takes years off his age. Isn't he turning twenty-seven this year?

I catch his eyes and speak with a serious tone. "I need to have a conversation with you, Melancton, about cleaning up something between us that has been bothering me for the past five years."

"Why don't we order a few cocktails before we begin this conversation," he suggests.

A part of me hesitates, since the conversation I intend to have deals with the subject of being present, but I choose to have a cocktail. As usual, I order a Sapphire tonic and sip quietly as Melancton gazes at me with a perplexed look on his face. If I didn't know better, I would say that Melancton has an idea of what I'm about to bring up.

"Melancton, I first want to say that I want to apologize to you for who I have been being since we first met. I need to take responsibility for my actions and how they have impacted you. Miscommunication has been the number one problem in our relationship and I want to take responsibility for that. I know it's difficult to understand who I am when I cannot even express myself directly, and that has put a strain on our relationship and our friendship."

"Fredy, it takes two to tango. You don't need to apologize at all for who you have been being with me," Melancton's eyes soften as he places his hand on mine. "You've had a hard life and I'm just happy to be there for you when you need me."

"I sincerely am full of gratitude to you for helping me when I needed it in New York, for supporting me at times when I felt I didn't have the strength to move forward, and for you just being you." I smile as the cocktail has its effect on me. "I lost my virginity to you, Melancton Vassiliadis, so I consider you my first true love."

Suddenly, Melancton's eyes darken.

"Didn't you lose your virginity to Jacob Lee?"

"No, Melancton."

"That's funny, I could have sworn you and Jacob had sex."

"Since we're on this subject, I have to be honest and admit that I still think you cheated on me with him," I reply. "I've already come to terms with it, but I need to hear it from your mouth. I take full responsibility for who I was being in that period, so I can't hate or judge you if you did. Did you cheat on me, Melancton?"

"Fredy, I thought we put this behind us! I never cheated on you with Jacob. I don't know why you have it in your head that I slept with him. I'm not that kind of guy. I have a question for you. Did you cheat on me with John Michael Stutz?"

At the sound of John Michael Stutz's name, I nearly drop my drink.

"I can't believe you would ask me that about John Michael Stutz," I reply. "He passed away a year after you and I broke up."

"I didn't know that, Fredy. I apologize." He takes a swig from his drink.

Sitting there in silence, I recall how I met John Michael Stutz at Club Faith in San Francisco when I first turned eighteen. He was my mentor and taught me the parameters of what it entails to be a young gay man; he would always pick me up and take me everywhere with him. I remember how soft his hand felt in my palm; how at the age of thirty-two he looked handsomely fit and could pass for twenty-five; how I tried to persuade him to take my virginity, but he wouldn't do it; how he revealed to me that he was disowned by his family after he came out, thereby leading him to change his name and losing out on inheriting a fortune—his family owned one of the biggest steel companies in America. And how on October 8th, 2003, I walked into Starbucks, picked up a newspaper, opened it to the obituary section, and saw John Michael Stutz's name printed there.

"John Michael Stutz was my mentor and friend and nothing sexual ever occurred between us," I say calmly. "He was to me what Roger Haryana was to you."

"What about that weekend when you left with him to Yosemite? You knew I didn't want you to go, but you still went with him. And you're telling me nothing sexual happened between you two over that weekend?" His voice is laced with anger.

Sighing, I think to myself that this is exactly what I wanted to avoid. I never should have ordered that cocktail.

"Nothing sexual happened that weekend. If it satisfies you to know, he held my hand throughout the drive to Yosemite. I did give him a massage once, but that's the closest we came to doing anything physical. And that massage happened before I met you. In fact, it was our inside joke, because I

begged him to let me give him a hand job, but the only hand job he'd allow me to give him was that massage." My eyes darken and mist up as I hear John Michael Stutz's laughter in my head and for a second I imagine him whispering, *You mean a lot to me, my friend.*

"I still can't believe you chose to go with him on that trip instead of being with me."

"Melancton! Do you know how difficult it was for me to tell John Michael Stutz that I couldn't see him anymore because my relationship with you prevented it? I chose you over him, Melancton," I say bitterly.

"It sounds like you're still emotionally invested in him, Fredy," he pries.

"He's the only gay man in my life who never betrayed me, never used me, never hurt me, never disrespected me. So, of course I still care about him."

What would my life look like if I had chosen John Michael Stutz over Melancton Vassiliadis?

"So, there we have it, Fredy. Neither of us cheated on the other." Melancton chugs the rest of the cocktail.

Why do I still feel he is lying to me? What of Jacob Lee? Didn't he confess to me at his going-away party, or was that a complete fabrication? And if it was a fabrication, was it to hurt me for never reciprocating the love he felt for me?

If a man is his word, then I have to take Melancton's word for what it is and accept that he never cheated on me.

"Well, I'm happy that we can finally put this to rest, Melancton. I promise to never bring this up again. I choose to believe you." Batting away the phantoms of the past, I smile at Melancton and propose, "Let's rebuild our friendship. Let it be based on trust, integrity, and authenticity."

And for the first time in a long time, I feel free as I choose to believe Melancton. He never cheated on me; he has been telling the truth for the

longest time. And I know he loves me. Why else would he have helped me in New York? Why else would he have offered to pay for my flight back to California?

So that he could be with me!

∞

I LEAVE MY APARTMENT and step onto 24th Street at Castro in Noe Valley, San Francisco. With books in hand, I hurry down to Church Street to catch the J train to City College of San Francisco. Stopping at Starbucks, I dash in, order a raspberry white mocha, and then jet out.

Brimming with excitement, I think back on all I have been through and remind myself that my first dream of many dreams has come true. It feels good to return to the world of academia. I want to plant a tree in San Francisco, plant the seeds and wait for my prospects to grow.

Hopping onto the J train, I plop into a seat and watch the people around me through my white sunglasses. My smile evaporates as it dawns on me that maybe I am dreaming. How do I know what is reality and what is fantasy, I wonder, observing the minutest lines on people's faces around me. How can I tell if I'm alive? Of course I am alive, but how do I truly know?

Shaking my head, I force myself to recognize that my reality is indeed intact. I inhale deep breaths as my anxiety returns to a manageable level. Opening my drama book, I take out a script and go over the lines for my performance piece, whose intention is to exorcise the demons that have haunted me for so long. I want to exorcise the Devil from my life and release the darkness that has eclipsed my heart for the longest time.

Stepping off the train at campus, I make my way to my playwriting class.

After the class settles down, the professor asks if anyone would like to perform first.

I shoot my hand up and give copies of the script to a male actor and a female actor. I ask them to stand on opposite sides of the upper stage.

"This performance piece is titled *Risen from Ashes*," I announce, lying down at center stage. "Action."

A hard masculine voice booms across the stage toward the audience. "From the East, West, South, and North, I call upon angels to guide this manifestation as I beseech Lucifer to reveal himself to these masks full of cynicism and resignation."

"And from the North, South, West, and East, I call upon angels to guide this manifestation as I beseech God to make His divine presence known and heal this human being who lies sprawled before us," a soft feminine voice enunciates in a stage whisper from the opposite side of the stage.

Closing my eyes, I twitch and jerk on the floor as I imagine both energies moving through my body on this stage.

"Show yourself upon these sleeping humans who fear waking up! Show yourself to awaken the dead!" the man's voice demands as I begin to writhe, gasp, and heave on the floor.

"And may the forces of light eradicate the darkness as one by one human beings awaken and recognize their enslavement to a lie for most of eternity," the woman's voice declaims, heightening in urgency.

He screams, "And the fires of Hell shall sweep across this human's soul to exorcise the very demons from within, for surely Hell is but a state of mind from whence one must pass through the specter of fire to awaken!" I am cued to imagine the energy of fire burning at the soles of my feet and sweeping across my body.

Silence envelops the theater as his scream echoes.

And deep within, I touch the core of my anger, pain, and sadness as it yanks me into the depths of my inner Hell. As if choreographed, I convulse violently, my body agitating about and twisting in rapid movements, and I throw my hands into the air as the horror descends upon me.

Cued, the woman's voice cries out, "And allow the light to show you the

way through these fires as you awaken from the darkest tomb of death! Awake and set yourself free from yourself! Awake and rise through the veil of illusion! Awake and rise! Awake and rise! AWAKE AND RISE!"

Collapsing onto the floor, I break into tears. I open my eyes for the first time, jerk my head toward the audience, break through the fourth wall, and stare into a girl's blue eyes. I stretch my hand out to her and cry, "Help me!"

"Lucifer is among us!" The actor's voice lashes out. "Now is the crucial moment of your awakening! Break through the veil of illusion and destroy the mask of death, for no one can save you but yourself!"

Gasping, I drop my head back onto the stage and imagine peace rippling through me as I make the sign of the crucifix.

"You are resurrected and risen from ashes," the actress intones softly.

I lie there for a few seconds, then say, "End scene."

Stepping off the stage, I make my way to a seat behind the girl I unintentionally made eye contact with. Her straight blonde hair glistens beneath the lights and perfume lightly fills the space around her. She is decked out in a leather jacket, studded leather gloves, a fashionable tee, black leggings, and black stiletto shoes. Her name is Amanda Michelle Foschia and in many ways she reminds me so much of Albana Ferizi, my model friend from Pensacola.

When I tap her shoulder, she turns and demands, "What!"

"Oh, I wanted to say I'm sorry for breaking the fourth wall and making eye contact with you."

"Le Lord! This is too much to handle right now," she says, pivoting back to her original position.

∞

DEAD, I REST in peace, floating serenely like a ghost over the Atlantic Ocean. From afar I hear my name, whispering back and forth, stirring me to life.

"Wake up, Fredy Espinoza. Wake up!" It whispers as I become conscious and enter a state of confusion.

Suddenly, Golden Gate Bridge appears before me and I find myself being transported in a vehicle. A beautiful angel drives it across the bridge to San Francisco. Behind me, the New York skyline is enshrouded in darkness; lightning cracks and thunder rumbles all around me. I ask the angel where she is taking me and she shakes her head. Her mouth is taped shut with duct tape. She points to the side of the vehicle. Lightning reveals block letters printed along the side: FORRESTER KESSINGTON.

"But, I'm dead," I whisper in shock.

"No!" Forrester Kessington's voice echoes around me.

Suddenly, I am walking through a thick forest with graves and tombstones stretching for miles. The angel holds a scepter with a beam of light emanating from its tip. Hastening, she grabs my hand and we race past the tombstones. Urgency quickens and my pulse rises. Ahead, one tombstone stands in solitude on top of a hill.

The angel disappears, leaving me in darkness. I stumble onto my knees in front of the ancient granite tombstone. A bolt of lightning flashes directly above me, casting light on the tombstone.

"Here lies Forrester Kessington, the special caretaker of Fredy Espinoza," I read.

Forrester Kessington is dead...

Waking up with a start, I jump out of bed and take a quick shower. I promised Tyrone I'd meet him for breakfast and I'm already running late. Dashing out of the apartment, I jump onto the number 24 bus and head into the Castro.

Stepping off the bus, I see Tyrone patiently waiting inside Harvey's.

"Hey, Tyrone, I'm so sorry for being late!" I pull a chair back and sit at the table.

"No worries, Fredy. I already ordered. I hope you don't mind." He smiles as the waiter drops off his dish.

"Oh, I don't mind at all." I look over to the waiter and ask, "Can I just order your ham and cheese omelet? Thanks."

"From Fremont to San Francisco, I can't believe both of us are living here, Fredy." Tyrone bites into a vegan dish of sautéed mushrooms, onions and peppers, spinach, and tofu.

"I had the weirdest dream about Forrester Kessington," I tell him.

Tyrone puts down his fork and glances at me with a serious expression.

"I thought you were past being Forrester Kessington."

"I am, but this dream was too surreal. It's funny, Tyrone. I know I am Fredy Espinoza, but sometimes…sometimes I can't help but wonder who I authentically am. And I wonder about that night when you, Cliff, and I experienced that supernatural event." I glance around to ensure no one is near enough to hear us.

"Fredy, I don't want to talk about it. You're only feeding energy into it by doing so," he says with a frown.

"Just tell me I'm not crazy and that what happened between the three of us actually happened, Tyrone. I haven't spoken about this to anyone for fear that they'll think I'm crazy. I know we promised never to talk about this, but I had a dream last night in which I was dead, only to be awakened by Forrester Kessington, and I'm troubled."

Tyrone sighs.

He stares at me for several seconds before lifting his fork and taking another bite of tofu.

"That night is unexplainable, Fredy. You're not the only person who wonders what happened that night. And to answer your question, you're not crazy. I told a few people about it and one of them brought up the idea that maybe we experienced a moment of mass hysteria. But I don't think it was

mass hysteria when Cliff and I witnessed with our own eyes what happened in that room."

"What did you do afterward, Tyrone?" I inquire as the waiter hands me coffee.

After the waiter leaves, Tyrone replies, "I stopped seeing Cliff. He revealed to me that he belonged to a coven of witches who practice black magic. I told him I couldn't see him after that event, and I personally wonder whether what occurred that night wasn't entirely his fault. I met a spiritual psychic who gave me a cleansing with a bowl made from crystals. She told me that my third eye chakra had been blasted open after that event and that the cleansing would help close it so that I wouldn't attract malevolent spirits. And it helped. Seriously, Fredy, I thought I was losing my mind for awhile there. If it wasn't for that psychic, I think I might have gone mad."

Frowning, I say, "I felt like I died that night, Tyrone. And though I want to say Forrester Kessington is another being that possessed me, I feel as if I somehow created his personality to help me cope with the event. Can you recount the whole event to me from your perspective, Tyrone?"

"No, let's just drop this conversation about that night, Fredy. You recently saw your mom and dad right?"

"Yeah," I glance out the window and stare at a handsome gay couple strolling past. "Mom was so drugged up that I think she only noticed me being there once. And Dad still lives in Fremont with Edith and her children. He invited me for dinner next week."

"Are you going to go?"

"I'm thinking about it. My grandparents are flying in from Mexico and will be there." My nostrils flare at the welcoming aromas as my meal is delivered.

"Have you spoken to Eduardo, Bianca, or Alexander?"

My eyes darken as I think about my younger siblings.

"Eduardo is a revolving-door case. He's back in jail. Dad told me Eduardo exits jail only to return to it. He wouldn't tell me why he's back in jail but I think it has to do with breaking his parole. As for Bianca, she's in Utah and I haven't been able to get ahold of her. Alexander dropped out of high school and started hanging out with gangs, so Dad shipped him off to Mexico, where he's put to work every day for Edith's family. It's so depressing, Tyrone. And then there's Ricardo, whom I haven't seen in a long time."

Tyrone's eyes soften with empathy. "I forgot about Ricardo."

"Ricardo must be about five years old now. My mom's sister, Angelica, is raising him. It's funny. After Eduardo raped Mom, I thought that it might have been his baby, but it turns out Mom had already been pregnant for three months."

"Do you think Ricardo will ever know who his real mom is?"

"My cousin told me he's being raised to believe my mom is his mother. Ricardo was confused at first, but he now accepts that he has two moms, one who is sick and another who is his foster mom. It's funny, I saw a picture of Ricardo and he looks exactly like me when I was his age."

"Your dad won't admit that it's his baby?"

"Mom says the father is a guy named Ricardo. You and I weren't friends back then, when it all went down, Tyrone. Around the time Eduardo raped Mom, Dad had rented out a room to a nice Mexican woman and her two children. One of them was Ricardo, a scrawny seventeen-year-old guy. I guess Mom and Ricardo had sex while Dad was sleeping around with Edith. Dad met Edith through Ricardo's mother. It never dawned on me that when Edith came over to hang out with her best friend, she was also seeing Dad clandestinely."

"Are you going to see Ricardo?"

"He's currently in Mexico with my aunt. And so many years have passed

between us that I don't know if he would believe that I am his oldest half-brother. Tyrone, can you imagine growing up with the idea of your aunt being your mother and knowing that out there another family exists?"

"I don't know Fredy. After being through so many foster care parents, I think Ricardo has it lucky." He finishes eating.

"I personally believe that if there is an Espinoza curse, Ricardo may be the only child who has escaped it," I ponder aloud.

"Maybe you have escaped the curse too, Fredy... *If* there is a curse on your family." Tyrone smiles.

"I hope so, Tyrone. I hope so." I finish my cup of coffee and request another one. "Enough about me; what's going on in your life?"

"I hate my roommate. I seriously think he has an issue with me being gay, so I've been looking around for a studio downtown. As much as I love living behind City College, I can't stand living with a roommate who is constantly harassing me. You know, I think he broke my car window!"

"What?! You should report his ass if he did."

"I don't have proof," Tyrone sighs.

"Yeah, then it might be best if you move out. What are you doing after brunch? Want to come with me to Cafe Flore and have a few cocktails for Sunday funday?"

"No, I'm working after this."

"One day, neither of us will ever have to work for the corporate world," I say.

"I can't believe you called work and quit over the phone, Fredy," Tyrone says with a laugh.

"School is more important to me than working, Tyrone. With the scholarship money and the loans, I can live off that while focusing mainly on my studies."

"I wish I could do that, but I need to make sure I don't wind up on the

street."

"For sure, it's never a good thing to be homeless." A twinge of sadness enters my voice.

"Oh, I'm sorry I didn't mean to—"

"Don't apologize, Tyrone. I may have been homeless once, but I'll make sure never to be homeless again." I finish eating my omelet.

Departing from Harvey's, I hug Tyrone goodbye before making my way to Cafe Flore. Sitting down at a table along Noe Street, I order a mimosa. Opening my journal, I jot down the whole conversation I just had with Tyrone and then continue to write about Forrester Kessington.

And a thought strikes me.

Why not call upon my inner child, my future self, and Forrester Kessington and try to merge all these different selves into one complete human being? Setting down the pen, I smile at the waiter as he hands me a mimosa. Sipping it gently, I look to my left and imagine seeing the image of a frightened child, trembling in confusion, and always avoiding my eyes. To my right, I imagine what I would look like in the future: a handsome man full of light, love, and tranquility, with defined jaw and cheekbones, his eyes intensely wise, with an acute awareness of the many opportunities available to him. Across from me is a spitting image of myself, except he is Forrester Kessington, with green eyes. He smiles at me with the acknowledgement that this is my Now.

In my head, I feel the young child yearning and thirsting for attention. I turn to him and say, "Fredy, let me tell you that with or without adversity, you are an angel. Walk with fierce determination to my Now in this present moment and I promise you a future of gold awaits you. If you ever feel fear, just squeeze my palm. I will be your guide, always by your side until you meet me in this present moment."

The young child stops trembling and locks eyes with mine. He nods his

head and reaches for my palm. I clasp his hand and squeeze it to confirm that I will always believe in him, my inner child.

Then I glance over to Forrester Kessington and lock eyes with his green eyes.

"I am ready to accept my Now, Forrester Kessington. At the moment of my spiritual death, you took over, always nurturing and instilling within me amazing gifts to ensure I grow up to become the angel I was born to be. I sincerely thank you from the bottom of my heart. Because of you, I will manifest all my dreams into existence.

"When I came into being again in New York, I feared you. Who was this entity that had possessed me, I questioned. But now I see that you and I are one being. At the time of my possession, I died, only to have you rise out of the flames and take me as far away as possible from the site of my trauma. And like a phoenix, I have risen from ashes and reawaken into being. The dream I had last night is your way of telling me you have fulfilled your purpose."

Taking a bow, Forrester Kessington winks at me and disappears. A sense of courage uplifts me as I recognize that Forrester Kessington is just an aspect of me, is me, and will always be me.

Shifting my gaze to my future self, my knees buckle. I feel like a courtier in the midst of his presence. Luminous cappuccino-brown eyes twinkle at me and his rivulets of black hair are crowned with a golden diadem. He nods and laughs capriciously at my aloofness and strange habit of constructing such a mental delusion.

I snap back to reality, take another swig of the deliciously blended mimosa, and lose myself within the soft timbres of my future self's voice as I imagine him speaking to me from the future.

"You have so much to learn, Fredy Espinoza, but know that you are finally on the right path. Accept the moment you are living in and allow

yourself to just be. From this state of being, all your desires will be brought forth into existence. Harness your essence and be true to your word. I promise that by doing so, many will stand behind you as you move forward to fulfill your destiny. And just as you have promised to your inner child, I too promise to be by your side until you meet me in my Now. And what a beautiful reality you will create for yourself, Fredy Espinoza. Trust in your being."

He leans over to me and brushes his palm gently across my forehead, sparking a fire within. In the blink of an eye, he disappears, leaving me sitting alone in this reality I have constructed.

∞ CHAPTER XIV: FORBIDDEN FRUIT ∞

ROGER HARYANA RANDOMLY bumps into me later that evening in the Castro. He pulls me into his muscular arms and hugs me. His dark brown eyes light up with warmth as he repeats, "Oh, my God! Oh, my God! Oh, my God!" His jubilant voice is riddled with an Indian accent.

"Roger! It's been like, what, five or six years since we last hung out?" I laugh as I notice how masculine he looks with his slightly unshaven face.

"Fredy Espinoza! Oh, my God! I can't believe it! What are you doing here?! Last time I heard, you were still in New York!"

"I moved back recently."

"You look good, Fredy!" Roger laughs and he pulls me into another hug.

"Thank you," I reply, blushing. "You look handsome yourself."

"Here, let's grab a drink and catch up!"

Roger and I walk into Badlands on 18th Street. Madonna's music video of "Hung Up" blares out from several television screens. Making our way to the bar, we both order a round of drinks and head into the adjacent room.

Young cute guys mingle around us, their conversations overlapping one another. The more Roger and I drink, the more flirtatious he becomes and the more his eyes linger over my svelte body.

"So, you and Melancton are no longer friends," I say.

"Let's just say that after you left for New York we had a falling out. We haven't spoken since then."

"What happened?"

"I don't want to talk about it, Fredy," Roger says with an expression of distaste.

"I've been hanging out with Melancton since I returned."

"Oh? How is he doing?" Roger asks indifferently.

"He's good—living with Trevor, his partner of many years now."

Roger's voice spikes with curiosity. "Are you over Melancton?"

"I think I am complete with our history, but I still love him and will always love him, Roger."

"I was just wondering. You've really grown up into a hot guy, Fredy." Roger bats his eyes at me with a charming glint.

"Stop it, Roger," I chuckle, feeling my cheeks turn red.

He grabs my arm. "You know what? Let's celebrate your return! You deserve all the happiness in this lifetime after what you have been through. I'm going to buy us shots of tequila and meet you on the dance floor."

I head over to the dance floor and move my body to Britney Spears. Around me, hot young men dance gaily and voyeurs stand watching us along the metal counter that wraps around the dance floor. Roger finds his way through the crowd and hands me a shot. Toasting, we chase the tequila with slices of lime and set the empty glasses on the counter.

Laughing, I dance happily with Roger as he buys us more and more shots of tequila.

Then Roger leans over and kisses me.

Pleasantly shocked, I return his kiss.

"I want to fuck you," Roger tells me as he pulls me into his strong embrace.

"No! You're Melancton's best friend!" I cry in alarm, music blaring around us.

"He's my ex-best friend, Fredy," he reminds me.

Roger and I sway to the beat of the music. Hours pass, then the lights come on at closing time and we leave. I follow him to his car. We drive to Dolores Park.

"Let me go down on you, Fredy." Roger pants with desire as he parks the car alongside the park. Leaning over, he plants his lips onto mine. His hand slides along my chest as he feels me up.

"Fuck it," I whisper as I undo my pants and push Roger's head into my crotch.

Moaning, I push him away, undo his pants, and go down on him.

The windows steam up as we make out and go down on each other, fulfilling our carnal desire for each other. Finishing up, Roger leans back in his seat and whispers, "Melancton was a fool to let you go."

"Everything happens for a reason," I sigh as I it dawns on me I have broken one of my cardinal rules: never to sleep with an ex's best friend.

Some rules are meant to be broken.

∞

ANOTHER DISTURBING REVELATION comes to light as Roger Haryana calls me a few nights after our sexual rendezvous in his car.

"I'm sorry for pushing myself onto you that night, Fredy," Roger apologizes.

"We're both equally responsible. Let's make sure it never happens again."

"There's something that's been on my conscience, Fredy." He hesitates.

"I think it's time you knew the truth."

"The truth?" I sit up on my bed as my ears prick up with alertness.

"Your breakup with Melancton left you reeling in pain and I couldn't bring myself to cause you any more hurt." Roger sighs. "Remember how you came to me and asked if there was any truth to whether Melancton cheated on you with Jacob? Well, I told you the truth indirectly."

My hand tightens around the phone as the blood rushes from my head.

"What do you mean?" My voice thickens.

I get up from the bed and slowly pace as Roger's voice cuts the air with his words.

"Remember our conversation? You asked me, 'Is it true Melancton cheated on me with Jacob Lee?' and I said, 'The one with the seven-inch cock?' You said, 'Yeah, he told me they slept together behind my back.' And I told you it wasn't true, but in a way I said it was true, indirectly."

"Wait. I don't get it, Roger."

"Fredy, how would I know Jacob Lee has a seven-inch cock if I've never met him?"

"I see. So…" I pause for a few seconds as an acidic emotion cuts through my heart. "It is true, then. But why would he lie to me? Just the other day I had a conversation with him and he told me that he never cheated on me."

"That is the reason why our friendship ended. Let's face it, Melancton is a liar. Melancton is like a bank robber who robs a bank and later returns and gets a job at the bank, and he's worried over someone trying to cash a bad check for twenty dollars."

"I'm confused."

"Melancton says he's worried about your wellbeing and doesn't want anyone to hurt you, but it's okay for him to hurt you. And that's the worst thing a man can inflict on another, Fredy."

"I don't understand why Melancton would want to hurt me, Roger! What did I ever do to him? I loved him with my whole being!"

"Melancton purposely hurt you to get back at you for sleeping with John Michael Stutz."

"I never slept with John Michael Stutz!"

"Well, Melancton thought otherwise, and that's the truth, Fredy. I'm sorry for breaking it to you like this. The last thing I want to do is hurt you, but after you told me that you still had feelings for him, I felt it necessary to let you know."

"Thanks for telling me, Roger," I manage to say as hot tears burn my eyelids. "I have to go."

Ending the call, I throw the phone across the room and it smacks into the wall.

An unbearable pain bleeds again as an old wound is viscerally shredded open. I can't believe it's true. Melancton has been lying to me for these past five years. And to this day, he insists on his truth.

Breaking into an agonizing sob, I fling myself on the bed and bury my face deep in the pillow. Weeping, I think about John Michael Stutz and how innocent our interactions have always been; about Melancton and how his delusion of John Michael Stutz sleeping with me led to the very actions that spiraled me into a dark depression, causing me to believe I was nothing but a sex object. After awhile, I realize that this acidic poison only lasts for an hour. The truth takes root in me and slowly sets me free from Melancton's power over me.

I will not cast blame on Melancton; my hurt stems from a misunderstanding and miscommunication. I forgive Melancton and his deceitful deed against me. In fact, I will continue to foster my friendship with him, without him ever knowing what I learned.

I bit into the tempting apple of truth, and swallowed my fear.

I no longer fear you, Melancton.

<p style="text-align:center">∞</p>

DAD PLACES ENCHILADAS on my plate as I sit at the head of the table. Edith laughs in the kitchen, gossiping with my grandmother. My grandfather gazes intently at me as he mentally photographs every grain of my face. I haven't hung out with Dad's parents since I was a little child. I vaguely recall spending Christmas with them. Now here they are, in their nineties.

"You've done a wonderful job, Ambrocio, raising this young handsome man," my grandfather tells Dad.

"The genes run in the family, Dad." My father laughs as he sits down next to his father. Edith enters the adjacent room where the dining table is set and helps my grandmother to sit beside my grandfather.

"From what I can see, all seven of your sons and daughters are handsome and beautiful," Edith chirps. "Goodness, I don't know how you managed with so many children!"

"We believe in our Lord's command that his children bear as many fruit as possible. I believe we did our part," my grandmother says, looking lovingly at my grandfather.

My grandfather says, "It's a pity the rest of your children couldn't be here, Ambrocio. I was really looking forward to seeing Eduardo, Bianca, and Alexander."

"What a shame, Ambrocio," my grandmother chimes in. "I told you I wanted to see them one more time before we returned to Mexico."

Dad looks toward Edith uncomfortably.

"Ambrocio tried his best to round up the rest of the children, but none of them could make it except for Fredy." Edith says, covering up Dad's silence.

My grandmother smiles at my direction. "Oh, Fredy, you are the apple of our eyes. Such a wonderful grandson you are, dear."

"Thank you, Grandma," I reply. "Dad did a great job of raising me. Even when he worked so hard, he always found a way to make me happy and give me what I wanted." I take a bite of the tossed salad.

"I'm so grateful you're coming to Mexico to take care of us, Fredy," my grandfather says with immense joy.

Choking on my salad, I cough and my eyes bulge.

"Oh, dear child, are you okay?" My grandmother asks with concern.

"Wait, did you just say you want me to go to Mexico with you?"

"Ambrocio says you told him you'd be happy to take care of us in Mexico," my grandfather says. "We're getting so old and we need someone to take care of us. Your grandmother and I are no longer able to take care of the farm and it's wonderful that you're willing to come and be there for us."

I lock eyes with Dad for several seconds as I register what my grandfather is saying. Dad stares me down as if demanding I fulfill my grandparents' wish.

"There must be some confusion," I say slowly. "Of course I would love to return to Mexico to take care of you, but I failed to remind Dad that I'm back in college seeking a bachelor's degree."

My grandmother's eyes dart over to Dad. "Oh, dear! Ambrocio, you didn't tell us Fredy was in college."

"I'm certain Fredy can take a few years off and go to Mexico with you," he comments.

Edith remains quiet throughout the interaction and avoids my gaze.

"Actually, no I can't," I announce angrily, pushing the dish aside.

My grandfather's eyebrows rise as he watches my interaction with Dad.

"You can always finish schooling upon your return, Fredy," Dad says matter-of-factly.

"It's out of the question, Dad." I glower with silent fury as my teeth grind together.

"Oh, dear, maybe you have a girlfriend that we don't know of," my grandmother interjects. "That's why you don't want to come with us, isn't it, Fredy? After all, your grandfather and I both know about love—love is a beautiful gift from God. Tell us about your girlfriend." She tries to change the topic of conversation.

"I don't have a girlfriend, Grandma."

"Then there's nothing stopping you from coming with us, Fredy. I'm certain you'll find a woman in Mexico to marry and produce God's fruit. There's a wonderful church nearby and you can fulfill your dream of becoming a pastor." My grandmother is growing excited. "Oh, how my heart fills up with happiness whenever I recall you telling me that dream when you were a little boy."

"I'm shocked Dad never told you the truth."

"Truth? What is he talking about, Ambrocio?" My grandfather asks.

Dad's face turns deathly white.

"I'm a homosexual."

Everyone's attention swings to me and the dining room is swept into silence.

"That's right, Grandpa and Grandma. I'm a homosexual. And I don't believe in God."

"Jesus Christ, you're kidding, aren't you, Fredy?!" My grandfather looks at Dad aghast. "Ambrocio, tell me Fredy has your wicked sense of humor!"

Dad sits there silently staring at me.

"Fredy, you can pray it away, dear," my grandmother says. "God won't let any of His children go to Hell. I will not let the Devil win here, Fredy. Just come to Mexico and we can help you pray away this sickness."

"I am gay. Gay, gay, gay! A homosexual! I will never marry a woman and I will never become a pastor and I will never consider praying my *sickness* away!" I lash out as I get up from the dinner table.

FREDY ESPINOZA

My grandfather tries to assuage my anger. "There's no reason to get upset, Fredy." He turns to Dad with a look of shame. "Ambrocio, what kind of father have you been to allow this to happen to Fredy?"

Dad grimaces, as if my grandfather slapped him across the cheek.

"Poor Alma," my grandmother mutters beneath her breath.

Edith grimaces at the mention of Mom's name.

"It's obvious now that you never had any intention of coming with us to Mexico, dear," my grandmother asserts forcefully. "Please sit down."

Sitting down, I cross my arms across my chest and glare at Dad.

How dare he think I'd throw away my dreams so easily?

"It's a pity you chose this lifestyle, Fredy. We will pray for your soul every day," my grandfather says sorrowfully. "Jesus Christ died for your sins. Remember that."

Fuck Jesus Christ, I think.

I keep my mouth shut and ignore my grandfather for fear of triggering my anger even further. If there is one thing I hate hearing at dinner table conversation, it is being told that Jesus Christ can save my soul. My grandparents have no idea how much I hate religious ideology.

After several minutes of awkward silence, my grandmother clears her throat and says, "Well, there goes our dinner for the evening. Edith, let me help you clear the table."

"No, sit where you are. I'll take care of everything." Edith exhales gratefully as she gets up, grabs the dishes, and heads into the kitchen.

"I think it's time for me to leave," I say quietly, getting up from the table.

"Okay, dear. Thank you for taking time to see us. We will pray for you, Fredy," my grandmother replies as she gets up. She addresses my grandfather, "Get up and say goodbye to our grandson."

Kissing their cheeks and giving them hugs, I quickly make my way to the

door and say goodbye.

I don't even look at Dad.

∞

FORRESTER KESSINGTON, WHERE are you when I need you! As hard as I try, I can't summon Forrester Kessington. Returning to San Francisco, I make my way to the Castro, enter Badlands, and down three shots of tequila.

Suddenly, I feel *his* essence as a surge of sexual energy laced with anger consumes my body. Sticking my nose into the air, my eyes glaze with confidence as I charge sexually onto the dance floor. Dancing to Britney Spears' "Gimme More," I acknowledge that Forrester Kessington is my way of accessing anger without fear of being consumed by it. And right now, this anger fills me with sexual desire and a thirst for self-destruction as my eyes search for sex.

That's when I see him. Blue eyes, blonde hair, a poker face, muscular, and deliciously hot; I make my way to the middle of the dance floor and pull him into my arms.

"What are you on?" I say.

He smirks. "Cocaine."

"Give me some," I demand, grabbing his crotch. *Only Forrester Kessington has the guts to do this*, I think, smirking and brushing my lips against his.

He caves in. "Follow me to the bathroom."

I dash into the bathroom with him. Closing the stall door, he takes out a little baggie, opens it, hands me a key, and tells me to take a bump. Dipping the key into the baggie, I put a huge bump at the tip and say, "Here's to a prayer and a bump." I lift it to my nose and snort it.

He takes the key back and snorts a bump.

Within seconds, a feverish heat eclipses my heart.

"Fuck me," I demand.

Putting away the cocaine, he willingly drops his pants and whips out his

penis. I drop my pants, turn around, and feel him penetrate me.

Make me forget Roger's revelation and Dad's deception.

This handsome stranger pounds the deep-rooted pain away and I become immersed in the memory of Morgan Medeford. Oh, Morgan, how easy it is to lose oneself in self-destruction. I convulse as I ejaculate onto the wall. Behind me, I feel his body tense as he leans onto me, moans in my ear, and comes.

"Fuck yeah, breed me with that seed of yours," I moan.

We quickly clean up and dash back to the dance floor and lose ourselves within the beat of the music.

∞

THE FOLLOWING NIGHT, I find myself at Badlands again. Dancing, I make eye contact with a hot Puerto Rican. He smiles at me charmingly as I make my way to him.

"What's your name, cutie?" He asks.

"Fredy," I reply, smiling in return. "And yours?"

"Armando. Want to ditch the nightclub and come over to my house?"

"Sure."

I follow him outside.

"I live a few blocks from here."

At his house, we enter the living room. He takes out a pipe and fills it with weed. He lights it, takes a puff, and hands it to me. I take a hit and sit down.

"I'm positive," Armando says.

"Me too," I smile as I take another hit.

As we talk, Armando makes me feel like royalty as he flatters me with compliments and courts me. After awhile, the topic of medication arises and he mentions how he hates taking it.

"Oh, you're taking medication? Why are you taking medication?" I ask,

confused.

Armando looks at me incredulously. "I already told you, Fredy."

"You did?" I rub my finger against my temple, trying to recall the reason he gave.

"I'm positive," he reminds me.

"Oh. Ohhhh… You're *positive*." I laugh in embarrassment. "I thought you meant you were a positive thinker."

"You really are a blonde," Armando giggles. Then he suddenly becomes serious. "Does it scare you?"

"No, why should it?"

"Then come into my bedroom. I promise I won't bite," he says, flashing his smile.

Hypnotized, I take his hand and follow him down the hallway to his bedroom.

In the darkness, we undress and get naked.

Sound of a condom wrapper as he rips it open and slaps on a condom.

"Can I fuck you?" Armando breathes heavily.

"Yeah," I say passively.

"Why are you trembling?"

"I… I don't know," I lie as Armando slowly penetrates me.

I let out a whimper at the idea of the condom breaking.

"Are you sure you're okay?" Armando whispers, pulling out of me.

"I'm sorry, Armando. It's not you, it's me."

"Don't apologize, Fredy. Do you want to go home?"

"No, just hold me," I whisper.

What is it about Armando that I find spellbinding? He enchants me with his being. There's something dark and forbidden about him, which only makes him even more tempting. Of all the forbidden fruit in this world, Armando embodies the essence of the forbidden. What is it like to live with

HIV and always be considered forbidden fruit?

Armando is forbidden fruit to me; and I am forbidden fruit to Dad's pious family.

Will they ever accept me for who I am?

∞ CHAPTER XV: INTO THE WOODS ∞

THE ENCHANTMENT LASTS three weeks before I realize how toxic Armando is to me. I can only be spellbound for so long before waking up. I become aware that I cannot give Armando what he desires.

After seeing my bank account dwindle to practically nothing thanks to nights of binge drinking in the Castro, I set up an appointment with my financial aid advisor at City College. I tell him I desperately need housing since I can no longer afford to pay rent on my apartment in Noe Valley. Within a matter of minutes, Larkin Street Youth Services comes up in the conversation, a few phone calls are made, and they place me in the Castro Youth Housing Initiative. Larkin Street Youth Services provides the necessary services to ensure that San Francisco's most vulnerable youth are able to matriculate into society beyond life on the streets.

Carrying a duffel bag, I shuffle down Howard Street in the SOMA district.

Passing Lafayette Street, I notice a dilapidated yellow building. A Mexican restaurant, Taquería Reinas, plays salsa music from within. My stomach knots into pains of hunger as a waft of refried beans and fried steak reaches me. I slip past the restaurant, and a black-barred metal door with the numbers 1554 above it in gold catches my eye.

Suddenly, the door opens and a woman in her late twenties steps out. Her short blonde hair is cropped beneath a black hat and her blue eyes emit genuine kindness behind black eyeglasses. Her attire consists of slightly baggy jeans, a white polo shirt, and a light jacket.

"You must be Fredy Espinoza," she says, shaking my hand. "I'm Kasey Rosendale, your residential counselor. Here, come in so I can show you your new room."

Stepping into a tight hallway, we walk up a flight of stairs and make our way to a bedroom at the end of the hall. Kasey takes out a key, opens the door, and steps aside as I enter a single room occupancy. The room is barren, with the exception of a stripped-down twin bed beneath a window that faces Lafayette Street.

"My financial aid advisor said I would be placed in a studio. This does not look like a studio to me," I say, frowning in disapproval.

"There are many levels of housing in this program. If you are able to meet the requirements on a consistent basis, show us that you are taking action to get your life back together, and are able to follow the rules, then we move you into a bigger studio. You just have to prove yourself, Fredy.

"Here, I need you to sign these forms. It's basically a contract ensuring you understand the requirements: you need to find a job and work for a minimum of twenty hours a week, pay three hundred dollars of rent per month if you can, and maintain your goal of finishing your education. There are mandatory meetings you need to attend every Thursday evening at the LGBT Community Center."

I lower my head and a twinge of sadness wraps its arms around me. I quickly glance over the paperwork, sign it, and hand it to Kasey.

Kasey points at my duffel bag. "Is this all you have with you?"

"Yeah, I always move lightly." I drop the duffel bag on the bed.

"Every month you get a fifty-dollar card to help you with food and necessary things that you might need," she says. She glances at her watch. "You know what, I'm parked out front. If you want, we can head over to IKEA right now and shop for anything that you need."

"I would appreciate that a lot, Kasey." I glance at the room one more time before exiting. I force a smile on my face and remind myself that this is just a transitional phase to the next chapter of my life.

At IKEA, I reveal to Kasey my desire to write a memoir about all that I have been through. She smiles and listens patiently as I throw new sheets, a comforter, a pillow, a rug, and bedroom accessories into the cart. She asks me what the memoir would entail and I reply by telling her my life story on the way back to Lafayette Street.

"And even though I'm back in California, I still feel like an orphan, Kasey. I'm frightened of returning to living a life on the street as I did in New York." I say with a knot in my throat.

"I'm sorry to hear all that, Fredy. I can't believe all you've been through. Don't worry about ever living on the street again, okay? As your residential counselor, I will work with you to create a path of success for you. You just have to do your part and work with me."

Nodding, I glance out the window and notice the SRO across the street.

With my new belongings, I wave goodbye to Kasey and trudge to my new room. Making the bed with a polka-dotted brown-and-pink comforter and matching sheets, I sink onto the bed and stare out the window at a bright full moon. Down the hallway, the sound of a door slamming shut and the quick thud of footsteps penetrate the silence as someone clambers past my

bedroom.

Sighing, I close my eyes and sink into depression as tears fall forth from my eyes.

Is this what it feels like for you, Mom? Imprisoned in a room this size, with no one to see you, living all alone with no one to tell you how much you're loved? Is this what prison feels like for you, Eduardo, locked up in Santa Rita, unable to break free of the patterns that keep you locked in a tight cell? Will I ever know the meaning of home again? Will I always be an orphan without a real home, displaced from the possibility of finding love and creating a family of my own?

How could anyone love me if they knew my history word for word?

No, I will fight to create the reality I desire. I deserve love, a home, and a partner I can call family; my love is out there somewhere waiting for me.

∞

AT-RISK YOUTHS, ranging from sixteen to twenty-four, indulge in free pizza and soft drinks as I attend my first mandatory meeting at the LGBT Community Center.

I recognize my story in all of them.

With as little interaction as possible, I silently fill my plate with pizza, sit down, and keep to myself.

"How are you holding up, Fredy?" Kasey asks, sitting down next to me.

I smile. "Good. I got hired as a recruiter for a marketing research company."

"That's good to hear, Fredy! What company?" Kasey smiles widely at the news.

"Wharf Research on Pier 39," I answer.

"How much are you—"

"You think you're all that, but you ain't shit!" A girl spits out, stopping my conversation with Kasey short.

Thinking she's talking to me, I look up and see a young transgendered girl approach an effeminate gay boy on the other side of the room.

"You don't know what I've been through, so fuck you!" he hurls back, getting up from his chair.

Kasey gets up from the chair and steps between them. "Whoa, calm down guys. If you can't handle yourselves like young adults, then I will have to ask you to leave."

"Fuck this shit," the gay boy cries, storming out of the room.

"Fucking wimp," the transgendered girl calls after him, laughing.

"Watch it!" Kasey threatens. "Okay, everyone, settle down now. Let's get the meeting started. Everyone state your name and something you did this past week."

As the meeting commences, it soon dawns on me that the format is akin to group therapy. One by one, the ten of us reveal heartbreaking stories of being disowned, kicked to the curb, and abandoned, thanks to parents' inability to accept our sexual or gender orientation. Some kids talk about running away in fear of being punished for not accepting a parents' view of life, or about the tragic despair of feeling resigned from life after having lived homeless in the streets.

Hearing the length of time some of these teenagers had to deal with being homeless puts to shame my few day periods of homelessness over the course of three months. And even then, I was lucky enough to have the face and body to get a bed for the night.

You're minimizing, I hear Ms. Cunningham's voice say in the back of my head.

Depressed after the group therapy session, I head straight to the Castro and into the nearest bar, the Twin Peaks, and spend my last dollars on a couple of Sapphire tonics. A fleeting thought about a midterm for my Sociology II class flutters into my head, but I dismiss it—I have my own

problems to attend to. And what better way to attend them than downning these drinks.

I walk out of Twin Peaks and soon find myself on the dance floor at Badlands.

Taking my shirt off, I dance wildly and try to forget my problems.

I hear a girl's voice call out my name. "Fredy Espinoza!"

Turning, I see Amanda Michelle Foschia, the girl I made eye contact with during my performance piece in our playwriting class; she's decked out in another fashionable outfit. Four gay boys pose and sip flavored cocktails next to her. I wave and make my way over to them.

"Amanda!"

"Le Lord! Who knew I'd find you on the dance floor with your shirt off!"

"I enjoy showing my skin every now and then when I'm dancing," I reply with a laugh.

"Who are you here with?"

"No one," I say, putting my shirt back on.

"Meet my friends and hang out with us!"

I become a part of Amanda's entourage as the night progresses. We bar-hop all over the Castro. Her friends insist on buying me drinks. As the night winds down and the nightclubs close, I pull a Houdini and disappear on Amanda.

On the way to the subway station, I catch the striking blue eyes of a handsome forty-year-old man staring at me. He flashes a Hollywood smile that stops me in my tracks. His firm skin is smooth and a fitted shirt clings to his muscular body. Glancing down at his pants, I see a nice bulge in his pocket.

"You're hot," I smile at him.

"Thank you. So are you." He chuckles. "What are your plans for

tonight?"

"To get fucked by you," I assert with a mischievous grin.

"As much as I would enjoy fucking you, I can't allow that to happen," he says.

"Oh, come on, I can see your bulge. You're hard and you know you want to fuck me tonight," I insist, caressing his arm.

"I'm HIV positive."

"And? What matters to me is that you're hot," I say, undeterred.

"You don't care if you get HIV?" He asks, alarmed at how willing I am to jump into his bed.

"Oh, stop being silly, sexy boy," I chuckle. "Haven't you heard of safe sex? Just wrap a condom on that baby and ride me."

He glances me up and down and then hails a taxi.

I jump into the backseat next to him and place my hand on his bulge. He gives me a look of sexual lust and leans over and kisses me hard. The taxi driver steers the wheel with an aloof expression as if he's used to this.

His home is located near Corona Heights Park, overlooking the Castro district. Making my way into his bedroom, I can't help but notice he is loaded with money. Everything is custom made, with the newest technology. His luxurious king-sized bed is stacked with goosefeather pillows.

"So, what do you do?" I inquire.

He flashes his Hollywood smile at me again. "I'm a porn star."

"I've always wanted to be fucked by a porn star," I say. We undress and lie down on the bed.

His hands roughly massage my body as he feels me up. Intense sexual desire glazes his piercing blue eyes as he makes his way to my feet, sticks his tongue out, and licks me. Like a dog, he gets on all fours and licks every inch of my body; the attention he lavishes on me makes me feel wanted and needed.

"I want to eat your ass," he growls, lifting my legs into the air and sticking his tongue between my parting cheeks.

I let out a moan as his tongue thrashes like a tornado inside me.

Suddenly I let out an audible wet fart in his face.

Gasping, I open my eyes.

With a look of disgust, he gets up and heads to the bathroom to wash his face.

"Oh my God, I'm sorry!" I yell after him.

Embarrassed, I wait there as he returns with a wet towel and wipes my ass.

"It's okay," he mutters with obvious disdain.

I look at his penis and notice he has gone soft.

"Is it okay if I stay the night? I don't really have the money to take a taxi home and I'm too tired and drunk to move," I say, leaning back onto his soft pillow and closing my eyes.

Before giving him the chance to answer, I pass out into a deep sleep.

∞

AN EMPTY BED awaits me when I open my eyes. I grimace at the splitting headache and try to remember what happened last night. I have a flashback of running into Amanda, hitting the bars, meeting a handsome stranger, and the vague feeling of having done something embarrassing, but gaps of memory have been blacked out.

Getting out of bed, I dress and look around the spacious room. From somewhere in the house the sound of Anderson Cooper's voice carries into the bedroom and the smell of strong coffee lingers in the air. Making my way into the living room, I come upon a man busily working away on a laptop at his desk.

"You're up. Good. I need to be somewhere soon," he says shortly.

"I don't remember how I got here. Did we have sex last night?"

"No, you farted into my face," he says with a slight tone of disgust.

"Oh, how embarrassing!" I blush and let out a sigh of relief simultaneously.

"I don't mean to be rude, but I do need to leave very soon." He gets up from his desk, moves to the door, and opens it.

"Thank you for letting me—" The door slams behind me before I can utter the rest of the words.

Shrugging, I do the walk of shame to the Castro.

Stepping into Starbucks, I crave a coffee drink. With no money in my bank account, I consider using my debit card and dealing with the consequence of having my bank charge me a fee for spending money I do not have. I order a Venti drip and silently muse how I just spent thirty dollars on a two dollar cup.

Suddenly, I realize that I didn't make it to my Sociology II midterm. The clock on the wall says eleven and I imagine the last student turning in his midterm right now.

"Fuck, guess I'm getting an F on that one," I mutter, wincing.

I think about how irresponsible I have been, how close I have come to putting my life at risk again. First Armando, and now this guy—I am having too many close calls. What if I hadn't farted into his face last night and we wound up having sex? What if the condom broke?

Shaking my head, I let out a deep sigh as I consider and reconsider my actions.

The only way to break this pattern is to do the opposite. Sipping my coffee, I make the mental choice not to put myself in danger again. This entails not going out and getting drunk to the point where I become unconscious of my actions. And it also entails taking myself out on dates. Instead of feeling that I need men, maybe I should start coming from the position of needing myself. Last night was a wake-up call. I need to learn how

to put taking care of myself first.

The phone vibrates in my pocket.

Grabbing it, I see Melancton's name pop up in my caller ID.

Heart pounding, I wonder what he could possibly want. I haven't spoken to him for over a month now.

I answer the call. "Hey Melancton! How's it going?"

"It's been awhile since we last hung out. Can you talk?"

"Yeah, I'm at Starbucks right now in the Castro."

"I'm planning to go to Yosemite with Trevor and my friend, Chad this weekend. We're going to stay at my parents' cabin in the woods. Trevor and I were wondering if you'd like to join us. I remember you once said you wanted to make new friends and I thought it would be a great opportunity for you to hang out with Trevor and Chad."

"I would love to go, Melancton."

"Perfect. Pick you up at your place?"

"Sure. I live in SOMA now. Call me when you get near 11th and Howard. Thank you for thinking of me, Melancton."

"Yeah, sure. I'll pick you up around ten in the morning. See you then."

Ending the call, I remind myself of my intention to create a new friendship with Melancton, to have integrity with my word, and never to let him know that Roger told me the truth.

<p style="text-align:center">∞</p>

INTO THE WOODS we go as Melancton Vassiliadis drives his green jeep along winding roads, whipping around the bends, finally slowing down as we enter a village. We make a quick stop at a convenience store to pick up gin.

Arriving at his parents' two-story cabin, I jump out of the jeep and smell the fresh fragrance of sugar pine, white fir, and incense cedar. Entering his cabin, Melancton and I head to the kitchen, take the gin out of the bag, and make ourselves strong cocktails. Melancton gives me a tour of the spacious

backyard with plenty of firewood stacked up, the two bedrooms upstairs, and the bathroom.

"So, I will be sleeping in the guest bedroom, you and Trevor will be sleeping in your bedroom, and Chad will sleep downstairs on the couch?" I ask as we descend the stairs into the kitchen and living room.

Melancton looks at me. "I failed to mention that Chad texted me. He won't make it this weekend."

"Oh, so it'll just be you, Trevor, and I?"

"Nope, Trevor got stuck at work. It's just the two of us, Fredy." Melancton smiles and takes my glass, which is already empty. He fixes me another strong drink. "Can you imagine us at eighty years old, sitting on those rocking chairs in front of the fireplace, and you telling me many wonderful stories about our lives?"

I glance at the rocking chairs and silently think, *Fuck*. This is definitely a curve ball in terms of moving forward from the past. And drinking heavily will not help my situation.

"Melancton, I think I'm fine without another drink," I say, sitting down at the table.

"Fredy, don't be a poor sport. It's your favorite, Sapphire tonic." He hands me the drink. "You didn't answer my question, Fredy."

"I can see it happening, Melancton. But what about Trevor?"

"Trevor thinks you and I are just friends." He takes another swig from his drink. "And who knows, maybe it won't work out between Trevor and me. As long as I have you, Fredy, nothing else matters in this world."

Roger's voice flickers in the back of my head, *Let's face it, Melancton is a liar.*

"Melancton, we'll be sleeping in separate rooms tonight, right?"

He laughs. "Why are you playing hard to get all of a sudden?"

"I don't want to be the reason why your relationship with Trevor fizzles

out."

"It already is fizzling out."

"Wait, did you know in advance that Chad and Trevor both couldn't make it this weekend?"

"Yeah." Melancton giggles childishly, fixing himself another drink.

Sitting back, I watch him pouring a heavy drink at the kitchen island. His clean-shaven face takes off a few years and his brown puppy eyes sparkle with a mixture of joy and mischief. It's a look I recognize too well from our past sexual escapades. If Roger had never told me the truth about him, would I be falling for Melancton's ploy right now? What a silly question. I know the answer is yes.

"Look at that, it's nearing midnight," Melancton says softly.

I set the drink aside. "I don't think I'll finish this drink, Melancton."

"Do you want to head upstairs?"

"Sure, but I meant it when I said I want to sleep alone in the guest bedroom."

"You can sleep alone. Let's go upstairs and hang out for a bit in my bedroom. Be a good boy, tell me a goodnight story, and tuck me in," he teases me.

Getting up from the table, I glance out the window into the woods. History is repeating itself—I feel myself sinking into the arms of loneliness and vulnerability. It's too late to ask Melancton to take me back to San Francisco. The dark forest surrounding Melancton's cabin traps me without an escape route.

I catch Melancton's reflection watching me in the window.

Pivoting, I smile and follow him upstairs to his bedroom. It is nearly a replica of his bedroom back at his parents' house: Disney characters hanging off the walls, positioned on countertops, even lying on his bed. It registers that Melancton and I both have a strong attachment to the past of our

childhood dreams, unwilling to grow up into men, to commit our whimsical beliefs to the ground.

"Want to take a shower?"

"No, Melancton. I'm honestly tired."

"Here, take of your clothes. I want to give you a massage." He grabs me, pulls off my shirt, and undoes my pants. Resisting, I give him a look of confusion. His eyes burn holes in my chest. Becoming suddenly weak, I submit into his will and sink facedown on his bed with passive resignation.

I don't love you any more, Melancton, but why can't I find it in me to tell you?

His naked body hovers over me as his rough hands dig deep into my back.

"Fredy, you are so fucking hot. I want to make your dream come true and fuck you," Melancton says. He leans down and presses his smooth skin against mine.

"Don't fuck me," I whisper.

"Please," he begs.

He tries to kiss me but I turn my head.

Melancton slides into me and thrusts deeply.

"I've wanted you for so long, Fredy," Melancton whispers, nibbling my ear.

I lie motionless and vulnerable, like a porcelain doll, as Melancton fulfills his lust for me.

Quickly Melancton spasms, grunts, and collapses onto my back. He kisses my cheeks softly. I look back at him. His eyes reveal a depth of pain and sorrow for a few seconds before he snaps his gaze away from mine, rolls off me, and lies there in silence.

I can't give you what you want, Melancton Vassiliadis.

You're holding onto a dead dream.

All I desire is to escape into the woods, run away, and never return.

∞

THE FOLLOWING MORNING, I demand that Melancton take me home.

"But I thought we were staying here for the whole weekend."

"My boss asked me to come into work tomorrow to help recruit for a marketing research project on the pier," I lie.

Melancton mutters that he needs to take a shower first.

The drive back is awkward and mostly silent. Melancton glances at me a few times with a look of agitation. At one point on the road trip, he places his hand on mine, but I gently pull it away as I feign looking over my email on my phone.

Melancton drops me off at the SRO.

"I'm sorry about this weekend," he apologizes as I step out of his jeep.

"I'm sorry for cutting it short," I reply, avoiding his gaze.

I head toward the black-barred metal door. From behind I hear the jeep's engine still running as I take out my keys, insert them in the door, and disappear into the hallway.

∞ CHAPTER XVI: LOVE AT A COFFEE SHOP ∞

REIKI HEALING ENERGY is a Japanese technique for healing the physical and spiritual body of leftover dead energy created by trauma. The healing occurs when a Reiki Master moves the life force energy that flows in all of us through the chakras in the naked body.

Tyrone Botelho closes the blinds in his apartment, lights several incense sticks, and fills me in on how a Reiki healing treatment works.

"Reiki is made up of two words: *rei*, which stands for higher power, and *ki*, which stands for life force energy. I am going to administer this energy through you to remove any blockages you may have in your chakras: the crown chakra, the third eye chakra, the throat chakra, the heart chakra, the solar plexus chakra, the sacral chakra, and the root chakra." Tyrone motions to specific points on his body.

"And what do I do?" I ask as I strip my clothes off and lie down on his massage table.

"Nothing. You just lie there and clear your thoughts."

I close my eyes and my ears prick up as soothing music begins to play in the background. Tyrone places his palm very gently at the crown of my head. A lulling sensation overcomes my body and I fall into the arms of sleep...

Fierce orbs of fire flash above me.

Is this Heaven?

Oh, pearly gates—what a beautiful sight. Flash of lightning as the gates part open, leaving me breathless and filled with euphoria. My eyes feast upon a most glorious garden. I step into its mist, cascading over me with its white energy.

Ahead of me, I make out the tree of conscience. I float serenely toward its dark, chocolate-brown trunk, its vibrant and luscious green crown, its deliciously potent red apples of truth. At the base of the tree of conscience the most beautiful and enchanting serpent sleeps; white skin glistens across its breathtaking scaly body.

"Wake up," I whisper softly to the serpent.

A silent hiss escapes its mouth as his tongue flickers out and iridescent orbs of spellbinding purple hold my gaze.

"Thank you for allowing me to sleep for so long," his voice flashes in my head.

Angelic wings sprout forth from my back.

Amazed, I flex my wings as a burning bush of fire erupts within the chasm of my sacred heart. It showers forth from within and galvanizes me into a feast of exploding light. I shoot up into the sky, leaving behind flashing fires that consume the snake, the tree of conscience, and the ancient sacred garden. I soar higher and higher until I come upon a huge orb of fiery white light.

"Enter me," a voice commands me from within it.

Without hesitation, I fly directly into the fiery sun.

A golden-bronzed god appears before me and commences to tell me of many undiscovered secrets. He reminds me of my purpose, and I laugh in agreement as my wings stretch for millennia. I become conscious that although I understand completely what he tells me, our thoughts disappear paradoxically into nothingness, as the tongues we speak cannot be translated into any human tongue.

Grasping to stay awake in this eternal moment, I am suddenly yanked forth from the fiery sun and plummet to my earthly body. I plunge downward in horror, spiraling faster and faster, until I settle into my sleeping mortal body.

"Remember what you were born to do," a voice whispers. The command flickers back and forth…

Snapping my eyes open, I look over to Tyrone and notice his eyes are closed. One of his palms is placed over my heart chakra and the other hovers over my root chakra. He breaks into a quiet smile as his eyes flutter open and steps back from me.

Sitting up, I look around the room in pure amazement.

Tyrone's voice is relaxed and soothing. "How do you feel?"

"I feel so present and alive, as if I've awakened from a dead sleep. I'm so present to life right now that my eyes hurt from the energy all around me."

"It's amazing, right?" He smiles as he settles down onto his couch and gazes at me.

"What a beautiful paradox: I hurtle through life to my impending death with velocity, yet every waking moment feels eternally present. Is this the secret of the sphinx? The elixir of life the ancient gods and goddesses spoke of?"

"I don't know if I'd go that far, but yes, you're now awakened. I had a vision of you getting your wings back, Fredy."

My eyes widen as I recall the dream.

"I had a dream of being in an ancient garden and feeling wings sprout from my back. You know, Tyrone, I don't believe in Heaven or Hell, but whatever you did makes me believe that there is more to life than what we are led to believe."

"I think that event with Cliff shut you off from your gifts, Fredy. Maybe it's time you open up again and take on the role of being a healer of human beings."

"I think that's more your forte, Tyrone."

"Well, consider yourself awakened. It's a gift not many humans ever attain in their lifetime. It's only a matter of time before this healing energy manifests in your life and transforms it."

"Thank you." I smile and sit there for several minutes before finally getting up and heading home for the day.

Later that night, I take out my journal and jot down ten commitments I intend to manifest and adhere to:

1. I will mold my body into the form I mostly desire.
2. I will re-virginize myself.
3. I will live passionately.
4. I will live with integrity.
5. I will allow my artistic nature to evolve.
6. I will seek knowledge.
7. I will expand my spiritual awareness.
8. I will evolve into my next phase of self-actualization.
9. I will live a life of fully empowering choices.
10. I will live by these principles and never compromise them due to negative circumstances.

"I will return to my roots of steely determination, tenacious actions, and unrelenting adamancy. I realize my worth and have a purpose in creating my destiny," I declare. I slam my journal shut and take my first step of action.

"I'm going to take myself out on a date, romance myself, buy a bottle of wine, and just be."

Smiling, I look into the mirror on the wall and stare contently into my brown eyes.

"I have a confession to make. I must admit I have fallen deeply in love with myself. All over again."

Dropping the journal onto the bed, I spray on cologne and descend into

the night.

∞

PRESENCE AND BEING confounds me as I yearn to be more present in my life. From Eckhart Tolle's *The Power of Now* to Jean-Paul Sartre's *Being and Nothingness*, I find myself seeking meaning in my life.

Finishing a grueling workout at Gold's Gym in the Castro, I quickly get dressed, ignoring the naked bodies around me, then grab my journal and Sartre's *Being and Nothingness*, stroll out of the gym, and head to my favorite coffee shop: Starbucks at 18th and Castro.

Usually I order a coffee and head off to Dolores Park, but today, I sit down on the upper level. Opening Sartre, I find myself baffled and confused by the notion that all existence arises from nothingness. I close the book and take a sip of coffee as I ponder this idea.

It's now midsummer—July 17th, 2007, to be exact—and I feel proud for keeping the ten commitments I made a few months back. I pushed myself to finish the semester without dropping out, took on grueling workout sessions at the gym, and took myself out over and over again without once slipping into fulfilling a sexual act with another man.

Suddenly, the door opens and a young nerdy-looking boy gets in line and orders a drink. His sparkling blue eyes capture my reflecting gaze as I immediately look away. He reminds me of Harry Potter, I muse picking up Sartre again and immersing myself in it.

"What does he mean that our desires arise from nothingness?" I whisper to myself as I close the book and drop it onto the table.

Turning my head in a reflective manner, I notice the Harry Potter doppelgänger sitting at the table next to me. His face puckers into a serious expression as his eyes go over a lengthy study guide.

Suddenly, he glances up and makes eye contact with me.

Pretending I don't notice him, I avert my eyes to the book, take another

sip of my coffee, and remind myself of the commitment I have made. I quickly process the reasons to why I am not in the space to become sexually involved with a man: I am perfectly satisfied being on my own, I have no desire to be romantically involved, nor do I believe in the Victorian ideal of love, and I need to focus on my goals in order to get to the top. And this guy is just another distraction from my path to freedom.

Feeling his eyes on me, I glance over again and catch him staring at me. It is hard to discern whether he is looking at me or just deep in analytical thought over his study guide. His soft steel-blue eyes remind me of an Alaskan Husky: intelligent, wise, thoughtful, present, and intuitively perceptive. His pupils shift slightly as he notices me gazing into his eyes. His dewy white alabaster skin shines with a thin veil of perspiration and his mouth parts into a smile, revealing perfect white teeth.

Snapping my eyes away, I frown and chastise myself for allowing this guy to become aware of me being conscious of him. Picking up Sartre again, I return to the passage about desire and passion and how these two impulses can spark anything to arise from nothingness.

Sighing, I put the book down and make eye contact for the third time.

"Hi, what are you studying there?" I ask, thinking that it doesn't hurt to be friendly.

He smiles. "Studying Wills and Trusts," he says. "What are you studying there?"

"I'm reading *Being and Nothingness*, by Jean-Paul Sartre. It's actually a summer book outside my curriculum. To be honest, I am stumped by one of his ideas."

"And which idea is that?"

"Something about how desire allows being to arise out of nothingness," I reply, finding myself completely at ease with this guy. "Wills and Trusts—is that law?"

"Yeah, I'm a law student and have a final this weekend. All work and no play makes Jack a dull boy," he says jokingly.

"Whatever it takes to get to the top, right?" I laugh.

He smiles again. "Michael Ethan Lillegard, pleasure to meet you."

"Fredy Espinoza," I smile back.

"No middle name?"

"For some reason, my parents chose not to give me one."

"I bet *Louise* would fit you well." He chuckles. "Yeah—Fredy Louise Espinoza."

"If you say so, Michael Ethan Lillegard. I like your name. It has a nice ring to it."

"I have Norwegian blood in me," Michael says, scooting closer.

"I love Norway."

"Oh, isn't Norway wonderful! Especially during the winter, when it's night for days on; it's better than the summer, when the sun is up for, like, twenty-two hours." Michael grimaces.

"I mean, I love the idea of Norway. I actually have never been." I smile sheepishly for making him think I've visited Norway.

"So, what do you do?"

"I'm penning a memoir," I say. His eyes widen and I nod my head. "And I just finished writing my first one-act play, titled *Whisper in the Wind* about a paranoid schizophrenic mother who kills her first-born daughter by the end of the act. It's not completely done. The protagonist is a fourteen-year-old boy who winds up committing suicide at the end of the play. I intend for it to be a three-act play one day."

"That's dark. Where did you get such an idea for a play?" He sits back, interested in our conversation.

"My life." I look away as I suddenly feel tears spring to my eyes. That's funny, I never get so easily emotional. Blinking them back, I glance over at

Michael and he gives me an endearing empathetic look.

"Do you want to talk for the rest of the evening? I feel peaceful around you, Fredy."

"Strange, I feel comfortably at ease talking to you, Michael."

And for the next five hours we talk nonstop, jumping from one topic to another. Closing down Starbucks, we head over to a Thai restaurant next to Badlands and continue our conversation until we close that restaurant as well.

By the end of the night, I feel as if I have known Michael Ethan Lillegard for over a lifetime and I have the phenomenal sensation of having returned home.

<div align="center">∞</div>

FOR HIS TWENTY-THIRD BIRTHDAY, Michael Ethan Lillegard takes me to Picaro's Tapas on 16th at Valencia Street in the Mission District. Ordering delicious tapas, we laugh and cajole each other as Mariachi music plays in the background.

"I feel honored that you want to spend your twenty-third birthday with only me."

"Well, there's a reason for that," he says, blushing as he takes off his glasses and sets them down on the table.

"Reason?"

"You asked me if I wanted anything for my birthday and I said no. But I would like the gift of you going steady with me as my boyfriend." He blushes again.

"I would love to be your boyfriend, Michael!" I gush as my face breaks into a huge grin.

Leaning forward, we kiss softly.

Gazing into his eyes, I realize I am falling deeply in love with Michael. And this love is different from any love I ever felt for anyone in my life. It isn't the same as what I felt for Melancton Vassiliadis or Daniel Hansen or

Eric Morrison. The love I feel for Michael Ethan Lillegard is pure, innocent, and authentic.

"Michael, I will never harm you, and if I did, it would be unintentionally. You are my lion, my lotus flower, and my sweet inspiration. I will always strive to live in a space of vulnerability, trust, and complete, unconditional love. I love you authentically, Michael Ethan Lillegard. There is no man on this earthly plane who moves my being so, and I believe no man ever will," I tell him, falling into his ocean-blue eyes.

"I too am falling deeply in love with you, Fredy," he replies. "As you once mentioned, Fredy, all we have is the present, our words, and the meanings behind our actions. I hope to continue along this path with you for as long as I am meant to traverse it—whether it's for a day or for eternity. With you, I will enjoy and seize every moment, for every moment with you is a rich treasure, so pleasurable, edifying, mesmerizing, interesting, and fulfilling that it is almost decadent."

I smile as I place my hand on his. "You're so romantic, Michael. Stop it before you bring tears to my eyes."

Smiling, he continues, "The reason it took me awhile to make this choice to ask you to be my boyfriend is that I needed time to get grounded in what I feel for you, untainted by past encounters, and to ensure that whatever I have with you is built on a strong foundation. And the more I get to know you, the more I see the true, gorgeous, beautiful person that is your essence, your core.

"Fredy, you truly make me more alive, more in touch with myself, and I feel as if you guide me on the correct path I am to take in life, rather than stagnating or diverting into realms that will surely destroy me. You truly do have a beautiful, sweet, and amazing presence that is a privilege to experience. In my eyes, you will always be perfect and complete, and I hope you continue to shine this beautiful soul into our world, showing your true and strikingly mesmerizing self to the world. You inspire me, and you complete me."

He leans in and kisses me more gently, more softly, and more passionately.

Holding his kiss for a few seconds, I reply, "And you complete me too."

∞

IN THE DARKNESS, Michael Ethan Lillegard and I walk side by side as I show him to the BART station. As we descend onto the platform, a crowd of people pushes us apart. Separated from Michael, I freak out, searching desperately for him. Suddenly, I see Michael's father leaning against a column.

"Follow me," he says, motioning to me. I clasp his hand and follow.

"Where are you taking me?"

"Back to Michael," he answers.

We come upon Michael searching in vain for me at the other end of the platform. The three of us talk for over an hour. Then, needing to leave, Michael's father looks at us with a proud smile and departs.

Leaving the BART station, I notice a restroom and rush to it.

Washing my hands, my ears perk as I hear Michael psychically crying out for me. An image of him is implanted in my head: I envision him in a tight ball of anxiety, bawling over having lost me for good.

Dashing out of the bathroom, I come upon Michael frantically sobbing and running in a frenzy, searching for me on a deserted grassy plain. Sprinting to him, I grab him, embrace him, and comfort him as I assuage his fears.

"It was never my intention to leave you, Michael. There, don't cry, my lotus flower. I'm right here." I plant kisses all over his face streaked with tears.

"Fredy, promise me… Promise me you will never leave me," he whispers as he leads me over to the tree of conscience.

"I promise you this, Michael Ethan Lillegard: never to leave your side again." I smile as his body fills up with warmth.

"Instead of returning home, can we lie down beneath this tree and gaze at the night sky?"

"For you love, anything you desire..."

Waking up, I kiss Michael's neck softly and hold him in my arms.

"I promise never to leave your side, Michael," I whisper as he mumbles softly in his sleep.

Lying in bed, I think about my dream and pray that it never comes true.

May I never leave Michael.

After another hour of treasuring having Michael sleep next to me, he wakes up. We shower, get ready, and head over to the Castro. We both enter Gold's Gym, work out, and then stroll over to the Starbucks where we originally met. Ordering coffee, we sit down on the upper level in the same spot where we met.

"Do you always push yourself so hard at the gym? You were running like hell on that treadmill," Michael says.

"There's a fire inside me, Michael. I don't know what it is, but it propels me to the point of no return."

Michael stares at me for several seconds before replying, "I think you're still running from yourself—whatever and whoever makes up the essence of who you are, Fredy. I can see that you fear this person, because in the past you have been rejected for being you, which is an awful and stupid thing."

"Maybe I am still running away from myself," I mutter beneath my breath. His words ring true. Michael has a keen ability to strike at the core of every matter. Often I feel grateful for it, but at other times, a part of me yearns not to hear the truth.

"Honey, you have to see that who you are is a lovely and beautiful person," he says warmly. "And I hope that you are able to create the true you in the center of yourself. I believe that you know who this 'you' is, but you run from even beginning to find it and from healing the pain that causes you to become Forrester and other manifestations."

"Michael, how can you be so perceptive?"

He smiles sheepishly, leans in, and kisses me. "Well, I did major in psychology."

"The more I spend time with you, the more I feel as if you know the real me," I reply. "And for the first time in my life, I yearn to find out who that person is, Michael. I feel that you are the only one who can help me in this process. And I hope I can help you in return." I finish my hazelnut latte.

Gazing over to Michael, I see my future husband.

And it's all due to this Starbucks in the Castro.

It is true that one can find love at a coffee shop.

∞ CHAPTER XVII: ROSE PETAL BATHS ∞

MICHAEL ETHAN LILLEGARD is attending his first day of the Landmark Forum. I hope that this course changes his life as it has done for me. Stepping out of the store, I quickly dash to my studio at 1169 Market Street in Civic Center. Carrying a bouquet of a dozen stemmed roses, several candles, a prepared dinner, a bottle of red wine, and Michael's favorite cookies, I smile as the warm cool October air caresses my face.

Inside the studio, I turn on Mozart, heat up dinner, pour two glasses of red wine, light the candles, and wait for Michael's text to let me know he is on his way. A few minutes later, it comes, *"Ten minutes away babe! Love you!"*

Dashing into the bathroom, I turn on the faucet and fill up the bathtub with warm water. Grabbing the bouquet of roses, I take off every petal and place them gently on the water.

I hear the door close to the studio. "Fredy?" Michael's voice surprises me.

"Michael!" I cry in joy as I dash out of the bathroom, close the door, and

jump into his arms. "How was your first day at the seminar?"

"It's very mentally exhausting, but I see what you mean now about living in the present moment. I never made so many phone calls in my life. What's going on here, babe?"

"Because you took the initiative of taking the Landmark Forum, I wanted to do something special for you tonight. This is all for you, my lotus flower. Tonight, it is all about you. Here, have this glass of wine and follow me into the bathroom."

"What's in the bathroom?" Michael asks me suspiciously.

"You'll see," I reply, smiling mischievously.

Opening the door, I look at Michael. His face lights up with so much emotion. His expression of surprise and happiness plants itself in my memory.

"Fredy, is that a rose petal bath?"

"Yeah, have you ever had one?"

"No, I never have had one. I didn't even know people took rose petal baths." He embraces me and kisses me for a minute.

"Well, tonight I want you to experience your first rose petal bath. Here, take off your clothes, babe. I want you to relax, lie down in the bathtub, and bathe in the essence of your being." I speak softly with notes of pure joy as I help him get undressed. "I took my time with every petal, Michael; as each petal dropped into the water, I infused it with the intention of unconditional love and acceptance for you. I want you to fall unconditionally in love with yourself this weekend, Michael."

"You're amazing, Fredy. I am truly blessed to have an angel sent to me." His blue eyes sparkle with an intensity of love as his radiant smile shines across his Norwegian face.

As he dips into the water, I step out of the bathroom and finish preparing dinner. Bringing his plate into the bathroom, I hand it to him,

lower the toilet seat, sit down, and watch him with a serene calmness in my being as I slowly sip from my glass of wine.

"Michael, ever since the first day I met you, I felt a connection, an electric charge, and an unexplainable feeling of having come across my soul mate. Ever since I was a little boy, I have had a dream that my soul mate's name would be Michael. And I believe you are the one, my lotus flower." I smile lovingly as Michael takes a sip from his glass of wine.

"I feel the same way for you, Fredy Louise Espinoza," Michael whispers. His eyes become slightly misty.

"I may not be rich or have a job with a safety net, Michael, but what I do know is that I want to build a long-lasting solid foundation and a future with you. I want to continue to grow with you, share my experiences with you, laugh, cry, run crazily amok, and just be with you. I see myself in your future, Michael. I desire to always learn more about you, every hope, desire, fear, embarrassment, even in those moments when things seem not to be going right."

"Fredy, you know how many times I've told you that money means nothing to me. I'm actually glad we're both on the same level, love. In fact, I think I would actually feel uncomfortable if you had a lot of money because I would feel that you were looking down on me for not having money. Or that I couldn't take you to places, or afford to go to places, to which you are accustomed. I would prefer that we grow our wealth together, both romantically and monetarily." He reaches for my hand and gently squeezes it.

"I never thought this day would come, Michael. I'm so blessed to have you in my life." I get up from the toilet seat, kiss him softly on the lips, and take his empty plate and exit the bathroom. I grab his favorite cookies and reenter the bathroom.

"You got me my favorite cookies in the whole world! You're the best partner ever, Fredy." Michael munches happily on the cookies. "Here, have a

bite."

"No, they're specifically for you."

Michael gazes into my eyes and we stare at each other in silence.

We sit there basking in our love for each other.

"I love your brown eyes, Fredy; the way their mocha brown has a way of capturing my soul while looking so sedate and at peace."

"May my eyes always capture your soul, Michael."

∞

MICHAEL ETHAN LILLEGARD descends onto my bed. Our bodies become one as he gently penetrates me. Moving slowly, he looks into my eyes and kisses me. His soft skin feels warm against my body. He takes his time. We make love beneath the full moon, our bodies moving in quiet unison, in peaceful rhythm, and in sweet harmony.

"I choose you, Fredy Espinoza, because I choose you, Fredy Espinoza," Michael whispers lovingly into my ear.

"And I choose you, Michael Ethan Lillegard, because I choose you, Michael Ethan Lillegard," I whisper back as I stare into his tiger-blue eyes.

As Michael pulls out of me I break into a sob.

He kisses my tears away. "What's wrong, honey?"

"Michael, I feel as if I just had sex for the first time in my life. I feel like you just took my virginity," I cry softly.

"Love, don't cry. I will always be here for you, I promise."

"I feel at home with you, Michael."

"I will always be your family, Fredy, as long as you continue to choose me to be your family. Don't yearn for what never was, but instead, let's create and appreciate what is and will be. Let's always be true and honest with each other, because how can we be a true family if we don't show those we love who we are?"

"You always know what to say, Michael. I love you so much." I lean into

him in the darkness.

"I love you, Fredy. I know you've been hurt in the past, but you no longer have to fear losing me. And my family cares about you. They know all about you and look forward to meeting you this Christmas."

"All I ever wanted was to have a family and a place to call home, Michael. Do you really think your family will love me? I'm scared that they will hate me and think of me as worthless. If they ever knew my history, all of it, would they bless my love for you?"

"Shhh… Nonsense—don't be silly, love. I know my family will love you and accept you as one of their own. In my eyes, you will always be a Lillegard. And I hope to always be an Espinoza."

"Hold me, Michael Ethan Lillegard," I whisper. "I feel extremely vulnerable right now. Just hold me all night long."

Fresh tears fall from my eyes.

<div align="center">∞</div>

STROLLING LEISURELY THROUGH the Castro, I gasp in surprise and shock as I bump into Daniel Hansen.

"Daniel!"

"Fredy! Oh Lord, I had a feeling that I'd run into you here, if anywhere."

"You're in San Francisco!"

"Well, it's good to see you too." Daniel laughs.

"I'm sorry, it's just that I never expected to run into you here. The last I knew you were still back in Pensacola."

"I moved here a few months ago, Fredy," he reveals.

Knots of anxiety form in my stomach as his revelation haunts me.

"Why?" I ask, hoping he doesn't say that he made a mistake and wants me back in my life.

"The Lord works in mysterious ways, Fredy," he says with a laugh, as if talking to an old friend. "I went to New York for vacation, just like the first

time I met you, and I met another guy and fell in love with him. I moved to San Francisco to be with him. In fact, we're meeting for a cocktail. You should join us for a drink."

"Oh, I can't. I'm meeting my boyfriend in an hour for dinner at Coté Sud. I'm actually on my way right now to find a gift for him."

"Want to hang out sometime, Fredy?" Daniel asks me suddenly.

"No," I lash out.

"I understand," Daniel says, glancing away from my pained expression.

"I mean, I can't. Michael and I have a commitment with each other regarding ex's."

"Oh, his name is Michael? I hope he treats you well," Daniel says softly as his eyes get distant.

"He treats me very well," I reply. "I'm sorry, Daniel, but I have to run." I grimace as the interaction between us becomes awkward.

Turning away, I jet hastily across the street and calm my nerves.

It's too much of a coincidence to have run into Daniel Hansen.

Why now?

I run into the store and find the item I noticed a few days back. Grabbing it, I look around me, afraid that Daniel will suddenly pop into the store. I buy it, asked for it to be gift-wrapped, and make my way to Coté Sud through crowds of strangers, past bars, and drunken revelers.

Michael and I enter the restaurant and sit down on the patio. I tell Michael about the random encounter with my ex. The conversation only lasts a few minutes, then we move on and have the most romantic dinner. A French waiter serves us as Michael and I laugh, giggle, and share the joys of what it means to be in each other's lives. Toward the end of the night, I pull out my gift and hand it to Michael.

"A gift? Honey, what for?"

"Just because."

Michael unwraps the gift and gasps. He places a yellow music box on the table and winds the spring. The soft notes of a familiar melody sound in the cool night air.

"I recognize this song," Michael says, his brow furrowing as he tries to identify it.

"It's the theme song from *Love Story*," I say, beaming. "I believe our love is encapsulated in the lyrics of this song, Michael. And to quote from the movie, my favorite love movie, 'Love means never having to say you're sorry.' I love you, Michael Ethan Lillegard. And no matter what happens in our lives, love means never having to say you're sorry."

"But what if I want you to say you're sorry, Fredy," Michael says, raising his eyebrows.

"Sorry won't mean anything when I pass over into the arms of death, Michael—all I will remember of our love is the joy you brought into my life. When I am on my deathbed, all I will remember is the great love story that we both shared in this lifetime, and nothing you can do will take away my love for you."

"I love how dramatic you can be, Fredy Louise Espinoza." Michael opens the music box. "Oh, there's a picture of us in it!"

Later that night, Michael surprises me with an oil massage.

"I want to show you how much you mean to me, Fredy." He bends down and kisses me softly. "You deserve a man who treats you the way you treat him."

His hands feel good against my warm skin as he lathers oil over my back.

When the massage is over, Michael disappears into the bathroom. I hear the sound of water rushing into the bathtub. Rising in bed, I glance to the bathroom with a curious look and wonder why Michael would be taking a bath so late into the night.

Getting up, I open the door and gasp as Michael finishes lighting the last

candle.

"Michael, you shouldn't have." I choke back tears as I come upon a rose petal bath.

His eyes shower me with love. "I love you, Fredy Louise Espinoza."

"I love you so much, Michael Ethan Lillegard."

As I slip into the bathtub, the fragrance of fresh rose petals fills my nostrils. Michael slips out of the bathroom and returns with two glasses of wine. He hands me one and we toast to each other's presences.

∞ CHAPTER XVIII: REQUIEM ∞

A HIGH-RISE TOWER penetrates the dark sky two hundred floors up. Lightning and thunder flash around it, sending rumbles into my spacious and luxurious penthouse.

Sleeping peacefully on my neatly pressed Egyptian satin sheets, I flutter my eyes open at the sound of scraping metal. Getting up from the bed, I float in the direction of the sound.

As I enter the kitchen, I see a butcher knife levitating high above the kitchen sink.

Mesmerized, I move slowly to the knife and reach out for it. My jaw drops in horror as a pulse of dark energy sparks from it and shoots at me.

"BIANCA!" I scream in terror...

"BIANCA! BIANCA! BIANCA!" I scream, kick, and thrash beneath the blankets.

Suddenly, Michael pulls me into his arms and cries, "Fredy, honey, it's okay. You're just having a nightmare, that's all. I'm right here, love. You have nothing to fear."

I break into anguished sobs and choke out, "Bianca... Bianca... Bianca."

The nightmare fills my soul with so much horror that I shudder, slowly

regaining consciousness of my surroundings. Turning over in the bed, I bury my face in Michael's chest. Trembling, I close my eyes and have flashbacks to when Bianca and I were children.

I will be attending our grandmother's funeral tomorrow evening. She passed away a few days ago and I never got the chance to say goodbye. My cousin contacted me a few weeks ago relaying her wish to see me, but I gave an excuse, as always, because I didn't feel ready to be surrounded by Mom's side of the family. I wonder if Mom will be at the funeral service.

Lying buried in Michael's chest, I feel him fall back into a deep sleep.

From the clock across the room I make out that it is a few minutes past three in the morning. It is always around three in the morning that I am plagued with nightmares.

Maybe it's because Mom tried to kill me around that time.

<div align="center">∞</div>

DRESSED IN BLACK from head to toe, I arrive at my grandmother's wake. Stepping into the aisle, I make my way to the first pew. Everyone pivots and stares at me as I pass, jaws agape, gasping silently. Whispers dart back and forth.

"Is that…"

"No, it can't be…"

"It's Alma's son, Fredy…"

"Fredy is here…"

"That's Alma's son, Fredy, her oldest son…"

"I never thought the day would come when we'd see him again…"

"Poor Alma…"

"She's the one who went crazy…"

"What a pity…"

"Look at him, all grown up and so handsome…"

"He looks just like his mother…"

I hastily pass everyone, and sit down next to my cousin in the first pew. Transfixed, I feel everyone's attention on me. Across the parlor, I see Mom's two sisters, teary-eyed and lost in the heaviness of the moment.

A beautiful casket lies open in front of us.

From this vantage point I can make out my grandmother's face.

And for whatever reason, I break into the most anguished and horrific sobs.

One of my aunts quickly gets up, crosses the parlor, sits down next to me, and buries me in her arms. Heaving, I let it all out as my pain comes undone at my grandmother's wake.

My aunt caresses my hair. "There, there, mijo, it's okay now."

Calming down, I get up and make my way to the casket.

Leaning over, I kiss my grandmother goodbye.

I'm sorry for not coming to see you, Grandma, when you wished to see me. It's just that I always carried the pain of you calling me a *creatura* when I was ten years old. I thought you were calling me a creature and for the longest time I held it against you. I shake my head, knowing now that when you told Mom to take care of her *creatura* in Spanish, you meant her child. And because of this misunderstanding, I lost the opportunity to have a close relationship with you.

Returning to the pew, I make eye contact with several family members. Then across the room, I make eye contact with the uncle who molested me. I dismissively glance past him, searching to see if Mom is present among everyone.

Leaning over to my cousin, I whisper, "Where's Mom?"

She replies, "We felt it more appropriate not to have her here, Fredy."

"Does she even know that Grandma passed away?"

"No," she replies.

One by one, people approach the casket and pay their dues as they recall

memories of my grandmother. On the wall behind the casket, a slideshow of snapshots of my grandmother plays. Around me, people mourn together.

Being back in the presence of Mom's family, I find myself an anxious mess as old wounds resurface from the past. I have flashbacks of my religious uncles and their wives coming to my house for nights of endless prayers; and I recall the exorcism when my grandmother sprinkled holy water all over the house in hopes of exorcising the Devil.

∞

A FEW MONTHS later, Eduardo and I reunite when he visits me at my studio. He throws his arms around me and embraces me fiercely in a tight bear hug. Stepping back, we take each other in, studying each other's faces.

Eduardo could easily pass for someone in his mid-thirties. Greasy long curly black hair dangles past his shoulders. He wears thick black frames, a baggy red shirt, and baggy pants that hang off his ass. His face is pudgy from the excess weight he has gained over the years.

"Bro! Fuck, man, it's been years now!" He laughs with joy and suddenly embraces me again.

"It's been six years," I tell him.

He glances to a picture of Michael and me.

"Who's this guy?"

"That's Michael Ethan Lillegard, my boyfriend," I answer.

"Cool. I'm cool with it now. Cool, yeah cool," he repeats, becoming quiet. I notice him clenching his fist and fear strikes my heart as I recall all the times he physically abused me.

That's the past; I need to let it go.

"How long have you been out of jail, Eduardo?" I ask, moving to the kitchen counter to prepare us some sliced fruit.

"Two weeks. Fuck, dude, where does time go? Yo, Dad's been asking about you." He saunters over to me and helps himself to fruit.

"And?" I ask bitterly.

"He wants you to attend our cousin's going-away party."

I throw a strawberry into my mouth and bite it. "I'll consider it," I say wryly.

"You looking good, bro. So, tell me—tell me about you, bro! Come on, bro, let's catch up! Tell me—tell me!" He repeats himself, causing me to wonder if he is high on something.

I call him out on it. "You're not high, are you, Eduardo?"

"Nah, man. I haven't touched shit since the last time they put me in jail, bro. I've been taking medication, bro."

"Medication?"

"I'm being treated for bipolar schizophrenia," Eduardo confesses.

"I'm sorry to hear that, Eduardo." The mental illness strikes another family member. My anxiety spiking, I drop the knife into the sink and look at Eduardo sympathetically. Oh, my poor brother—poor Eduardo.

"Hey, bro, want to go catch a flick with me?" Eduardo asks out of the blue.

"Yeah, I'll go with you," I say, sadness blanketing my heart.

Leaving the studio, I text Michael and let him know that I will not be available until later in the evening. I also ask him if he can free himself from any errands, since I will need someone to lean on after this encounter with Eduardo.

"What movie do you want to see, Eduardo?"

"*Iron Man.*"

Hopping into a taxi, we shoot off to downtown San Francisco.

Whereas at sixteen I cared about what others thought of me when it came to the people I surrounded myself with, today I hold my head up high as Eduardo and I make our way into the theater. I sense people thinking what an odd pair we are; a well-kept attractive gay guy hanging out with a straight-

edged overweight hard-core guy.

As we sit watching the movie in darkness, I feel my brother's emotional ups and downs. In the darkness, I allow my tears to flow freely as I force myself to be present with a brother I never had growing up. He was always the scapegoat in our family; now, seeing what has become of him, all I desire is to cry for him.

I yearn to cry for all of us.

∞

I ACCEPT EDUARDO'S invitation to attend our cousin's going-away party. The drive to San Jose is awkwardly silent; Dad and Edith keep themselves busy with their own ghosts. I don't bring up how our last encounter ended, nor does Dad. We revert back to the times when we would just not talk about it.

Arriving at the park, I surrender into an intense ball of anxiety. Cousins I have not seen since my early teenage years huddle together on the field in two separate teams as a volleyball swooshes back and forth across the net.

Just as Mom's family all pivoted in their pews at the funeral, Dad's family immediately notice my presence among them. A smile freezes on my face as I make my way around, saying hello. I take note of my piously religious Born Again Christian family members, who huddle apart from everyone else. I wave, making sure not to get near them.

"Fredy, how have you been? Have you seen your mother? How is she?" Aunt Christina asks me. Three other aunts in the vicinity crane their necks and eavesdrop on our conversation.

"I'm good! Been working on a memoir, back in school, and living in San Francisco. Mom's doing well. She's in a halfway house for the mentally ill. To be honest, she's become very ugly," I state matter-of-factly.

All four aunts break into nervous laughter, unable to tell whether I am joking or telling the truth.

"Your poor mother; she was always the jealous type. She always had it in for us, huh, girls?" Aunt Christina glances over at my other aunts and they all nod in agreement. "I always knew she'd end up in the nuthouse. It was only a matter of time, Fredy. She was always crazy. I even told her myself. I remember when you were born, you guys moved into our house for awhile. Your mom walked in on me laughing with your dad one time and she lost it. Just went ballistic! She threw herself at me, smacked my face a few times, pulled at my hair, and threatened me under my own roof! Ha! I wouldn't have any of it. I told her, 'You're crazy, Alma! Tu eres loca! Just watch, one day you will be locked up in a straitjacket!' And, well, there she is."

"Your mom hated my guts," another aunt chirps in. Everyone breaks into more nervous laughter.

As I stand there listening to them, a silent rage boils in me. I want to scream out at them that they are attacking a woman who is holed up in a decrepit room, without any visitors, with no one to see her, no one caring to redeem her from her misdeeds. I want to shout, Where is your empathy for a woman who is imprisoned within her own insanity? Is it too hard for them to acknowledge that a woman's life was stolen because she is paranoid schizophrenic? And that she, in turn, stole all our lives? But how could they know? They didn't witness the horrific acts that catapulted each of my siblings and myself down the path of darkness.

"Yeah, she's crazy, alright," I chuckle. I excuse myself and sit down at a picnic table.

Three of my cousins immediately flock to the table and join me. I barely recognize these three young women. They ask me about Bianca and Alexander.

"I haven't seen Bianca or Alexander in over six years now. So I really don't know how they're doing." I murmur.

"So, why did Eduardo go to jail?" Adriana asks.

"He raped his mom," Michelle says beneath her breath.

My cousin plays dumb, widens her eyes, and glances at me to confirm it.

Nodding, I say, "Yes, it's true. He raped our mother while under the influence of a horse tranquilizer."

"No shit," she whispers.

Suddenly, Eduardo strolls up to the picnic table.

His thick black-rimmed prescription glasses look huge on his face. He sits down and stares at us intensely for a minute; then he lets out a huge belly laugh. His brown eyes shift colors as a range of emotions flicker in them as if turned on by light switches. As he gets up and leaves the table, another burst of laughter erupts from his mouth.

"Isn't it true that your mom forced you into a Christian marriage at the age of fifteen?" I ask Adriana.

Her eyes darken as I remind her that no one is perfect.

Focusing my attention on Eduardo, I see him join the guys for a game of volleyball.

What thoughts race through his head? Does he ever wonder about the night he had sex with our mother? Does it haunt him as it haunts me? How does it feel to have that hanging over your head? What does it feel like to know that you will carry this dark act for the remainder of your life? How do you sleep at night, my poor, poor brother?

Sadness once again settles softly across my heart as I blink back tears.

No one will ever understand what I have been through in order to survive Mom's mental illness and what it cost me. Indeed, my life can only be understood backwards, but hopefully I find the strength in me to move forward.

Gazing at Eduardo, Dad, and my religious family, it dawns on me that the nightmares of the Devil desiring my soul is my way of coping with what befell Mom. The Devil is her mental illness and I am deathly afraid of waking

up a paranoid schizophrenic.

What would my life look like if the Devil, disguised as Mom's mental illness, never appeared before her? This mental illness that swiftly arrived in a bejeweled golden chariot full of fire and brimstone and whisked me away into its dark embrace, consuming my soul and leaving behind a whisper...a haunting whisper that to this day flickers in the wind, churning in angst, and mourning over stolen childhoods, displaced dreams, and lost innocence.

The Devil left behind a requiem.

∞ Epilogue ∞

AN ANGEL GLOWS vibrantly in front of me as I bend down on one knee on a jetty that stretches forth from Waikiki Beach. The sun sets behind me, releasing breathtaking hues of dashing turquoise, deep purple, and iridescent orange. The opulent city encloses Michael Ethan Lillegard and me in the shape of an ephemeral crescent moon.

"Michael Ethan Lillegard, I love you with all my heart. Will you marry me?"

"Yes," he whispers as tears well up in his eyes.

I slip a sixteen-karat white gold ring on his finger.

As he helps me to my feet, I lean forward and seal our fate with a passionate kiss.

Around us, the ocean sprays a fresh Hawaiian mist in our faces.

No matter what becomes of us, I will always love you, Michael Ethan Lillegard.

I once heard it said that only by destroying yourself can you truly

discover the greatest power of your spirit. I admit it—I succeeded in destroying myself almost to the point of no return, but Michael's love brought me back to life.

I feel as if I have regained my lost innocence.

Michael, you resurrected me from death.

And now, I am home.

I am truly home.

ABOUT THE AUTHOR

Fredy Espinoza graduated from University of California, Berkeley with a degree in Film and Media Studies. He resides in San Francisco, California.